Critical Decision Making

Critical Decision Making

A New Theory
of Social Choice

David Collingridge

St. Martin's Press, New York

© D. Collingridge 1982

All rights reserved. For information write:
St. Martin's Press, Inc., 175 Fifth Avenue, New York NY 10010
Printed in Great Britain
First published in the United States of America in 1982

ISBN 0-312-17418-7

Library of Congress Cataloging in Publication Data

Collingridge, David.
   Critical decision making.

    1. Social choice -- Decision making.   2. Decision making. I. Title.
HM73.C58 1982   302'.13   82-6017
ISBN 0-312-17418-7   AACR2

To
Jenny

Contents

PART I: THE JUSTIFICATIONIST MODEL — 1

1. The Justificationist Model of Decision Making — 3
2. The Scope of the Justificationist Model — 21
3. Problems of Individual Values — 34
4. Problems of Social Values — 43

PART II: THE CRITICAL MODEL — 67

5. The Critical Turn — Popper's View of Science — 69
6. A Critical Theory of Preference — 82
7. The Criticism of Decision Maxims — 97
8. Flexibility — 141

PART III: COMPARISONS — 153

9. Critical and Bayesian Decision Theory — 155
10. Critical Decision Theory and Partisan Mutual Adjustment — 173

Preface

This book considers the problem of how collective or social decisions ought to be made. The issue is the perennial one of how a group of free individual agents can come to agree rationally upon some course of action, even when it appears to be counter to the interests of some of them. Not only has this proved to be a challenging theoretical question, but attempts to tackle it continue to have profound practical consequences for the conduct of affairs.

Most current attempts at solving the problem of social choice try to show how at least some such choices may be *justified*. Underlying these attempts is a nest of assumptions about the nature of decisions which I refer to as the *justificationist model* of decision making. The model is examined in Part 1 which is an attempt to collate various criticisms which have been made against standard views of social choice. I make no claims of originality here and many readers will no doubt be quite familiar with the points raised, although the use I have put them to may have some novelty.

The second part develops a radical alternative to these standard views in the critical tradition which owes so much to its chief champion, Sir Karl Popper. It is held that no decision may be justified, so that any individual decision may be discovered to have been mistaken after it has been made. The rational way for an individual agent to proceed is therefore to make choices whose errors, if they exist, can be detected quickly and remedied rapidly and without unduly high cost. This provides the clue for the treatment of collective decisions. Making a social choice is not finding some reasonable compromise between the fixed values of the individuals concerned. On the contrary, disagreement is resolved by some of the people involved in the decision changing their views about what their interests are, realizing that their original opinions about what the group should choose were mistaken. Each person tries to convince those in opposition to him that the option which really serves their individual interests is the one which he thinks serves his own. Thus *debate* and not *compromise* is the key to the making of social decisions. This is the core of the conception of social choice to which this book is dedicated, and hence its title *Critical Decision Making*.

The third part of the book shows how some of the intractable problems which plague standard views of social choice can be happily resolved by the new critical theory. It also shows how the new theory subsumes the important work of the political scientist Charles Lindblom. This gives the new view far greater practical significance than standard ones; it can criticize social institutions in a way quite impossible for earlier conceptions of social choice.

The book should be of interest to three groups: those philosophers who welcome the recent increase in the attention their discipline pays to problems of social choice; decision theorists who are looking for an escape from mathematical sterility and those students of public policy who feel the need for some deeper level of analysis. All authors learn to their cost the impossibility of pleasing all of their audience all of the time, and this is especially true of the present work whose intended readership is so varied. If some simple point seems over elaborated and a complex one too compressed, a forgiving reader will gain some comfort from the thought that others may complain in an exactly contrary way.

This work has had a long gestation and was in draft some time before its logical sequel, *The Social Control of Technology* (London, Frances Pinter, 1980) saw the light of day. I am deeply grateful for the support, assistance and inspiration I received during this time from my colleagues and students at the Technology Policy Unit, University of Aston in Birmingham, and to Jerome Ravetz of Leeds University and Keith Taylor of UKAEA for their many kindnesses. A special word is due for Gill Crawford who prepared an immaculate typescript. Beyond all this, however, is the debt this work owes to my wife Jenny, about whose help and encouragement words of mine can do no justice — many, many thanks.

PART I

THE JUSTIFICATIONIST MODEL

1 The Justificationist Model of Decision Making

The concern of this book is normative rather than descriptive; it considers how decisions of various kinds *ought* to be taken, not how they *are*, as a matter of fact, taken. The book's thesis is that the standard view of how decisions ought to be taken, or of what constitutes a rational decision, is fundamentally flawed and in urgent need of replacement by a rival conception to be developed in its later chapters. All the problems of the standard view that are discussed in the following three chapters are a consequence of the view's attempt to show how at least some kinds of decision may be *justified*, and for this reason I shall refer to it as the *justificationist model* of decision making. In its place the present work proposes a *critical model* of decision making, which holds that decisions cannot be justified but that they ought to be submitted to criticism and revised if they are found wanting. This chapter outlines the justificationist model and considers how it has been articulated in Bayesian decision theory and in welfare economics.

The Justificationist Model

In the real world the variety of circumstances under which decisions have to be made is endless. The only way of coping with such richness is to anchor on some particularly simple and transparent decision problem and to develop an account of how decisions of this sort ought to be taken. The decisions and the description of how they are to be tackled are likely to be artificially simple and may bear little relationship to the muddle and confusion that so often characterizes real decisions, but their purpose is not so much to solve everyday decision problems, rather it is to provide a base from which to approach the solution of realistically difficult and messy decision problems. For this reason, the selected simple decision problem and the way of solving it are best seen as a *model*, and not as a practical tool for making decisions. Once the model has been developed it may be extended so as to cope with ever more complex decision problems, which bear an increasingly close resemblance to those encountered in the real world. The model may therefore be judged on two criteria, its internal consistency and its scope of application. In what follows I hope to show that the justificationist model, which underlies most of conventional thinking about decision making, is severely flawed on both counts; it incorporates serious logical inconsistencies and, even if these are ignored, its scope of application is inherently limited to a very small and relatively unimportant class of decision problems.

At the centre of the justificationist model is the claim that a decision is rational to the extent that it can be justified by the person who makes it. Decisions that cannot be justified may sometimes have to be taken, but they can only be made in an arbitrary way. Wherever he can, the rational man will make decisions that he can justify making. A decision is justified by being shown to be the best of all the options available to the decision maker. The decision maker is, therefore, called upon to rank the options open to him in order of preference. How is this to be done? The model stipulates that the value of an option is determined exclusively by its consequences, so that one option is preferred to another if and only if its consequences are preferred to the consequences of the other. An option has no intrinsic value, only that which accrues from its consequences. The decision maker can therefore rank the options he has in order of preference if and only if the following three conditions, which together form a rationality postulate, are met:

(i) For all pairs of options, the consequences of option A are preferred to the consequences of option B, the consequences of B are preferred to the consequences of A, or the decision maker is indifferent between the consequences of A and of B.
(ii) One and only one of these three cases is true for any pair of options.
(iii) Preference over options is transitive so that if the consequences of option A are preferred to the consequences of option B, and the consequences of B are preferred to those of C, then the consequences of A are preferred to the consequences of C.

If any of these conditions is broken a 'money pump' may be applied. Consider, for instance, a person Q whose preferences fail to satisfy the third, or transitivity, condition. Imagine that he prefers A to B, B to C and C to A and that he possesses A, B and C being the property of some trader. The trader may suggest a deal by which Q exchanges A for C, and since Q prefers C to A he will be prepared to pay the trader for the exchange. This leaves Q with C and the trader with B and A, but since Q prefers B to C, the trader may extract more money from Q by exchanging B for C. This leaves Q with B and the trader with A and C, but since Q prefers A to B he will pay the trader to exchange A for B. This restores the original position, Q having A and the trader having B and C, and so the game can continue until all of Q's resources are transferred to the trader. This cautionary tale is a good reason for transitive preference orderings.

But how does the decision maker know that he prefers one set of consequences to another? If his selection of an option is to be justified then he must have some way of knowing what his preferences are which carries no possibility of error. The justificationist model therefore ascribes to the decision maker a privileged access to his own preferences. If a person tells you that he is in pain then (provided he is not drunk, lying, misusing language etc.) it is absurd to question his claim, because he knows about his own pains in a direct and immediate way not open to you. In other words he has privileged access to his own pains while everyone else must rely upon inferences from his behaviour or utterances. Whatever a person says about his own pains cannot therefore sensibly be questioned by someone else because his knowledge is superior to anyone else's. The justificationist model adopts a similar view of preferences. If a person states a preference for one thing over another, then (provided he is not drunk etc.) it is pointless to question his claim because he knows what his preferences are directly. Anyone else must infer what his preferences are from what he says and does, and in doing so there is room for error. The person's own insight into his preferences is not, however, open to error. If his preferences for the consequences of options satisfy the three rules above and are sincerely avowed, then these are indeed his preferences and nothing can show him to be mistaken. He may later change his preferences, that is true, but this can never be the result of discovering that the original preferences are erroneous. A person's pains may fade or move from one limb to another, but this does not mean that the sufferer originally thought that the pain was more severe than it really was, or thought that it was in the wrong limb.

The justificationist model naturally selects as its particularly simple starting place decision problems where there is a single decision maker who knows all the options that are open to him and who knows all the consequences which each option would have if chosen. Such decisions are spoken of as being under *certainty*. The justificationist model has little trouble in providing an account of how decisions under certainty ought to be taken. The decision maker should:

(i) list all the consequences of each of the options which are open;
(ii) place the consequences of the options in order of preference, using the privileged access he has to his own preferences and following the three rules for weak ordering;
(iii) choose the option with the most preferred consequences.

Having shown how the justificationist model applies to decisions under certainty, which must be admitted to be rare to the point of non-existence outside the covers of textbooks, the aim of the model's proponents is to gradually expand the type of decision problem with which it can cope until the model can illuminate the complex problems which arise in the real world. The expansion occurs in two directions; the model must be stretched to cope with decision problems with more than one decision maker, and to handle problems where there is less information about the consequences of options than in the case for certainty. Some of these extensions will be considered below where the model's articulation in welfare economics and in Bayesian decision theory are discussed.

The Justificationist Model in Welfare Economics

Welfare economics concerns itself with the desirability of different economic states, each state being defined by a set of consumables distributed in a particular way among a group of consumers. The theory claims to be descriptive of the behaviour of consumers but maintains that, as a matter of fact, each consumer chooses a bundle of commodities for his consumption in accordance with the rules of rational choice laid down by the justificationist model of decision making. Each consumer is seen as facing a decision problem under certainty. He can purchase a whole range of commodity bundles, and has full knowledge of the constitution of each bundle and of the effects of consuming each bundle. It is assumed that each consumer is concerned only with his own consumption, having no interest in what bundles are consumed by his fellows. A choice of commodity bundle in accordance with the justificationist model requires that each consumer is able to list all possible commodity bundles in order of preference, which requires a 'postulate of rationality' which is basic to welfare economics. For every consumer:

(i) For all pairs of commodity bundles, the consumer prefers bundle A to bundle B, bundle B to bundle A, or is indifferent between A and B
(ii) One and only one of these cases is true for any pair of commodity bundles.
(iii) If the consumer prefers bundle A to bundle B, and bundle B to bundle C, then he prefers bundle A to bundle C.

Although one might exist somewhere, I have never seen a discussion of how the consumer knows that he prefers one bundle of commodities to another. It is assumed to be too obvious to warrant explanation. The consumer, of course, is attributed privileged access to his own preferences, so that he knows immediately and directly that he prefers this bundle to that one and so on.

The justificationist model of decision making has had a tenacious grip on the minds of welfare economists. Despite the strength of the above postulate of rationality, for many years it was not seen fit to test it empirically. By now, however, a considerable body of convincing experiments shows that breaches of the postulate must be extremely common (Edwards, 1954, 1960; Kahneman and Tversky, 1979; May 1954; McCullock, 1948; Rose, 1957; Slovic and Tversky, 1974; Tversky and Kahneman, 1974) and yet the only response from economists has been the casual aside that, of course, their theories contain many working assumptions and so demand charity in the interpretation of empirical results. Very little work has been done to adjust the theory to the results of experiment (Hutchison, 1977; Scitovsky, 1971 chapter II; Von Neumann and Morgenstern, 1974; Weinstein, 1968).

Having ranked the commodity bundles in order of preference, the consumer may assign to each a number on a scale of *utility*. The scale is ordinal, so that bundle A has a greater (smaller, equal) utility than bundle B if and only if A

is preferred to B (B is preferred to A, the consumer is indifferent between A and B). The absolute value of the numbers, their differences and ratios are without significance, only the order giving information. Since the consumer is supposed to act in accordance with the justificationist model he will choose the most preferred commodity bundle (i.e., the one with the highest utility). Thus the behaviour of a consumer may be summarised in what proves to be a mathematically useful way by saying that he *maximizes his utility*, a notion which will be encountered later in various forms. It is now orthodoxy that welfare economics requires only ordinal, as against cardinal, utility measures. (For a brief history of cardinal utility in welfare economics see Dobb, 1969, chapter 45; Ellsberg, 1954; Nath, 1973.)

The Justificationist Model in Bayesian Decision Theory

Welfare economics does not attempt to expand the justificationist model to cover decision problems where information about the consequences of options is less than that demanded for certainty, but this task is undertaken by Bayesian decision theory. The first class of such decisions to be considered are ones under *risk*. These are decisions where the consequences of at least one of the options are not known with certainty, but a list of possible consequences may be drawn up and assigned a probability distribution. Estimates of this probability distribution may be tested by sampling of some kind, and revised in the light of the information so gathered. For such decision problems the ordinal utility scale adequate for conditions of certainty no longer works and a cardinal scale must be employed. Its employment calls for a postulate of rationality somewhat stronger than that used in welfare economics (see Von Neumann and Morgenstern, 1947; several other versions of the axioms exist). If the axioms of the postulate are followed, a decision maker's values may be determined by presenting him with a series of lotteries. The idea here is very simple. Suppose there are three choices to evaluate, A, B and C, of which A is best and C worst for a particular person. What we want to know is how close the value of B is to either extreme for this person. We present him with a choice between having B for certain and having a lottery ticket which gives him a chance P of winning A and a chance $1 - P$ of getting C. P is then adjusted until he is indifferent between the two options, B for sure and the lottery ticket with $P = P^1$. If the person values B just below A, then P^1 will be large — if B is valued equally as highly as A, P^1 will be 1 (i.e., the person will be indifferent between having B for certain and A for certain). On the other hand, if B is valued close to C, then P^1 will be small — if B is valued equally to C, then $P^1 = 0$ (i.e., the person is indifferent between B with certainty and C with certainty). In this way the individual's evaluation of a set of items can be made and his utility function constructed. It is unique up to a positive linear transform.

The value of an option to the decision maker is then taken as its expected utility (i.e., the sum of the utility of each possible consequence multiplied by the probability of the consequence occurring). This follows directly from the axioms of the rationality postulate. As before, the decision maker is justified in choosing the best option, which is now the option with the highest expected utility. The decision maker operating under risk ought, therefore, *maximize his expected utility*. Following the axioms of the rationality postulate is, moreover, not an arbitrary restriction, because an argument similar to the money pump of the previous section can be constructed to show that deviation from the postulate can lead to unending losses. (For a review of the methods for the determination of utility functions in practice see Hull *et al.*, 1973.)

The term Bayesian comes from the use of Bayes' theorem in making decisions under risk. If there are n mutually exclusive and exhaustive uncertain events, $\theta_1 \ldots \theta_n$, with probabilities estimated to be $p(\theta_1) \ldots p(\theta_n)$ and if X is some item of information relevant to the uncertain events ($p(X) \neq 0$), Bayes' theorem, which is an elementary consequence of the probability calculus, states how the probabilities of the events are to be revised in the light of X since:

$$p(\theta_j, X) = \frac{p(\theta_j)p(X, \theta_j)}{\sum_{i=1}^{i=n} p(\theta_i)p(X, \theta_i)}$$

The *prior* probabilities, $P(\theta_1) \ldots P(\theta_n)$, are therefore revised to the *posterior* probabilities, $P(\theta_1, X) \ldots P(\theta_n, X)$, in the light of additional information X, so that the decision maker may adjust his calculations of expected utility in the light of X, possibly finding that this is now maximized by a different option. The decision maker may continue to gather information, revising his probability estimates accordingly, and as information accumulates the probability of one of the events will tend to unity, the others to zero whatever the prior probability distribution. In practice, however, the gathering of such a quantity of information may prove prohibitively expensive. Where information has to be paid for, the decision maker can calculate the expected value of further information and compare this with its cost. Information shows decreasing marginal returns, the value of, say an additional random sample, decreasing with the number of earlier samples, so that eventually the expected value of the decision maker's next item of information is sure to be below its cost. At this point to acquire more information is to throw money away, so the decision maker may make his decision, maximizing his expected utility using values for the probabilities of the outcomes revised using Bayes' theorem and all the information he has found it worthwhile to acquire.

In this way the justificationist model of decision making is extended to decision problems where all possible outcomes are known and can be assigned a prior probability, where all options and the utility from any option/outcome pair are known, and where sampling information can be acquired which can lead to the revision of the prior probabilities. There is, however, an important class of decision problem that even the extended model cannot accommodate. The extended model demands statistical information for the determination of prior probabilities and for their revision using Bayes' theorem. In many cases where information of this sort is possible it may not exist and, worse, for many decisions the information is not even possible. Consider, for example, a company's decision whether to launch some novel product where the outcomes are various market shares. Because the product is new, there can be no appeal to the market share achieved by earlier products to determine the prior probabilities of the new product's market share reaching various levels. Nor can there be sampling information before the decision is made, because sampling requires the launching of the product which pre-empts the decision, so that prior probabilities, even if they could be assigned, could not be revised through Bayes' theorem. A decision of this sort is said to be under uncertainty, although for reasons that will emerge later it is best to qualify the term here, speaking of *restricted uncertainty*. The next extension of the justificationist model of decision making is made to cope with decisions of this sort. It involves the adoption of a subjectivist view of probability and the drawing of an analogy between decisions under risk and under uncertainty.

Exponents of the model stress that a decision maker operating under uncertainty does not do so without information. The managing director of the company above, for example, can be expected to have considerable knowledge relevant to deciding the market share to be achieved by the new product, but this is not in a convenient statistical form. The problem, then, is to see how a decision maker in this position could use non-statistical information in something like the way statistical information can be used when operating under risk. If this analogy is to be sustained, decisions under restricted uncertainty must somehow be able to be based on probabilities without supporting statistics. A subjectivist view of probability is, therefore, adopted which holds that a person's ascription of probability to an event reflects the degree of belief that they have in the event's occurrence. Degrees of belief cannot be distributed arbitrarily. If a money pump is to be avoided, then they must be distributed in conformity with the calculus of probability. Having made this step decisions under restricted uncertainty may be made in exactly the same way as those under risk. The decision maker should assign prior probabilities that reflect his initial degrees of belief in the various outcomes. These should then be revised in the light of further information worth acquiring (i.e., whose expected value exceeds its cost). The revision of prior probabilities and calculation of the expected value of information will not, of course, involve statistical computations, but will reflect changes in the decision maker's degree of belief. When this information has been obtained and digested, the expected utility of each option should be calculated and the option with the highest utility chosen.

The justificationist model of decision making has been extended in many other ways, for example, to give an account of games of various sorts (starting from Von Neumann and Morgenstern, 1947), but our summary may end here. All of these further extensions require acceptance of the Bayesian methods of dealing with risk and restricted uncertainty. Any criticism of these methods therefore strikes so near to the core of the justificationist model that it is also criticism of all the further extensions of the model which have been attempted. The following three chapters aim to provide such criticism.

Supplement to Chapter 1 – A Decision Theory Primer

Decision theory and philosophical ethics have developed with very little cross-fertilization. For this reason decision theory has been able to proceed upon philosophically naïve assumptions about knowledge of preferences that have gone largely unchallenged, and philosophical discussion of problems of choice and action has been carried on in an unhealthy isolation from decision theory. One aim of the present work is to overcome this curious insularity; to show that marriage of the two bear considerable fruit in the form of an exhibition of the shortcomings of Bayesian decision theory and the suggestion of a new approach to the problem of rational choice which, being more philosophically informed, marks a decided advanced upon existing ideas. Most philosophers are, however, less than well acquainted with decision theory and may find the offered prospect a little daunting. Whilst nothing worthwhile in philosophy is easy to digest intellectually, I think that such fears are largely misplaced. Part 1 of the present work is a criticism of Bayesian decision theory, but one which attacks the foundations of the theory. Like many theories, this one has a foundation of great simplicity, but many of the developments arising from this elegant base are of considerable complexity, abstractness and close technical detail. Criticism of these developments would indeed require philosophers to master a daunting heap of technicalities, but criticism directed at the foundations of the theory is much easier to understand. A second word of encouragement may be added. My criticisms of Bayesian decision theory are mainly philosophical. Thus in chapter 3 I shall argue that the theory incorporates a mistakenly simple view about knowledge of preferences and my arguments there ought to be appreciated by philosophers with no previous acquaintance with decision theory. In chapter 4 I shall discuss the problems which beset traditional decision theory in providing an account of social values which are needed for making social decisions, and this should present no greater difficulty. It includes, for instance, a discussion of Rawls' theory of value which is now familiar to all philosophers. The arguments of chapter 2, however, are less philosophical, but even so they do not involve technicalities of decision theory. The criticism offered in this chapter is that Bayesian decision theory has a very narrow scope of application, so that readers more concerned with the philosophical meat will miss little by accepting the conclusion (provisionally of course) with a skip through the chapter. To calm any fears which may still exist, I offer the following primer of Bayesian decision theory.

Bayesian decision theory is normative; it considers how decisions of various kinds *ought* to be made, not how they are actually made in the real world. A starting place for understanding the theory is provided by decisions under certainty. Here the decision maker knows the consequences of each of the options that are open. The value of an option is assumed to be determined solely by its consequences; no option can have 'intrinsic' worth. If the consequences of the various options can be placed in order of preference, then the rational decision is to choose the option whose consequences are most preferred. Placing the consequences in order of preference requires that three conditions be met. Writing /Z/ for the consequence of option Z, then for any pair of consequences /A/ and /B/, /A/ is preferred to /B/, /B/ is preferred to /A/ or the chooser is indifferent between /A/ and /B/; one and only one of these conditions holds; and that if /A/ is preferred to /B/ and /B/ is preferred to /C/, then /A/ is preferred to /C/ (transitivity). This is called a rationality postulate because it is fundamental to making a choice under conditions of certainty. If it is broken, then a money pump may be constructed to empty the chooser of all his resources. An example has already been given earlier in the chapter where the pump could be applied because of a breach in transitivity.

It turns out to be mathematically convenient to employ a measure that reflects the decision maker's preferences known as *utility*, for decisions under certainty nothing could be easier because an ordinal scale of utility is all that is needed. If the consequences of option A are preferred to those of option B, A may be assigned a utility of any magnitude, provided that it is greater than the number assigned to the utility of B. Where A and B are indifferent, they are assigned the same number on the utility scale. There are therefore an infinite number of utility scales of this sort, but they will all agree in the order in which they place the options. Suppose that there is a choice between three options A, B and C, and that the consequences of A are preferred to those of B, and that the consequences of A are preferred to those of C, and that the chooser is indifferent between the consequences of B and C. The three conditions of the postulate of rationality are met so that a rational agent will select the option with the most preferred consequences, namely A. Table 1.1 gives four possible utility scales for the choice. The rational decision maker is now seen as one who seeks to maximize his utility as measured in this way.

We may now turn to the somewhat more complicated case of decisions under risk, where not all the consequences of each option are known. An example might be useful here. Consider a bus operator who is considering whether or not to expand his fleet of buses. For simplicity, it may be supposed that there are just two options open to him; 'expand fleet', and 'do not expand fleet'. If the operator expands his fleet and finds that this corresponds to an increase

Table 1.1 Ordinal utility scales

Option	Utility			
	Scale 1	Scale 2	Scale 3	Scale 4
A	100	100	5	4
B	50	−10	3	3.7
C	50	−10	3	3.7

in demand for his services, he will do very well, but there is a risk; the operator does not know for certain that there will be an increase in demand, and if there is not then expanding his fleet will have been an expensive waste of resources. Again for simplicity's sake we may think of the problem as incorporating just two possible consequences, or states of the world as they are sometimes called; 'demand increases' and 'demand static'. Nothing will be lost by these two simplifications. It may be supposed that the operator has access to statistics about the demand for buses in the past, and that they lead him to assign a probability of 0.6 to demand increasing and 0.4 to static demand. There are, therefore, two decisions which the operator may make, and the pay-off he receives depends upon two states of the world, so there are four *outcomes*: expand fleet/increase in demand; expand fleet/demand static; do not expand fleet/increase in demand and do not expand fleet/demand static. Before deciding on an option, utilities must be assigned to each outcome. The problem, however, is that the ordinal utilities which prove sufficient for decisions under certainty are not adequate here. The rational decision maker will select the option which maximizes his *expected utility* (that is the sum of the utility multiplied by the probability of receiving it). Table 1.2 gives two ordinal utility scales for the consequences. The first of these may be placed in the *decision matrix* of Table 1.3(a) when the operator should maximize his expected utility by expanding his fleet. But if the second utility scale is used Table 1.3(b) shows that the reverse is true; utility on this scale is maximized by not expanding the fleet.

Table 1.2 Ordinal utilities for bus operator's choice

Outcome	Utility	
	Scale 1	Scale 2
Expand fleet/increase in demand	10	3.5
Do not expand fleet/increase in demand	3	2
Expand fleet/demand static	1	0
Do not expand fleet/demand static	5	3

THE JUSTIFICATIONIST MODEL OF DECISION MAKING 13

Table 1.3 Decision matrices for bus operator's choice using ordinal utility

Option	State of World		Expected utility
	Increase in demand $(p = 0.6)$	Demand static $(p = 0.4)$	
(a) Using ordinal scale 1			
Expand fleet	10	1	$10 \times 0.6 + 1 \times 0.4 = 6.4$
Do not expand fleet	3	5	$3 \times 0.6 + 5 \times 0.4 = 3.8$
(b) Using ordinal scale 2			
Expand fleet	3.5	0	$3.5 \times 0.6 + 0 \times 0.4 = 2.1$
Do not expand fleet	2	3	$2 \times 0.6 + 3 \times 0.4 = 2.4$

There is no way to distinguish scale 1 or 2 as the correct ordinal measure of the bus operator's utility, so the lesson is that some other way of measuring utility is needed; a way which does something more than reflect the order of preference. In short a *cardinal* utility scale is required. Suppose that there are three items to evaluate, L, M and N, of which L is the best and N the worst for the chooser in question. We could write down any number of ordinal utilities to reflect this, but a simple device enables us to go beyond that and to say something about the relative intensity of the chooser's preferences. The chooser may be presented with a choice between having M for certain and having a lottery ticket with a chance π_i of winning the best, L, and a chance $1 - \pi_i$ of gaining the worst, N. This is known as a standard alternative, and the lottery as a π_i lottery. The value of the probability π_i may be adjusted until the chooser is just indifferent between the two alternatives, M for certain and a lottery ticket with a chance $\pi_i = p$ of winning L and a chance of $1 - p$ of winning N. If M is valued nearly as much as L, then p will be large, while if M is valued nearly as little as N, then p will be small. In this way a cardinal utility measure may be constructed which says something about the decision maker's intensity of preference.

Let us see how this applies to the bus operator's decision problem. The best outcome is expand fleet/increase in demand which may be arbitrarily assigned the cardinal utility 1. The worst outcome, namely expand fleet/demand static may similarly be assigned the number zero. The operator's utility of the intermediate outcome, do not expand fleet/demand static may be found by presenting him with an imagined choice between this outcome and a lottery ticket with a probability of π_i of gaining expand fleet/increase in demand and a probability of $1 - \pi_i$ of gaining expand fleet/demand static. We may suppose that π_i is then adjusted, when it is found that the operator is just indifferent between do not expand fleet/demand static for certain and a π_i lottery with $\pi_i = 0.3$. He is indifferent, in other words, to having the outcome do not expand fleet/ demand static for certain, and a lottery with a probability of 0.3 of gaining the best outcome and 0.7 of gaining the worst. Then 0.3 may be taken as the cardinal utility of the outcome do not expand fleet/demand static. In a similar way we may suppose that the lottery method shows that the bus operator's utility for the outcome do not expand fleet/increase in demand is 0.4. These values may then be placed in the decision matrix of Table 1.4, when it is clear that the operator can maximize his expected utility by expanding his fleet.

Table 1.4 Decision matrix for bus operator's choice using cardinal utilities

Option	State of world		Expected utility
	Increase in demand ($p = 0.6$)	Demand Static ($p = 0.4$)	
Expand fleet	1	0	$1 \times 0.6 + 0 \times 0.4 = 0.6$
Do not expand fleet	0.4	0.3	$0.4 \times 0.6 + 0.3 \times 0.4 = 0.36$

There is, of course, no guarantee that things will turn out well for the bus operator just because he has gone to all this trouble of measuring utilities. The operator may decide to expand his fleet only to find that demand is static, but maximizing his expected utility in this way is claimed to be the rational way of balancing the risks in the case, because following no other decision rule will provide him with a greater pay-off, at least in the long run. This is reinforced when it is realised that the expected utility rule follows immediately from the perfectly reasonable axioms which have been suggested for π_i lotteries.

The attribution of 1 and zero to the best and worst outcome is arbitrary, so there are clearly an infinite number of cardinal utility scales. It can be shown that if the utilities in Table 1.4 reflect the bus operator's preferences, then so do any set of utilities which are formed from them by a positive linear transform (a multiplication of the original numbers by a given number followed by the addition of some number). Thus if the utilities first entered are 1, 0.4, 0.3, 0, then multiplying by 2 and adding 10 yields 12, 10.8, 10.6, 10, which is also a useable utility scale. The reader should check that placing these utilities in the decision matrix still favours the bus operator expanding his fleet. We shall see later that this raises problems about comparing utilities between different people.

We may now turn to the problem of the value of information. The simplest case is so-called perfect information, which tells the chooser what state of the world will be realised. In the bus operator's case, for example, he might be able to conduct extensive enquiries into people's future travelling intentions, which would tell him for certain whether demand was going to increase or be static. The trouble is, of course, that such information is difficult and costly to acquire, and so its value in helping him with planning his fleet might not be worth the trouble of collecting it. If the findings of the survey are that demand will increase, the operator will obviously expand his fleet, achieving a utility of 1. The probability of this result he estimates at 0.6. There is similarly a probability of 0.4 that the survey will reveal a static demand, whereupon the operator will not expand his fleet, achieving a utility of 0.3. The expected utility of choosing once the survey has been conducted is therefore $0.6 \times 1 + 0.3 \times 0.4 = 0.72$. The expected utility of deciding to expand the fleet in the absence of the survey we have found to be 0.6. The survey therefore increased the expected utility of the bus operator by $0.72 - 0.6 = 0.12$. This is a measure of the value of the survey; in general, it is the expected value of perfect information. The calculation shows the operator that it is worthwhile suffering a loss of utility of 0.12 in order to gain perfect knowledge about future demand for his services, but no more than this. If the proposed survey were to involve a loss in utility of more than this, its cost would be prohibitive.

This account can be expanded to cover information such as weather forecasts, which is less than perfect, and it is here that Bayes' theorem comes into operation. This is a straightforward consequence of the calculus of probability. If there are n mutually exclusive and exhaustive uncertain events, $\theta_1 \ldots \theta_n$, with probabilities estimated to be $p(\theta_1) \ldots p(\theta_n)$ and if X is some item of information relevant to the uncertain events, Bayes' theorem shows how the probabilities of the events are to be revised in the light of X since:

$$p(\theta_j, X) = \frac{p(\theta_j)p(X, \theta_j)}{\sum_{i=1}^{i=n} p(\theta_i)p(X, \theta_i)}$$

The *prior* probabilities, $p(\theta_1) \ldots p(\theta_n)$ are therefore revised to the *posterior* probabilities $p(\theta_1, X) \ldots p(\theta_n, X)$.

To see its role in decision making, an interesting example is provided by Lindley (1971), concerning diagnosis of illness. Before seeing a patient a doctor will have some idea of what is wrong, based on his knowledge of the incidence of various illnesses in his practice. In an urban practice for example, the probability that the next patient to be seen has farmer's lung can be put as extremely low, whilst his having backache or a cold will be given a much higher probability. The doctor may, therefore, assign prior probabilities to various diseases. For simplicity, suppose that there are only three illnesses (or else think of them as classes of illness), $\theta_1, \theta_2, \theta_3$, which may be regarded as mutually exclusive and exhaustive. θ_1 is common, θ_3 rare and θ_2 lies somewhere in between. On his knowledge of past consultations the doctor puts the prior probability of a patient having them at the value given in Table 1.5. Suppose the patient complains of having symptoms X. X occurs rarely with θ_1, but is quite common with the other illnesses, θ_2 and θ_3. Again using his experience the doctor may say that the probability of having symptoms X, given that the patient has disease θ_1 is 0.2; that is that in a sufficiently long run sample of sufferers of θ_1, 20 per cent of them will show symptoms X. This is the *likelihood* of X given θ_1, written $p(X, \theta_1)$. Likelihoods for the other diseases are given in Table 1.5.

Table 1.5 Bayes' Theorem diagnosis of illness

Disease	Prior probability $p(\theta_j)$	Likelihood $p(X, \theta_j)$
θ_1	0.6	0.2
θ_2	0.3	0.6
θ_3	0.1	0.6

The doctor has ascribed prior probabilities that the next patient he sees will have various diseases; the patient has then provided additional information by complaining about symptoms X, and the doctor must now revise his original probabilities to incorporate this. Looking at Bayes' theorem

$$\sum_{i=1}^{i=3} p(\theta_i)(X, \theta_i) = 0.6 \times 0.2 + 0.6 \times 0.3 + 0.6 \times 0.1 = 0.36.$$

$$p(\theta_1)p(X, \theta_1) = 0.2 \times 0.6 = 0.12$$

so by the theorem

$$p(\theta_1, X) = \frac{0.12}{0.36} = 0.33.$$

Similarly, $p(\theta_2, X)$ and $p(\theta_3, X)$ may be calculated to be 0.50 and 0.17 respectively. Thus the symptoms reduce the probability that the patient has θ_1, and increases the probability that he has one of the other diseases.

We may now turn to the problem of the value of money. It is commonplace that the value of money to an individual depends upon the wealth possessed by the person. To a tramp who possesses next to nothing, £1 represents a great deal: it can improve the quality of his life very considerably, so that he places a high value on this amount of money. Give the tramp £1 000 000, however, and his judgement is transformed. To a millionaire, an extra £1 means very little: it enables him to do virtually nothing which he cannot already do, so that he places a much lower value on this amount. The more money a person has, the less an additional £1 means to them; the lower it will be valued. This is known as the *declining marginal utility of money*. In Fig. 1.1 A–B and C–D represent the same quantity of money, but moving from A to B obviously gives the individual in question a much greater improvement in utility (from W to X) than that obtained from moving from C to D (when utility moves from Y to Z).

Suppose someone with such a declining marginal utility for money is offered a bet, by which they have a 50:50 chance of winning £50 and losing £50. Will

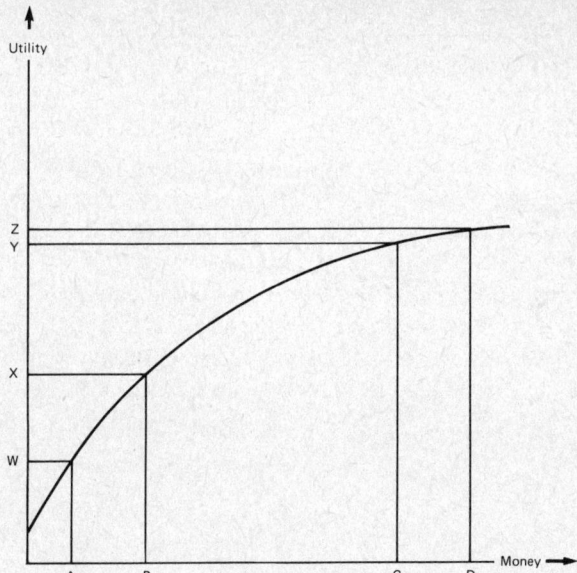

Fig. 1.1 Declining marginal utility of money

they accept the bet? The bet is undoubtedly fair in monetary terms, but because the value of money declines with wealth the bet will not be accepted. Suppose that the potential gambler has £100 (any other figure will do equally well) so that he has a probability of 0.5 of finishing with £150 and the same probability of ending with £50. If the utility of having £50, £100 and £150 respectively is U_3, U_2 and U_1, then the gamble may be represented by the decision matrix of Table 1.6.

Table 1.6 Decision matrix for gamble

Option	State of world		Expected utility
	Win (p = 0.5)	Lose (p = 0.5)	
Gamble	U_1	U_3	$\frac{1}{2}(U_1 + U_3)$
No gamble	U_2	U_2	U_2

If the gambler's utility for money shows declining marginal utility, such as in Fig. 1.2, then clearly

$$U_1 - U_2 < U_2 - U_3$$

re-arranging yields

$$\tfrac{1}{2}(U_1 + U_3) < U_2$$

In other words, the expected utility of not gambling will exceed the expected utility of gambling, so the bet will not be accepted, even though it is fair when considered in purely monetary terms. The gambler is said to be *risk averse*. Most people, when offered lotteries of the kind described earlier reveal themselves to be risk averse, at least for sufficiently high stakes. A minority, however, are *risk seeking* and will accept bets which are unfair to them in money terms. For such people the marginal utility of money, at least over the range in question, is increasing rather than decreasing. A gambler is said to be *risk neutral* if he accepts only bets which are fair in money terms, and for such a person the utility of money is directly proportional to the quantity of money.

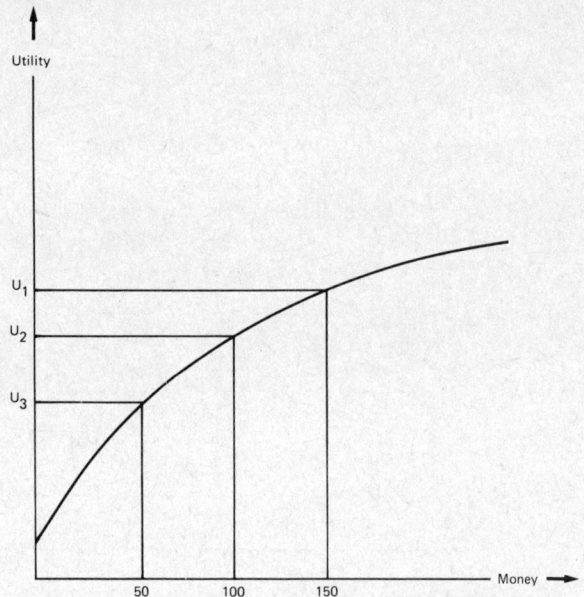

Fig. 1.2. Bet by gambler who shows declining marginal utility for money

The third category of decision that must be mentioned here are those under *uncertainty*, or what we have earlier agreed to call *restricted uncertainty*. To return to the doctor's diagnosis of the patient showing symptoms X; there the decision is said to be under risk because the doctor has statistical information, which enables him to assign prior probabilities and likelihoods. This information may be in the doctor's head, or may have been acquired by a systematic collection of statistics, but this is not the important point. What is significant is that the data is there to collect; exactly when it is collected and who collects it is secondary. Faced with the decision problem, the doctor could have examined his past records to assign prior probabilities, and consulted his own and perhaps other doctors' records to determine the likelihoods. The doctor's handling of the problem will therefore be acceptable whatever view of probability is taken; whether it is seen as a disposition, as a statement about long-run sampling, or as a reflection of degree of belief, or any other interpretation consistent with the calculus of probability. Nothing needs to be said about these rival interpretations as far as decisions under risk are concerned.

But this is quite otherwise for decisions under (restricted) uncertainty. There are many decisions, such as the one facing the company director about launching a new product discussed earlier, where in the nature of the problem it is impossible to acquire statistical data. The answer lies in adopting the view that statements of probability refer to the agent's degree of belief in the proposition. Thus, if the managing director says that he thinks the probability of achieving a 20 per cent market share for the new product is 0.4, he cannot be saying that in the long run 40 per cent of all products launched will be found to achieve a 20 per cent market share, but he can be understood if he means that his degree of belief in the proposition 'the new product will achieve a 20 per cent market share' is 0.4. Once probability is interpreted in this way decisions may be approached in exactly the same way as those under risk. The distinction between risk and (restricted) uncertainty is therefore this; that in the first statistical information may be found so that the machinery of decision making in no way depends upon adopting a particular view of probability; while in the second case statistical data cannot be acquired so that the machinery only works if probability is seen as degree of belief.

References

Dobb, M. (1969) *Welfare Economics and the Economics of Socialism*, Cambridge University Press.
Edwards, W. (1960) 'Behavioural decision theory', *Annual Review of Psychology*, **5**, 473–98.
Edwards, W. (1954) 'The theory of decision making', *Psychological Bulletin*, **51**, 515–53.
Ellsberg, D. (1954) 'Classical and current notions of measurable utility', *Economic Journal*, **64**, 528–56.
Hull, J. *et al.* (1973) 'Utility and its measurement', *Journal of the Royal Statistical Society, A136*, 226–47; reprinted in G. Kaufman and H. Thomas (eds.), *Modern Decision Analysis*, Harmondsworth, Penguin, 1977.
Hutchison, T. (1977) *Knowledge and Ignorance in Economics*, Oxford, Basil Blackwell.
Kahneman, D. and Tversky, A. (1979) 'Prospect theory', *Econometrica*, **47**, 263–91.

Lindley, D. (1971) *Making Decisions*, Chichester, Wiley.
May, K. (1954) 'Intransitivity, utility and the aggregation of preference patterns', *Econometrica*, **22**, 1–13.
McCullock, W. (1948) 'A recapitulation of the theory', *Annals of the New York Academy of Sciences*, **50**, 263–75.
Nath, S. (1973) *A Perspective of Welfare Economics*, Basingstoke, Macmillan.
Rose, A. (1957) 'A study of irrational judgement', *Journal of Political Economy*, **64**, 394–402.
Scitovsky, T. (1971) *Welfare and Competition* London, Allen and Unwin (2nd edn).
Slovic, P. and Tversky, A. (1974) 'Who accepts Savage's Axiom?', *Behavioural Science*, **19**, 368–73.
Tversky, A. and Kahneman, D. (1974) 'Judgement under uncertainty', *Science*, **185**, 1124–31.
Von Neumann, J. and Morgenstern, O. (1947) *The Theory of Games and Economic Behaviour*, Cambridge, Mass., Princeton University Press.
Weinstein, A. (1968) 'Individual preference transitivity', *Southern Economic Journal*, **34**, 335–43.

2 The Scope of the Justificationist Model

Two things are required of a model of decision making; first of all the model must be coherent and free from contradiction and if this hurdle is passed it must be applicable to a wide variety of decision problems. This and the following two chapters submit the justificationist model to scrutiny, its scope of application being considered here and its logical consistency in the subsequent chapters. The discussion of scope will concentrate on Bayesian decision theory, as this makes claims to be of assistance in the making of many types of decision, although some reference will be made to welfare economics. The conclusion of the chapter is that the justificationist model of decision making, as it exists in its most highly articulated form, can only hope to have application to a very narrow class of decision problem.

The justificationist model of decision making calls for a *synoptic view* of the decision problem before the model can be applied. (For an attack on a somewhat different account of decision making called 'synoptic' see Braybrooke and Lindblom, 1963.) The structure of the problem, the relevant facts and values, the relationship between the decision and the whole network of future decisions and the nature of the information that might be made available all need to be known in great detail before the justificationist model can be applied. Such a counsel of perfection is only practically useful if it also tells us what to do when perfection cannot be attained. Indeed, this is why the justificationist model has been articulated to cover decisions under risk and restricted uncertainty. The model's first form, which deals with decisions under certainty, is so demanding as to have virtually no application in the real world, despite the fancies of welfare economists. It is, therefore, of some urgency for the upholders of the model to give advice to those who have to make decisions under less happy circumstances, and this they have done. What I wish to argue in this section is that although the scope of the justificationist model has been expanded in this way, it can still operate only under very restricted conditions so that it can be applied to a limited variety of decisions. When some of these conditions are not met, the model can occasionally suggest some way of circumventing the ensuing problem, but this is possible only rarely, and even then the additional scope of application won for the model is very small.

It is now time to pursue the argument in more detail by considering what conditions must be met for the application of Bayesian decision methods. These are discussed below.

All States of the World must be Identified

This, of course, is a necessary condition for the application of Bayes' theorem; the states of the world considered must be mutually exclusive and exhaustive. In using the theorem in making decisions under risk or uncertainty there must be some way, therefore, of identifying all the states of the world as such. There may be a finite number of such states or an infinite number, but in either case there must exist some rule which tells the decision maker which states of the world are relevant to his decision and which are not, and which also tells him when he has a complete list of such states. Without the assurance provided by such a rule the decision maker would be in jeopardy from the exclusion of states of the world which he should have considered, in which case Bayes' theorem will not be applicable.

Textbooks minimize the problem by telling us that there are just two urns containing different fractions of coloured balls for sampling, or that the managing director of the firm knows that he will make such and such a profit if the market share of his new product is greater than x, and loose so much if it is less than x. Many real world decisions are not, however, so straightforward. In many, the problem is not how to ascribe probabilities to states of the world, but rather to identify what states of the world are relevant to the decision. This is particularly true where the decision has a considerable lead time. In the notorious case of energy planning, for example, decisions have to be made now whose main effects will only begin to be felt 20, 40 or even 50 years in the future. The states of the world which will determine the pay-offs from the various options now open are just impossible to perceive over such lengths of time. The sorry history of forecasting shows this to be a very common feature of decision problems. Where even quite modest lead times are involved, it is impossible to predict what factors will determine the pay-offs of today's options when they arrive in the future with sufficient confidence to apply the Bayesian approach. For an assessment of forecasting problems see Collingridge, 1979, chapter 9.

This is a serious constraint on the application of the justificationist model, because there seems no way of breaking it. Where it is impossible to identify all the relevant states of the world the model is silent, giving us no clue about how to proceed in such trying circumstances.

All Options must be Identified

At first this may seem a little strict. Even if only some of the options open to the decision maker have been identified, Bayesian methodology may be applied to determine which is the best of those which have been identified, and since the other options have escaped scrutiny it seems reasonable enough to adopt the best of those considered (i.e., it seems reasonable to adopt the decision rule: where not all options have been identified, choose the identified option which has the highest expected utility). This is, however, only reasonable when the time between the decision and its implementation is negligible. Where this is not so there is time for the decision maker to discover an option that is even better than the one chosen. If he is free to do so, the decision maker may thereupon revise his original choice so that he has an even better expected utility. The freedom he has to do this, however, is a function of his original choice. If he has selected an option that cannot be revised at all, or can be revised only at a cost greater than the improvement he can achieve from the newly identified option, he must stick with a decision he knows to be suboptimal. On the other hand, if the first option chosen is easily revised, he can improve his decision. To give a colourful illustration, getting to the ground by the option of jumping from the window is much less easily revised than the decision to use the stairs, if the upper storey seems the better place to be when halfway down.

What this means is that a decision maker who has not considered all the options open to him should place a premium on options that are easily revised so that he may improve his decision if a superior option is discovered in time. This is an additional factor to the conventional one of expected utility, and some trading between ease of revision and expected utility may be required. It is very difficult to see how this could be accommodated within Bayesian methodology. In the nature of the case it is impossible to calculate the expected utility of making a revisable choice, because the revisions that might be called for are not yet known. The only hope would seem to be the restriction of Bayesian methodology to desicisions where all the options can be identified, so that the decision maker has no need to guard against the discovery of options superior to the one first chosen.

As before, the theory is silent if this condition is not met. Where a superior option may exist it cannot be correct to tell the decision maker to select the best of those options which have been considered, irrespective of how easy it will be to revise this option. But if ease of revision is to be a factor in the decision maker's choice, he must go beyond Bayesian methods to accommodate it.

If the decision maker's use of Bayesian decision theory depends upon the identification of all the options that are open, the often glossed-over question of how such a complete set of options is to be determined takes on a new importance. Any decision is taken against a background of facts and institutions and ways of doing things that are regarded as more or less fixed, at least as far as the decision maker is presently concerned. In theory, the decision maker has a huge, and sometimes an infinite, number of options that he might take, but the human mind is so limited that they cannot all be considered. Indeed, it would be irrational to consider too many options, since the cost of the investigation might well outweigh any likely benefits from good decision making. Any decision maker, therefore, considers a tiny sub-set of all possible options before him, rejecting the others out of hand as obviously inferior or else beyond his concern at the moment. In this way the problem is reduced to picking the best option from half a dozen or so. Many of the options not considered are not deliberately rejected by the decision maker, because they never emerge into his consciousness through lack of imagination or a shrewd intuitive eye for the impossible.

An example might be helpful here. A typical text book simplication is from Moore (1976). The example concerns a firm, which has to decide between launching a new product and not launching it. Best estimates yield the decision matrix shown in Table 2.1, according to which expected monetary value, used as a surrogate for utility, is maximized by launching the new product.

Table 2.1 Decision matrix for launch of new product

Decision	Pay-off (£000)	
	10% market share (0.7 chance)	2% market share (0.3 chance)
1 Launch product	100	−50
2 Drop product	0	0

The decision is obviously represented as one under restricted uncertainty (or even risk, depending upon how the probabilities were estimated). A little reflection, however, soon reveals that any decision maker considering a problem similar to the example will have before him an enormous number of options and not just the convenient pair of launch product/drop product. The whole firm could cease to market anything, sell its equipment and invest the resulting capital in an enormous number of different ways. The firm could also be sold as a going concern, at a variety of prices, and the money invested as before. Or, again, the plant needed for the new product could be burned down and the fire insurance embezzled by the managing director. And why look at the possibility of launching only one product; why not wait until a pair, or trio, of products can be launched, perhaps to save on advertising. The calculations of the marketing director presumably rest upon assumptions about pricing, distribution, packaging, advertising, retailer and wholesaler margins, and a host of other things. Even altering these in combination opens up a host of alternatives. In the example we are offered, however, all these options, and the many more which may be imagined, are suppressed, leaving us with a simple pair. What is really a situation where there are so many options open that a decision maker can hardly be aware of them all is magicked into a choice between two options.

This is, as I have said, a perfectly typical example of how decisions are simplified. The reason for this, of course is that the human mind cannot hope to compare any more than a handful of options and that the expense of doing more is likely to exceed the benefits derived from any decision analysis. In the hypothetical marketing example, for instance, nobody has suggested liquidating the firm, or selling it; these, and many other options are simply not under scrutiny. The firm has restricted the problem to make it amenable to discussion and eventual resolution at modest cost. The need for such restriction is a truism. The limitations of the human mind are matched only by the limitations of the human pocket. It is quite impossible and crazily expensive to consider a huge number of options in detail, which no-one can deny. What can be asked, however, is under what conditions are such simplifications in order if Bayesian methods are to be applied to the simplified decision problem?

This is best examined by expanding the example of the product launch. Suppose that another pair of options, sell the firm/keep the firm, are imposed on the first pair. There are now four options;

1 launch the product and keep the firm;
2 drop the product and keep the firm;
3 launch the product and sell the firm;
4 drop the product and sell the firm.

The first two of these are equivalent to the original options. Imagine that the net present monetary value of the firm's activities in the future are £9 million and that this is independent of the fate of the new product. The firm has something of a false reputation and so can be sold for £10 million if the product launch is successful. If the launch fails, however, inefficiencies in the organization will be uncovered which will reduce the price to £8 million. If the product is dropped, the sale will realise £9.5 million. The matrix is shown in Table 2.2.

Expected monetary values for options 1–4 are, 9055, 9000, 9400 and 9500 (£000) respectively. Option 4 should, therefore, be favoured; the product being dropped and the firm sold. This, of course, is quite contrary to the conclusion reached when only options 1 and 2 are considered, when launching the product is favoured.

Table 2.2 Decision matrix for launch of product and sale of firm

Decision	Pay-off (£000)	
	10% market share (0.7 chance)	2% market share (0.3 chance)
1 Launch product–keep firm	100 + 9000	−50 + 9000
2 Drop product–keep firm	9000	9000
3 Launch product–sell firm	10 000	8000
4 Drop product–sell firm	9500	9500

The example is, of course, generalizable. As we have seen, when a restricted number of options is considered, choosing the best of them may preclude choosing the best from an expanded set of options or the best from the complete set of options. A set of options is complete where the choice of an option has no effect on the pay-offs obtainable in any other decision. In the example, the decision launch product/drop product has an effect on the pay-offs of the decision keep firm/sell firm so the two decisions must be considered together in the expanded matrix of Table 2.2. In the same way, any other decision whose pay-offs are dependent upon which of the four options of Table 2.2 is chosen ought to be considered together in an even bigger matrix. The decision to paint the managing director's door green or vermillion may, however, be regarded as a totally separate one because the pay-offs from the choice of colour is not influenced by, and has no influence on, the pay-offs from launching/dropping the product or selling/keeping the firm.

The conclusion is that the application of Bayesian decision methods requires the identification of a set of options that are complete in the above sense. The reason for this may be expressed in two ways. If an incomplete set of options are employed, allowance must be made for the discovery between the decision and its implementation of a new option, superior to all of those so far identified, by favouring revisable options in a way which cannot be accommodated by Bayesian decision theory. Alternatively, consideration of an incomplete set of options may lead to the necessity of making sub-optimal decisions in the future, optimal choice being prevented by the choice of the best of the incomplete option set. This is a severe restriction on the applicability of Bayesian decision theory, because it is notoriously difficult to foresee the complex interactions between decisions taken at different times, a requirement which is necessary for drawing up a complete list of options. Indeed, it is often stated that, in reality, all decisions are sequential.

The lesson from this discussion has some parallel with the problem of the second best which plagues welfare economics (Lipsey and Lancaster, 1956). If the decision of Table 2.1 had no effect on the pay-offs in Table 2.2, then an overall optimum is obviously achieved by optimizing each decision separately. If, however, there is interaction, the pay-offs in the second decision depending upon the choice made in the first, then it is generally wrong to choose the option that gives the optimum in the absence of interaction. Thus, considered in isolation, the best option in the first decision is to launch the product, but when interaction with the second decision is taken into account the best option is now dropping the product. Piecemeal optimization is therefore impossible when there is interaction of this sort between decisions, and the entire set of interacting decisions must be examined as a whole before Bayesian theory points to a choice.

In welfare economics, it can be shown that a number of Pareto conditions must be met for the maximization of a consumer's utility, namely that for each pair of commodities the rate of commodity substitution is equal to the rate of product transformation. This enables piecemeal optimization of markets, each one being adjusted until the relevant Pareto conditions are met, there being no need to consider interactions between markets. When markets interact in such a way that one or more of the Pareto conditions cannot be met, the best cannot be achieved and so the second best must be sought (i.e., the consumer must maximize his utility subject to the constraint that these Pareto conditions cannot be met). It can be shown that, in general, none of the Pareto conditions should now be met. No market should now be adjusted until the relevant Pareto conditions are met, so that all markets can be expected to deviate from their adjustment by piecemeal optimization. To determine the adjustment of any market now calls for detailed knowledge of how it interacts with all the other markets, and piecemeal optimization is no longer possible.

All Pay-offs must be Known

To apply the Bayesian decision matrix, all the pay-off entries must be known. This involves the double task of identifying the outcome of each option under each state of the world and then assigning a utility value to each outcome. This is made difficult because of the interactions between decisions discussed in the previous section. Calculation of pay-offs for one decision is only possible where all decisions that have pay-offs affected by the first decision can be identified. This, of course, calls for the expansion of the first decision into one with a set of options that is complete, and subsumes all these affected decisions. Pay-offs can be known, in other words, only if a set of options that is known to be complete is considered.

The problem this poses is not quite so bleak as the others considered so far, because there are ways of applying the Bayesian approach even when the condition is not met. If all options and all states of the world have been identified and all but one pay-off is known, sensitivity analysis may be employed. It may be said that if the missing pay-off lies within such and such limits, then one option is best, that if it lies elsewhere another option is best and so on. In practice, the pay-off may be known to fall into one of these regions with a high probability, although its absolute value may be unknown, so that the best option may be discovered. If there is more than one missing pay-off, however, this approach rapidly deteriorates and the decision maker is told less and less, until it becomes impossible for the best option to be found. Sensitivity analysis is, therefore, a crude way of extending the scope of Bayesian theory, and achieves little in this direction. The need for information about pay-offs is, therefore, a severe restriction on the scope of Bayesian theory, and so on that of the justificationist decision model that underlies it. Not only must the set of options be complete, and all states of the world identified, but a utility must be assigned to every option/state of the world pair, except where sensitivity testing can marginally reduce the severity of this condition.

All Relevant Information Must Be Collected

We may say that an item of information is relevant if its expected value exceeds its cost. In applying Bayesian procedures to decisions under risk, such as the standard urn problems, information is obtained at fixed cost by sampling. Information has a decreasing marginal expected value and so there must come a point where further sampling fails to justify its cost. The decision maker can then stop collecting information and can choose, using what information he has found to be worth collecting. Decision making under uncertainty, however, may involve non-statistical information, and it may prove impossible to be sure that all information that is relevant has been collected. Bayesian methods are nevertheless often applied to such decisions, using what relevant information has been identified. I wish to argue that this is mistaken, my argument being a *reductio ad absurdum*. I shall begin, therefore, by assuming that it is proper to apply Bayesian methods in this way. In other words, we begin by accepting the decision rule: when not all relevant information is identified, gather all information known to be relevant, apply Bayes' theorem, and select the option which maximizes expected utility.

The problem arises when time is required for the decision's implementation. Additional relevant information may be discovered and gathered during this period and application of the above decision rule may lead to an option different from the one originally chosen being favoured. If he is free to do so, the decision maker may then incorporate this additional information into his calculations and alter his choice. The freedom he has to do this, however, is a function of his original choice. If he has selected an option that cannot be revised at all, or can be revised only at a cost greater than the improvement he can achieve by shifting from the option originally chosen, then he cannot take into account the new information and he must stick with a choice which, according to the above decision rule, is sub-optimal. On the other hand, if the option first chosen is easily revised, he can exploit the additional information and so improve his decision.

What this means is that a decision maker who cannot be sure that all significant information has been gathered should favour options that are easily revised, so that he may improve his decision if more information is discovered between him taking it and its full implementation. This is an additional factor to the usual one of maximizing expected utility. It may happen that there is no conflict between these two criteria; the option with the highest expected utility as calculated from the information originally available being also the most easily revised option. But this is a happy accident which cannot be expected to happen. In general, there will be conflict between the two criteria, the option with the highest expected utility as calculated from the information originally available being different from the option that is most easily revised, so that trading will be necessary in the choice of an option. It is very difficult to see how this

THE SCOPE OF THE JUSTIFICATIONIST MODEL

trading could be accommodated within Bayesian methodology. In the nature of the case, it is impossible to calculate the expected utility of making a revisable choice because the revisions that might be called for are prompted by the discovery in the future of information that is not known at the moment.

Where some significant information may be discovered between a decision being taken and its full implementation it is, therefore, wrong to tell the decision maker to select the option with the highest expected utility as calculated from the information that happens to have been identified and obtained up to the time of the decision. The decision maker should retain an ability to respond to the discovery of additional information by favouring easily revised options, so that trading between these two requirements is necessary. This is, of course, contrary to the decision rule that has been assumed. The rule's adoption therefore generates a contradiction. It follows that Bayesian methods may only be applied when it is known that all relevant information has been discovered, so that there is no need to worry about having to revise an option once chosen. In practice, this would seem to confine these methods to decisions under risk, where information is from sampling, and to the most simple of decisions under uncertainty.

All Interpretations of the Data Must Be Examined

Bayesian decision theory adopts a very simpleminded view of the nature of the information that is available for the estimation of prior probabilities for states of the world and their adjustment through Bayes' theorem. The classical example of deciding under risk concerns a set of urns each containing balls of different colour in various proportions. An urn is selected at random and samples withdrawn in order to decide what proportion of balls of the various colours it contains, using Bayes' theorem in the normal way. By concentrating on such simple cases of sampling a distinction which it is vital to understand where more realistic decisions are concerned is overlooked. This is the distinction between *data* and *information* (see, for example, Loasby, 1976, chapter 6). Data is the raw, unanalysed observation, which becomes information when analysed and interpreted. Concentrating thought on sampling coloured balls from urns tends to collapse this vital distinction, with disastrous consequences for more complex decision problems. The distinction can, nevertheless, still be made even in such simple cases. The data from sampling is the series of subjective impressions, which the withdrawn objects — to call them 'balls' requires an interpretation to be placed on the data — make in the sensory apparatus of the sampler. Transformation of this data into information that can be employed in statistical calculations requires an interpretation to be placed on these raw impressions — that they are produced by objects that are solid balls and whose surfaces have such and such a colour. We are so accustomed to such straightforward interpretations that the transition from data to information in these examples easily goes unnoticed. Its presence becomes clear, however, if errors of interpretation are considered. Suppose, for example, that a ball in a sample looks midway between the colours involved; perhaps one of those awkward shades that could be blue or could be green. Or suppose the sampling is done under lighting conditions that vary in such a way that the colours of the balls change, or that the sampler has eye defects where fatigue produces distortions of perceived colour. In cases like these the process of interpretation of the data suddenly becomes intrusive and obvious, unlike sampling in clear daylight of balls of unmistakeable colour, by a sampler with consistently perfect vision, where interpretation is easily overlooked.

For any set of data there are always many, mutually incompatible interpretations. In the case of sampling coloured balls, one interpretation which is consistent with the data is the straightforward one — that coloured balls are being viewed under normal illumination, with no perceptual distortion. But by various hypotheses about the illumination and the presence of perceptual distortions, many other interpretations can be made consistent with the given data. Maybe, those that are given the straightforward interpretation of red balls are really white balls viewed under red light, or those that are counted as yellow balls in the straightforward interpretation could also be regarded as white balls under daylight illumination viewed by a jaundiced sampler. These interpretations are, however, easily tested and if they fail the test they may be rejected. For example, the spectrum of the illumination could be examined and the sampler's blood tested for jaundice, but their ease of elimination should not prevent us grasping the logical point that even in sampling coloured balls more than one interpretation of the data is possible, because in more complex decisions this may become a more difficult problem.

This is exactly what happens. When we move from risk to uncertainty, problems of interpreting data become much more important. Data is no longer subjective impressions from observing samples, but can be much more complex. In an example I have given considerable attention to elsewhere (Collingridge, 1980, chapter 11), the problem was whether to remove lead additives from petrol in the USA. Data here was reports of scientific investigations and findings covering an enormous area, and, as data, it was accepted by those wishing to remove lead (in particular the Environmental Protection Agency) and by those wishing to continue its use (notably the Ethyl Corporation, a major manufacturer of the additive). The data may have been agreed upon, but the two sides offered very different interpretations of it. The Environmental Protection Agency interpreted the data as showing that lead from vehicle exhausts impaired the health of children, while the Ethyl Corporation offered the interpretation that lead from this source poses no health hazard to any group of the population. Surprisingly, both of these obviously incompatible interpretations were reasonable and could be defended with some vigour.

This feature of decision making is, however, overlooked in standard Bayesian accounts of decision making under uncertainty. As we have seen, attention to information from such things as samples of coloured balls when deciding under risk tends to hide the possibility of data being given different interpretations, and failure to attend to this point is carried over to decisions under uncertainty. But for these decisions, rival interpretations of data may not just be theoretically possible but may be a central feature of the decision problem, as in the case of health hazards from lead in petrol.

How easily can Bayesian decision theory accommodate the existence of many interpretations for one set of data? The problem, of course, is that the favoured option may be sensitive to what interpretation is placed on the data. This was certainly true in the lead-in-petrol case, where the acceptance of the Environmental Protection Agency's interpretation meant the removal of lead from petrol, which indeed is what happened, and acceptance of the Ethyl Corporation's rival interpretation would have meant continuing with lead additives. If the decision maker's choice is sensitive to the interpretation chosen, then how can he be sure that he selects the best interpretation of the data? This will be a point of some interest later on, but for now let us be generous and grant the existence of some set of rules that show when one interpretation of the data is better than another. Knowing these rules, the decision maker can compare the interpretations which have been made of the data to select the best of them, but can he then use this best interpretation to make a decision in the way advocated by Bayesian theory? Unfortunately, the answer is no. The best of the interpretations known to the decision maker may not be the best of all interpretations, for he may be quite unaware of a whole series of interpretations. If a decision has to be made, then an even better interpretation may be discovered between the choice of an option and its full implementation, and this new interpretation may lead the decision maker to favour a different option. If the option first chosen is not revisable, then the decision maker cannot make use of the new interpretation, and has to make do with a suboptimal decision. If, however, the decision can be changed relatively easily, he can accommodate the discovery of an even better interpretation of the data by selecting the option which it favours.

As before, this means that ease of revision must be a factor in the decision as well as the more usual maximization of utility or expected utility. We have also seen, however, that this dual criterion cannot find a place within Bayesian theory. There is, in the nature of the case, no way in which a probability can be assigned to an as yet unknown interpretation of the data being discovered superior to any existing interpretation. The use of Bayesian methods, therefore, requires that the decision maker be sure that the interpretation of the data that he is using is the best of all possible interpretations. There is then no need to guard against the discovery of superior interpretations by placing a premium on easily revised options, so the only criterion is the normal Bayesian one.

In practice, this is a serious limitation on the scope of application of Bayesian theory, because in all but very simple decisions under uncertainty or risk, the interpretations that may be placed on the data available are open-ended, so that there can be no assurance that the best has been found.

Conclusion

Chapter 2 offers no fundamental criticism of Bayesian decision theory, and the justificationist model of decision making. What it has tried to do is to determine the conditions that must be satisfied before Bayesian methods of decision making can be applied, assuming that such methods contain no logical flaws. The conclusion must be that the scope of application of these methods is extremely limited. In detail, the following are necessary conditions for the employment of Bayesian decision methods:

(i) All states of the world can be idientified.
(ii) All options can be identified.
(iii) All pay-offs are known.
(iv) All relevant data has been gathered.
(v) All interpretations of the data available are known.

Where one or more of these conditions is not met, Bayesian methods cannot be applied, and there seems no way in which any modification of these methods consistent with the justificationist model of decision making could extend their scope to cover decision problems where the conditions do not hold. The narrow scope of Bayesian theory might not be so worrying, except that there seems so little room for its expansion. This, of course, is a direct result of the synoptic view of the justificationist model of decision making from which Bayesian theory springs. It insists that decisions are rational only if they can be justified, but justification calls for such extensive knowledge of options, states of the world, pay-offs and so on, that it has little reality beyond the covers to textbooks.

The situation is made murkier than it needs to be by the use of the term 'uncertainty' to include all decisions where there is insufficient information to assign objective probabilities. Thus, a decision meeting all the above conditions and needing subjective probability assessments is said to be under uncertainty, as well as a decision where one or more of the conditions fails to hold. This obscures the essential point that the first may be able to benefit from Bayesian decision methods, but the second has no chance of this. I therefore propose extending the usual spectrum of certainty/risk/(unrestricted) uncertainty to certainty/risk/(restricted)uncertainty/*ignorance*. Ignorance covers all decisions where Bayesian techniques cannot be applied because the conditions considered in this section do not all hold. Restricted uncertainty covers decisions where subjective probabilities may be employed and where all the conditions are met, so that Bayesian methods may be used. The lesson of this section is that all but the very simplest and well-structured decision problems are under ignorance and that it is, therefore, of the greatest importance to develop theories of how decisions ought to be made that are powerful enough to cope with decisions under ignorance. This, as we shall see, calls for the rejection of the justificationist model of decision making.

References

Braybrooke, D. and Lindblom, C. (1963) *A Strategy of Decision-Policy Evaluation as a Social Process*, Basingstoke, Macmillan.
Collingridge, D. (1979) *The Fallibilist Theory of Value and Its Application to Decision Making*, PhD thesis, University of Aston, Birmingham.
Collingridge, D. (1980) *The Social Control of Technology*, London, Frances Pinter/The Open University Press.
Lipsey, R. and Lancaster, K. (1956) 'The general theory of the second best', *Review of Economic Studies*, 24, 11–32.
Loasby, B. (1976) *Choice, Complexity and Ignorance*, Cambridge University Press.
Moore, P. (1976) *Case Studies in Decision Analysis*, Harmondsworth, Penguin.

3 Problems of Individual Values

The previous chapter made no attempt to question the logical coherence of the justificationist model of decision making, but merely sought to show that even if the model is consistent, it can only ever hope to apply to a very restricted range of decisions. This chapter will extend the criticism of the justificationist model by arguing that it is not only limited in scope but logically flawed. The flaw lies in the account offered of how the decision maker is to determine his preferences. Since this affects all decisions, whether they are under certainty, risk or restricted uncertainty, nothing will be lost by confining the discussion of the present chapter to the simplest case of decision making under certainty.

As described in chapter 1, the justificationist model of decision making insists that some decisions may be justified, and this calls for finding some way in which the values used in such a decision may be justified. It is no use trying to justify a decision if an essential component like the values of the decision maker cannot be justified. Attempting to justify values in this way generates two philosophical problems, which are discussed in the following two sections.

The Regress of Reasons

The sceptical arguments of this section depend in no way upon a special characterization of value judgements. If my arguments are correct, then whatever analysis or description is offered of value judgements, no such judgements can be justified. Similarly, the arguments in no way depend upon a particular view of justification. Whatever account is given of the exact nature of justification, scepticism about the possibility of justifying value judgements is inevitable. This enables the sceptical arguments to be couched in a very general way. The central element in the argument which I wish to deploy against the possibility of value judgements being justified is what I call a *regress of reasons*. Imagine that a value judgement of some kind, call it J, is to be justified. Reasons for regarding J as justified must be brought forward. As far as the arguments go, there is no need to specify what kinds of things may be used to justify a judgement such as J; it suffices that reasons of some sort are necessary if J is to be justified. What kinds of things may justify value judgements, and, in particular, whether these must be other value judgements, factual sentences, commands or other imperatives need not, therefore, detain us. Neither need we show concern for the exact nature of the relationship of justification. Reasons are needed for the justification of a value judgement; once this much is admitted, we have enough. Suppose R_1 is proposed as a reason that justifies J. Whatever account is given of justification, it must be admitted that R_1 justifies J only if R_1 is itself justified. If R_1 is not justified, we have no reason for accepting it, and hence no reason for thinking J justified. Suppose, therefore, that R_2 is produced as a reason justifying R_1. As before, this is only possible if R_2 is itself justified, which will lead to the invoking of a further reason, R_3, and so on. The regress $----R_3, R_2, R_1, J$ I shall call a 'regress of reasons'.

The next step is to show that J can only be justified if there is some non-infinite regress of reasons leading to J. Imagine that the regress of reasons above is infinite, so that the need to provide reasons never stops. In that case any attempt to justify J must be conditional (i.e., all we can say is something like 'if R_4 is justified, then J is justified'). This, however, does nothing but raise the question of the justification of R_4. If R_4 is justified, then so too is J, but if R_4 is not justified, we have no reason to think J justified. There can be no more assurance about J than there is about R_4, but once the question of R_4's justification is raised, we are back into the regress. In other words, the sort of conditional justification which an infinite regress of reasons permits is no justification at all.

If J is to be justified, it follows that there must be some regress of reasons leading to J, which terminates at some point so that it is non-infinite. If justification of J is possible, there must exist some reason, R_F, which can be justified without appeal to further reasons. Such a reason I shall call a *fundamental* reason, avoiding the confusion that might result from the use of such words as self-evident, *a priori*, certain, self-certifying and so on. The word fundamental is appropriate here. A value judgement is justifiable only if there exists some fundamental reason that justifies it, though perhaps through a chain of intermediate reasons. It is natural, therefore, to see such fundamental reasons as providing a basis for values, or as having authority in evaluative questions, or as a source for proper values.

This much will be familiar to most people having a nodding acquaintance with ethics and the search for fundamental reasons has been one of the main driving forces in the development of ethical theory, just as the search for a certain source of knowledge has been central to epistemology. The force of the present section is that the search for such reasons in ethics has been a search for the impossible. Before seeing why this is so, it will be useful to list the assumptions I have made thus far. To me there seem three:

A1 B is justified only if there is some reason supporting B.
A2 If A is a reason supporting B, then A is justified.
A3 No judgement B can be justified simply by a conditional justification of the form 'if A is justified then B is justified'.

These seem reasonable assumptions on any view of justificaton, so that the fine points of these views need not concern us.

Imagine that a value judgement J is held to be justified because there exists a regresss of reasons leading to J, which terminates at a fundamental reason R_F. R_F, being fundamental, is justified, but not by an appeal to further reasons, To press our sceptical intent we need only ask why R_F was chosen as fundamental rather than any other reason. This is not an idle question, because choosing some other reason as fundamental might lead to quite a different value judgement being regarded as justified, perhaps one contrary to J. In reply, it will be argued that R_F is fundamental because it has some special property, which we may call P. The next question, of course, is why it is that reasons with the property P and not some other property are fundamental. Seeking an answer to this question continues the regress of reasons that R_F was supposed to stop. A *reason* has been given for thinking R_F fundamental, that R_F has P, and a further reason — that all reasons with property P are fundamental — is obviously needed, but providing reasons for R_F in this way means that R_F cannot terminate the regress of reasons. The need for these reasons shows that R_F is not fundamental after all. Obviously, any attempt to stop the regress at some point beyond R_F will run into exactly the same difficulty, so the regress of reasons is an infinite one. Since the argument is stated perfectly generally, all regresses of reasons leading to J will be infinite and so J will be incapable of justification, as will all value judgements.

The point I wish to make is a very simple one, as the length of the argument shows. Philosophers have generally agreed that if a value judgement is to be justified then there must exist a regress of reasons leading to the judgement, which terminates somewhere. Many philosophers have, therefore, searched for a set of fundamental reasons, which can terminate regresses leading to value judgements. The selection of fundamental reasons cannot, of course, be arbitrary — reasons must be given why one set of reasons and not another is fundamental. But this leads to contradiction. On the one hand, there are to be fundamental reasons, which are justified without appeal to further reasons, and, on the other hand, it is necessary that reasons be given why these reasons, and not others, are fundamental.

It may be helpful to consider a brief example here, whose artificiality I hope may be excused on the grounds of clarity. Consider the view that all fundamental reasons that can lead to value judgements are commands of God, so that all such judgements rest ultimately upon God's commands. The relationship that exists between these commands and the value judgements they justify may be taken as entailment. Suppose the value judgement J is entailed by 'Do not cause unnecessary suffering', which is supposed to be fundamental. The regress of reasons leading to J, in other words, is supposed to terminate at the command 'Do not cause unnecessary suffering'. If we now ask why this command is singled out as fundamental we will be told that it is a command of God. Then, if we ask why commands of God are fundamental, we might be told that this follows from God's goodness. We may then, of course, ask how we know that God is good, and so on. The proponent of this view of value has tried to justify J by the finite regress:

$$\text{avoid unnecessary suffering}, \ldots, \ldots, \ldots, J$$

But the terminus of the regress cannot be arbitrary or else we could equally argue

$$\text{cause unnecessary suffering}, \ldots, \ldots, \ldots, \text{not-}J$$

Reasons must be provided for choosing the first terminus rather than the second and so we now have

..., ..., God is good, All God's commands are fundamental reasons, God commands us to avoid unnecessary suffering, avoid unnecessary suffering,..., ...,J

But this regress does not terminate at a fundamental reason. We can ask for reasons for thinking that God is good and thus continue the regress indefinitely. Thus the attempt to justify J by appealing to a fundamental reason fails. Reasons are needed for regarding 'avoid unnecessary suffering' as fundamental, and giving these reasons means that the regress does not terminate after all.

The above argument concerns the impossibility of terminating a regress of reasons because of the need to justify the claim that some set of sentences are fundamental. A second argument exists that is independent of the first, which can be shown by assuming that the difficulties raised above are unreal and that it can be shown that some kinds of sentence, say those with property P, are fundamental. If this is so, then a reason, R_F, can be known to be fundamental and justified without support from further reasons if it can be shown to possess the property P. But, of course, showing that R_F has P is something that demands reasons, and in demanding reasons, the regress of reasons that R_F is supposed to terminate begins all over again. R_F does not, therefore, terminate any regress of reasons, even if our earlier sceptical arguments are ignored. No regress of reasons leading to a value judgement, therefore, terminates and so no value judgement is justifiable.

The example of God's commands being fundamental may be used to illustrate this second sceptical argument. Let it be granted that there are no difficulties in justifying the claim that all God's commands are fundamental reasons. If it can be shown that the imperative 'avoid unnecessary suffering' is a God-given command, then it can be used to terminate the regress of evidence leading to J, but reasons are needed for believing that the imperative is so commanded. It might be held, for example, that God has revealed this command in the Bible, but then we may ask how this is known and so on and so on. The regress of reasons leading to J obviously cannot halt at 'avoid unnecessary suffering'. It must, in fact, be infinite as must any regress leading to J. J is, therefore, incapable of justification.

Decision theory has developed in a strange isolation from philosophical ethics, which also claims to illuminate aspects of evaluation, decision and action. It has therefore incorporated a naïve view of individual values, which was briefly mentioned in chapter 1. It is assumed that the decision maker has privileged access to his own preferences, so that he knows his preferences in more or less the same way that he knows about his own pains. It is easy to see, however, how this characterization is inadequate and runs foul of the two sceptical arguments developed above. Imagine a decision maker who adopts the view that X is preferable to Y. This is supposed to be justified because the decision maker intuits that X is preferable to Y, but this raises two problems each of which restart the regress of reasons. How does the decision maker know that his preference judgement is justified if it is intuited? Establishing this requires reasons, and so the regress reappears. Secondly, even assuming away the first problem leaves the question of how the decision maker knows that he is now intuiting that X is preferable to Y. To establish the truth of this requires reasons and so the regress seems unavoidable after all. But if the regress cannot be terminated, then ascribing privileged access about preferences to decision makers does not, contrary to the justificationist model of decision making, show how judgements of preference can be justified.

There may, of course, be some other view of individual values and their determination to overcome these difficulties and show how preference judgements may be justified. Elsewhere, I have reviewed many recent attempts in this direction from the literature of philosophical ethics and argued that none is satisfactory (Collingridge, 1979, chapter 2), and yet for all this some way may be found tomorrow, or maybe in the press at this very minute. But hope is no substitute for argument. What the discussion of this section establishes is that the view of individual values incorporated into the justificationist model of decision making fails to show how a decision maker's values may be justified so that the model itself cannot explain how decisions may be justified. And worse than this, such is the generality of the arguments used here that it seems very doubtful that any way of allowing a decision maker's values to be justified will ever be found, although this means an end to the justificationist model of decision making. What seems to be required is a view of decision making that can employ values which are not justified. But this is work for later chapters.

Facts and Values

In this section I wish to take a fresh look at the horny old problem of clashes between preferences. This is such a painful and obvious feature of everyday life that its existence requires no comment. What is needed, however, is a logical characterization of conflicting preferences, which will be useable in the development of a theory of decision making that is stronger than those based on the justificationist model. Consider an example where a person prefers eating an apple to eating an orange and also prefers eating things that do not make him sick to things that do make him sick. The first thing to observe is that there is no formal contradiction between these two statements of preference; they are not logically contradictory, and the person is not in breach of any of the rules governing the employment of 'preference', for example transitivity. To generate a clash between the two preferences facts are required (e.g., the fact that eating the apple will produce sickness and eating the orange will not). Given this fact, retaining both the original preferences now involves a breach of logic. Eating the apple is preferred to eating the orange, but the second preference and the fact about the digestibility of fruit entail that eating the orange is preferred to eating the apple. If the preferences are maintained, this means that a money pump may be applied. The person will swop the orange for an apple and because he prefers eating the apple, he will be prepared to pay money for the swop. But he will then be prepared to pay money for exchanging the apple for the orange, as he also prefers the orange. The game may be continued until he is bankrupted of all resources.

The person holds preference claims W and X below

W = Eating apple A is preferable to eating orange O.

$X = (x)(y)$ (x does not make me sick and y makes me sick $\supset x$ is preferable to y).

D = Eating apple A will make me sick and eating orange O will not make me sick.

The problem is that

$X \cdot D \to$ Eating orange O is preferable to eating apple A

so that

$$X \cdot D \to \text{not } W$$

Another way of viewing the problem is that the fact D falsifies the conjunction of the preference claims X and W so that the conjunction may be said to be *factually incorrect*.

$$X \cdot W \to \text{not } D$$

so that

$$D \to \text{not } X \cdot W$$

These logical relationships are not dependent upon a particular interpretation of preference judgements, for example the view that they have a truth value, but hold on whatever interpretation is given. Thus, if preference judgements are treated as imperatives, so that 'A is preferable to B', is rendered as the order, 'choose A to B', the relationships still hold. Consider the argument offered by Geach (1958).

If the 12.55 weather forecast says that it will be showery, then cancel the match.
Don't cancel the match
―――――――――――――――――――――――――――
not (The 12.55 weather forecast says that it will be showery)

Here two orders entail a factual statement, so that finding this to be false (i.e., that the forecast was showery weather) produces a clash between the two orders. At least one of the orders must in that case be regarded as inoperative.

These logical relationships are of some philosophical importance and I have explored them elsewhere (Collingridge, 1979, 1980, 1982). For now, the question is what they imply for decision making and theories of decision making. The lesson for the justificationist model of decision making is that justifying a decision requires justifying the preferences that it involves, but a preference judgement can be justified only if it is known to be immune from factual falsification. The decision maker must know that the preference claims being used will never require to be changed because of conflict with other preference claims and factual sentences. If the preference claims, on which the decision is based, are in jeopardy from factual falsification, they may one day have to be abandoned – and so cannot be viewed as justified. There are three ways in which immunity from factual falsification might be achieved. The first requires the conjunction of the preference claims in question with all of the decision maker's other preferences, to give all possible n-tuples of preferences. The factual consequences of all these n-tuples would then be deduced and compared with the real world for the assignment of a truth value. Where all the consequences are found to be true, the possibility of factual falsification has been exhaustively eliminated. In practice, this is a totally impossible task except for artificially confined, textbook problems. It requires the exhaustive listing of preferences, which is not possible in real decision making. The preferences of agents are never clear cut, well defined and closed, but always roughly formed, ill articulated and open-ended. (This does not matter very much provided these judgements can be made precise and definite when this is called for, but it is pointless to call for an exhaustive listing of sufficient precision to ensure immunity from factual falsification.)

The second way of safeguarding against factual falsification is to adopt preference judgements whose conjunctions yield no factual sentences. This is, however, possible only if a very weak set is adopted. For the sake of simplicity, consider only value judgements that ascribe some value to an object, and which we may write $Va = q$ (the value of object a is q as measured on some appropriate scale). These are preference judgements because they assert the agent's indifference between a and all other objects whose measured value is q. Now

$$Va = q$$
$$Vb = q'$$
$$\text{not } (a = b)$$

For example

$$\frac{\text{The value of the fastest steam engine in the world} = 3}{\text{The value of The Mallard} \qquad\qquad\qquad\qquad\qquad = 2}$$

not (The Mallard is the fastest steam engine in the world)

If the attribution of some numerical measure, as on a utility scale, is seen as suspicious, consider

$$\frac{Va > Vb}{\text{not } (a = b)}$$

For example

$$\frac{\text{The fastest steam engine in the world is more valuable than the Mallard}}{\text{not (The Mallard is the fastest steam engine in the world)}}$$

Confining ourselves to singular value judgements of the form $Va = q$, it can be seen that the only way to avoid factual consequences is to adopt a set of the form, $Va = q$, $Vb = q$, $Vc = q$, $Vd = q$ . . . . As soon as two objects are ascribed different values, a factual consequence emerges as I have shown.

If we now consider universal preference sentences of the form $(x)(Rx \supset Vx = q)$, a similar result appears. Thus

$$\frac{(x)(Rx \supset Vx = q)}{(x)(R^1x \supset Vx = q^1)}$$
$$\overline{(x)(Rx \supset \text{ not } R^1x)}$$

For example,

$$\frac{(x)(x \text{ is a Rolls Royce car} \supset Vx = 5)}{(x)(x \text{ costs more than £10 000} \supset Vx = 3)}$$
$$\overline{(x)(x \text{ is a Rolls Royce car} \supset \text{not } (x \text{ costs more than £10 000}))}$$

If numerical values are found objectionable they may be easily eliminated. As before, factual consequences can be avoided only be adopting a set of value judgements of the form $(x)(Rx \supset Vx = q)$, $(x)(R^1x \supset Vx = q)$, $(x)(R^2x \supset Vx = q)$ . . . As soon as two values appear in the set, factual consequences arise. Thus all sets of value judgements except of the very weak kind above, will be beyond justification. All but the weak sets above have factual consequences, and if these consequences may be discovered to be false then the preference claims cannot be regarded as justified.

A third way of trying to escape the possibility of factual falsification of preference judgements is for the decision maker to decide that those he has used in a particular decision are to be retained at all cost, other preference judgements being sacrificed to ensure their retention. We have seen that no single preference claim entails a factual sentence, but that a conjunction of such claims is necessary for this. It follows that a single preference claim cannot be factually falsified, and that when a conjunction is falsified there is always a choice of which preference judgement to reject. It is this choice that the present suggestion exploits, for the preference judgement Q is to be regarded as justified because wherever the conjunction of Q and another preference claim is factually falsified, it is the other claim which is to be sacrificed, Q being retained.

The problem is that this can only be known to be effective when one preference judgement is to be kept immune from revision. If it is hoped to keep both Q and Q^1 free from revision then the suggestion collapses. It may happen that

$$Q \cdot Z \to F \quad \text{and not } F \quad \text{so that } Z \text{ is rejected}$$

and also that

$$Q^1 \cdot \text{not } Z \to F^1 \quad \text{and not } F^1 \quad \text{so that not } Z \text{ is also rejected}$$

contrary to the law of the excluded middle. Thus, the decision maker's resolve to keep Q free from falsification may clash with his resolve to treat Q^1 in the same way.

In conclusion, there are no practicable means of ensuring that a particular set of preference judgements will not require to be rejected when some factual sentence they entail is discovered to be false. All sets of preference judgements are, therefore, in jeopardy from factual falsification, so that none may be regarded as justified. But if preferences are not justified, then neither are decisions based on them, contrary to the justificationist model of decision making. The model cannot hope to accommodate such a fundamental challenge. A radically new view of decision making consistent with the fallibility of preference judgements is demanded.

References

Collingridge, D. (1979) *The Justificationist Theory of Value and Its Application to Decision Making*, PhD thesis, University of Aston, Birmingham.

Collingridge, D. (1980) 'The autonomy of evaluation', *Journal of Value Inquiry*, 14, 119-27.

Collingridge, D. (1982) 'Evaluative reasoning and the factual falsification of value judgements', *Philosophy* (in press).

Geach, P. (1958) 'Imperatives and deontic logic', *Analysis*, 18, 49-56.

4   Problems of Social Values

The basic question in social philosophy is how a group of individuals, who may have widely divergent private interests, can come to agree on the evaluation of some item. When agreement is reached, we may talk of having arrived at a social value. The question is at its most forceful when the items to be appraised are courses of action. Until a decision is called for, the members of the group may happily tolerate the diversity of their individual values. Toleration, however, becomes logically impossible when a decision must be made. The private preferences of some in the group may lead them to favour one course of action, while those with other values may favour another course, incompatible with the first. Someone, it appears, must lose and someone must win. Any collectively taken decision, therefore, brings to the fore the problem of how a group of individuals with different private values can rationally agree about common social values, so that the gainers can justify their gains to the losers.

There are thus two related features of primary importance to social values; people with widely different private values are able to agree upon at least some social values, and social values are no less binding upon a person than his own private values, so that they guide the agent's actions in the same way as personal interests. This raises a pair of problems; how is agreement possible, and why should an agent's actions be guided by social values even when this runs counter to his private interests? Considerable effort has been exerted in trying to adduce answers to these central questions from the justificationist model of decision making. The problem is a severe one, however, because of the view of individual preference built into the model and examined in the previous chapter. Decisions call for preferences, but people have privileged access to their own preferences and know them in a way quite different from the way others can know them. The justificationist model, therefore, naturally starts with individual decisions involving the preferences of a single decision maker. This decision maker knows his preferences immediately, just as he knows of his plans, and there are no problems of how he is to determine the preferences of others, for these have no part in his decision. Economic man, for example, has no interest in the welfare of others; he is totally selfish. All important decisions, however, are public ones involving public values. Even where an individual such as a minister, managing director or vice-chancellor acts in the name of an organization, he does so in a way which he supposes reflects the social, public values of others in the organization, and does not employ the private values appropriate to his life outside the organization. The problem, therefore, is for the justificationist model to give some account of public decisions given its starting place, and in particular, to explain how agreement about such decisions is possible and why an individual's actions should be guided by public values in the same way as they are by his own private values. This chapter reviews the main attempts that have been made to articulate the justificationist model of decision making in this direction.

Welfare Economics

It will be useful to begin with welfare economics, which studies the distribution of wealth between consumers in an attempt to evaluate the social desirability of various economic states, or arrangements of economic activity and resources. It might, therefore, be hoped that welfare economics can shed light on the problem of forging social from individual values. Modern welfare theory has given up all hope of directly comparing the enjoyment or utility that one consumer received from his consumption with that received by another consumer. Instead, recourse is made to ordinal scales of utility. There are two reasons for this; the great difficulty found in making interpersonal comparisons of utility, and the realisation that the ability to make such comparisons would add only very little to the explanatory power of welfare economics — for brief histories see Ellsberg (1954); Dobb (1969, chapter 45) and Nath (1973). It is now an orthodoxy of welfare economics that it needs only ordinal measures of utility. The idea of such a measure is simplicity itself. The number x is applied quite arbitrarily to the utility of an object X for consumer Q and numbers assigned to the utility of other objects such that if Z is preferred to X, then the number is greater than x; if X is preferred to Z, then the number is less than x; and if Q is indifferent between Z and X, then the number is x. In this way the *order* of the numbers reflects Q's utility; the absolute magnitude of the numbers, the difference between them and their ratio being of no significance. Surprise is often expressed about the progress that is possible in welfare economics using this simple ordinal measure.

In seeing how social values can be based upon individual ones, the great restriction imposed by the use of ordinal measures of utility is that no interpersonal comparison of utility is possible. It is, therefore, impossible to make a direct comparison between the gains of the gainers and the losses of the losers. For this reason, a central idea in welfare economics is that of a Pareto improvement. If a change in economic state increases the utility of at least one person, but reduces the utility of nobody, then the change is said to be a Pareto improvement (Pareto, 1909, chapter 6, section 53 and 89). If the value judgement is made that the welfare of society is a function of the welfare of the individuals who compose the society, then the economic state after any Pareto improvement will be judged better than the earlier state — hence, of course, the term 'improvement'. It is very important to recognise that even at this early stage, welfare economics has to resort to value judgements in order to say anything about social values. The value judgement about the desirability of Pareto improvements may seem harmless enough, but there are imaginable conditions where it does not seem so acceptable — for example, when the community contains some group who we wish to see punished such as a conquered nation or ordinary criminals. We might well think that a reduction in the welfare of these individuals makes a positive contribution to social welfare. Sen has also pointed to the potentially extremely illiberal consequences of making all possible Pareto improvements (Sen, 1970a, chapter 6 and 6*; Sen, 1970b; see also Fine, 1978).

Unfortunately, very little progress is possible if all we have is the idea of Pareto improvement. When all possible Pareto improvements have been effected, the economy is said to be Pareto optimal (or Pareto efficient). In such a state no individual can be made better off without somebody else being made worse off. If there were only one optimum state, the original value judgement about the desirability of Pareto improvements would enable us to isolate one best economic state, which we could struggle to achieve. Unhappily, however, there are a vast number, and on some assumptions an infinite number of Pareto optimal states. Each state has a different allocation of economic resources to individuals, but once we have denied interpersonal comparison of utility, there is no way of selecting one allocation over others.[1] Moreover, a non-optimal state cannot even be judged inferior to all optimal states. It is essential, therefore, for welfare economics to provide some other, less universally satisfied, criterion for judging between economic states.

Before leaving the discussion of Pareto optimality, it will be useful to consider it in the light of how weights are to be attached to the utility of individuals in estimating social welfare. If it is assumed that social welfare is the weighted sum of individual utilities, then the principle of making all possible Pareto improvements can be restated as the principle of positive responsiveness. This says that weights must be attached in such a way as to make social welfare increase with an increase in the utility of any individual. Having made all possible Pareto improvements, optimal states can only be compared when we know what weights to apply. This, of course, necessarily takes us beyond Pareto.

One suggestion is due to Kaldor, in response to scepticism about interpersonal comparisons of utility expressed by Robbins and others in the 1930s. If one person's utility could not be compared with another's, then what hope was there for any comparison of different economic states? Kaldor proposed that questions of total consumption should be isolated from questions about the distribution of consumption. Thus, welfare economics was to consist of a scientific, objective part concerned with deciding whether one economic state could maintain a greater total consumption than another; and a second, political or ethical part concerned with how this total might be distributed (Kaldor,

[1] A very clear discussion of this is in Arrow (1963), pp 34–7 and 63–4.

1939; see also Hicks, 1939). Central to the first part of welfare economics was Kaldor's principle that an economic change produces an increase in consumption if those who gain from the change could compensate the losers and still be better off. It is easy to see that this is equivalent to saying that consumption increases if it is possible to make a Pareto improvement. This principle has great intuitive appeal, but cracks soon appeared. Scitovsky revealed an ambiguity in Kaldor's idea of compensation. For Kaldor, this was a flow of consumption from gainers to losers, but Scitovsky showed that it could also take the form of a bribe from the losers to the gainers, for the latter to forego their benefits. It is only possible to speak unambiguously of an increase in total consumption if the Kaldor criterion is satisfied and if this other form of compensation is not possible — the Scitovsky criterion (Scitovsky, 1941).

This proposals was, however, soon exploded. The problem is best seen by using the utility possibility curves shown in Figs. 4.1 and 4.2 below.[2] Such a curve shows the maximum utility which can be enjoyed by one consumer, A, given a fixed utility for another consumer, B (utilities being measured ordinally) for a fixed quantity of commodities. Each point on the curve represents a different distribution of commodities between the consumers. Figure 4.1 shows two utility possibility curves which do not touch. Commodities K may be distributed between A and B, and as A gets more B obviously gets less, reflected in the shape of the curve. The shape of the curves does not really matter for the argument, but it might be mentioned in passing that as A has more and more of K, a fixed addition to his bundle of goods increases his utility by less and less, so that he shows declining marginal utility of consumption. The same is also true of B. The question to be considered is whether the shift from K distributed at Q^-, to L distributed at Q^* represents an increase in social welfare. A has gained and B lost from the change. If A were hypothetically to give some of the goods he has at Q^* to B, the distribution of L could be shifted to Q_1^*. Here B is no worse off than before, but A's utility has increased, so that Kaldor's criterion is met. B cannot bribe A not to shift from K to L, even if he gives up everything. If A has the whole of K and B nothing, A is still worse off than he would be at Q^*.

If the two utility possibility curves cross, as in Fig. 4.2, then matters are not so simple. In the shift from Q_1 to Q_2 if the gainer, A, moves from Q_2 to Q_2^1 he can compensate B and still be better off than before. Hence the Kaldor criterion is met. As before, B cannot bribe A not to shift from M to N, so the Scitovsky criterion is also met. The transition from Q_1 to Q_2 would therefore seem to produce greater consumption. But now consider the move from Q_3 to Q_2. At Q_3 there should be exactly the same quantity of commodities as at Q_1, the only difference being in their distribution, so that the shift from Q_3 to Q_2 should represent an increase in total consumption. Nevertheless, there is no way in which A could compensate B. If A gives up all his consumption to

[2] The argument was developed in Samuelson (1950).

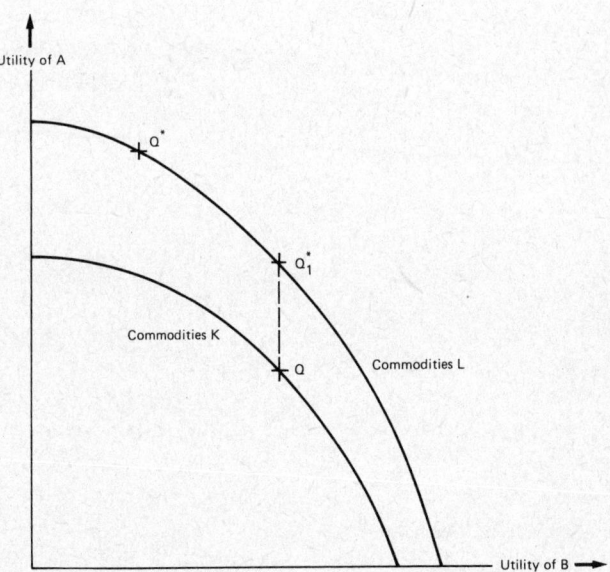

Fig. 4.1 Non-intersecting utility possibility curves

B, B is still worse off than he was at Q_3. The Kaldor criterion is not met, and so the transition from Q_3 to Q_2 does not represent an increase in total consumption.

It can be seen from this, that if the utility possibility curves intersect, then no meaning can be attached to increases in total consumption. Total consumption is relative to income distribution, and so the only unambiguous meaning that can be given to an increase in consumption is that there is an increase *for all possible income distributions*. This requires the non-intersection of utility possibility curves as in Fig. 4.1. Unfortunately, such non-intersection cannot be concluded from the usual index data of the economist. It can only be known to exist when the physical quantity of *all* goods shows an increase, something which is, of course, a trivial case. Attempts to sidestep difficult questions about the distribution of income and concentrate on measuring simply its total therefore fail. Any judgement that one economic arrangement is better than another can only be justified if the distributional differences can be shown to increase social welfare. This, of course, takes us right back to the problems we started from.

This is well illustrated by the use that is made of cost benefit analysis. As we have seen, measures of total consumption are relative to income distribution, and so it is customary to assume that its present distribution is optimal. This,

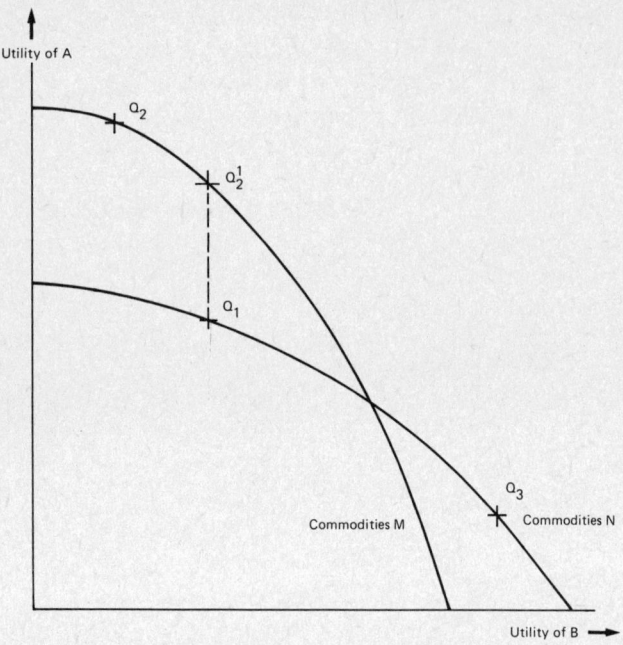

Fig. 4.2 Intersecting utility possibility curves

of course, is a value judgement. Once this is made, policies that increase total consumption, relative to this optimal distribution can be identified and adopted. Some other distribution could, it is true, be regarded as optimal, but calculations of changes in consumption can generally only be made on the basis of present income distribution, because the changes in prices resulting from a change in income distribution cannot generally be calculated. This can hardly be seen as a solution to the problem of rationally balancing one man's losses with another's gains, because the acceptance of a particular income distribution as optimal is totally arbitrary. No reason is generally given for the acceptance of present distribution as optimal, except that this distribution is the result of political decisions reflecting the preferences of legitimately appointed social decision makers. Apart from the element of mythology here, the question is whether these decision makers have acted reasonably or not. Can they be criticised for their views on income distribution, or can they justify their views by public reasons, which go beyond their own private tastes? We come, therefore, full circle, for these are essentially the same questions as those asked at the beginning of the chapter.

Utilitarianism

Having seen how the articulation of the justificationist model of decision making offered by welfare economics fails to give a satisfactory account of social decision making, a very different attempt in the tradition of utilitarianism may now be considered.[3] Harsanyi imagines a person who has the choice of joining several societies.[4] In order that the choice be fair, Harsanyi uses the well-known device of assuming that the chooser does not know what social position he will occupy in his chosen society. He does, however, know the utility enjoyed by people who occupy each social position in each society.[5] According to Harsanyi, the chooser in this situation is faced with a fairly straightforward decision under risk, so he must maximize his expected utility. If a society has n social positions, his chance of finding himself in any one of them, given his existing knowledge, is $(1/n)$. If the utility to be acquired from the occupancy of the jth social position is U_j, then the chooser's expected utility for this society is simply $\Sigma_j(1/n)U_j$. Thus the utility of a society for the chooser is simply the arithmetic mean of the utilities of all individuals in the society. He will, of course, choose the society with the highest utility so defined.[6] Moreover, his choice will be objective in the sense that anyone else in the same position would arrive at the same evaluation of the various societies.

Harsanyi's argument leads to the conclusion that social utility is a weighted sum of individual utilities and to the assignment of equal weights to all (the actual weight is irrelevant and functions only as a proportionality constant). It is, of course, a central tenet of utilitarianism that what determines social welfare is only the total amount of utility or happiness in the society, and not its distribution, so that increasing the utility of one person in the society increases social welfare by exactly the same amount as conferring that utility on some other person. I have five criticisms to make of Harsanyi's argument:

---

[3] According to Sidgwick (1902), utilitarianism begins with Shaftesbury (1711), though it achieved its clearest statement in Bentham (1789), Mill (1863) and Edgeworth (1888). For modern statements see Smart (1961) and Lyons (1965).

[4] Harsanyi (1953), (1955) and (1975a). It is interesting to compare the argument of Lerner (1944) from the equiprobability of individuals possessing a particular utility function. For two extensions see Samuelson (1964) and Sen (1973), pp. 83–5, and for a similar argument see Leibenstein (1965).

[5] A very similar argument is due to Vickrey (1960), except that he assumes that all the choosers have the same utility function, thus circumventing the problem of interpersonal comparison. The restriction is, however, highly artificial and for this reason Harsanyi's exposition is superior.

[6] Harsanyi has a second argument. First, social preferences and individual preferences are assumed to satisfy the usual axioms for utility. Secondly, the evaluative principle that if two social states P and Q are indifferent from the standpoint of every individual, then P and Q are socially indifferent is accepted. It follows from this that social welfare is a weighted sum of individual utilities. This is weaker than the first argument, which also tells us that the weights should be equal, and so I will not discuss it in detail. See also Pattanaik (1968).

(i) The first ciriticism concerns the determination of individual utilities by Harsanyi's hypothetical chooser. The chooser must determine the utility achieved by each individual in the society and, according to Harsanyi, this can be done by thinking himself into the life of each individual in turn; imagining that he has someone else's talents, tastes, liabilities, tasks, rewards, likes and dislikes. Harsanyi seems to see no difficulty here; the utility enjoyed by the other person apparently just emerges once this imaginative achievement has been accomplished (Sen, 1973, pp. 14–15). Underlying this belief seems to be a disturbingly naïve view of our knowledge of evaluation. We are aware of our own values because we know our own tastes, likes and dislikes, tasks and so on, and this gives us privileged access to our values. To discover another's values, all that is necessary is to acquire his tastes imaginatively etc., and we will have the same privileged access as before, but this time to *his* values. This is, of course, spurious. My estimation of another's values can, at best, be an intelligent guess, although one that I might be able to improve with greater knowledge. Things are not as simple as Harsanyi thinks.

(ii) The second problem for Harsanyi's account concerns the comparison of the utilities of different people. Harsanyi is quite correct when he says that we make such comparisons constantly, but the question is whether they can be made on the scale and with the precision that his method requires (see Little, 1957, chapter 4). The chief problem here is that even if cardinal measures for utility are used, such as those of Von Neumann and Morgenstern, the measure is unique only up to a positive linear transform. The utility function of a person is, therefore, not unique, but can be represented by an infinite set of functions. For an individual decision maker this is no problem since all functions lead to the same ranking of alternatives, but if interpersonal comparisons are to be made, there must be a way of selecting just one function from the infinite set belonging to each individual. When the utility functions of all the individuals in the society have been scaled in this way, they may be compared.

Vickrey has explored ways of scaling utilities (Vickrey, 1960; see also Hildreth, 1953). The zero point is not needed, since what is being measured are the differences in the utility of individuals. All that is required, therefore, is a suitable interval. Vickrey suggests finding two social states A and B such that everyone prefers B to A, and employing those scales which assign a utility of zero to A and 100 to B. It is easily seen, however, that this leads to contradiction. Imagine that 1 and 2 form a two-person society and that their preference for four possible social states is as follows:

1 B pref D pref C pref A
2 D pref B indiff C pref A

Where 'pref' and 'indiff' stand for strongly preferred and indifferent. This suggests two ways of scaling the individual utilities since both people prefer B to A and D to C. Scale S will use the first pair and scale S^1 the second, in the manner proposed by Vickrey. Suppose that the utilities of 1 and 2, as measured by, say, a Von Neumann–Morgenstern scale are as follows; then the scaled utilities are as shown in Table 4.1.

Table 4.1 *Utility Scaling*

		Unscaled utility	Scale S	Scale S^1
1	A	40	0	−100
	B	80	100	300
	C	50	25	0
	D	60	50	100
2	A	10	0	−100
	B	20	100	0
	C	20	100	0
	D	30	200	100

If we now aggregate utility in the way proposed by Harsanyi, scale S tells us to select social state D, with an aggregate utility of 250, whilst scale S^1 tells us to choose B, with an aggregate utility of 300. The scaling proposed by Vickrey will, therefore, be disastrously affected by the choice of calibration points. Indeed, any way of scaling will suffer from the same defect.[7] The problem might disappear if some other way of measuring utility were used, but none of these seem to hold out any promise.[8]

(iii) The third problem facing Harsanyi is the demands his method of measuring social welfare makes on factual information. Harsanyi seems to think that his account can be used for relatively small problems and not just those affecting the structure of the society, such as tax rates, rates of saving and so on (this will be seen to be important later when we discuss Rawls). But this is to overlook the vast amount of information his method requires. First of all, representatives of each social position must be chosen and their utilities measured. But this only gives their present utilities. Any estimation of social welfare must obviously take into account the future levels of utility likely to be enjoyed by the society's members, and so this must be estimated in addition. Some way of comparing present and future utilities, such as a discount rate, must also presumably be used. In the light of these problems it seems a little rash to suggest that the method might be used in real world decision taking.

[7] See Pattanaik (1968) and (1971, chapter 9), Arrow (1963, pp, 31–3) and Sen (1969). It might appear from this that interpersonal utility comparisons are impossible, but this might be too sweeping. Sen (1970c, 1972, 1970a, chapters 7 and 7*) suggests that comparison is a matter of degree.
[8] These are based on just discernable differences in utility. See Armstrong (1951); Fleming (1952); Kemp and Asimakopulos (1952); Goodman and Markowitz (1952); Ng (1975) and Rothenberg (1953) and (1954). Objections to these measures are well known see Arrow (1963, pp. 115–18), Pattanaik (1971, chapter 9), and Sen (1970 a, pp. 92–4).

Harsanyi does, however, suggest a remedy when the above information is not available. He tells us to treat social welfare as a weighted sum of individual utilities, the weights being arbitrary and the utilities being our best guesses. This is, however, a counsel of despair, for there is no reason at all to suppose that decisions made in this way will lead to genuine improvements in social welfare, any more than decisions made in a completely intuitive way.

Problems of information become pressing when one tries to apply Harsanyi's utilitarianism to the problem of setting an optimal tax rate. Here the theory is under two opposing influences. Decreasing marginal returns on consumption imply that a shift of consumption from the wealthy to the poor will increase total welfare, but the loss of incentives for the rich to produce results in a decline of total consumption. There is, therefore, a tension between justice and efficiency, a tension which has been known for many years.[9] Harsanyi tells us nothing about the resolution of this tension, and this is due to ignorance about the effects of incentives on total production and the sharpness of the decline in marginal utility. Without a great deal of additional knowledge, Harsanyi's theory is impotent here.

(iv) Several commentators have criticized Harsanyi in the grounds that the estimation of social welfare he proposes reflects the attitude to risk of the original chooser (Arrow, 1963, p. 10; Pattanaik, 1968; Rawls, 1972, sections 27–8; Sen, 1970a, chapters 7 and 7*). If the chooser likes taking risks, then he will give greater weight to those individuals with high utility than those with low, and vice versa if he is averse to taking risks. In each case his estimate of social welfare will be different, and the difference may be sufficiently large to alter his choice of social state. Harsanyi assumes that his chooser is risk neutral, so that he weights all utilities equally. In reply, Harsanyi has argued that attitudes to risk are a perfectly proper component of social welfare, any social welfare function reflecting the balance between acquiring high utility and the risk of ending up with a low level of satisfaction.[10] But despite Harsanyi's defence, the influence of attitudes to risk is enough to demolish his version of utilitarianism. This occurs in two ways. First, Harsanyi supposes that his chooser's estimate of social welfare is objective because anyone in the same position of ignorance would make the same estimate. Everyone will, therefore, agree on the ranking of social states and the final choice of one of them. But this will only be the case if everyone shares the same attitude to risk. This, of course, is a quite unrealistic hope and, in general, different people have markedly different attitudes to risk. If this is so, then as indicated above, there will be no unanimity about estimates of social welfare or the ranking of social states, or even the selection of the best social state — this is recognised by Pattanaik

---

[9] At least since Sidgwick (1893). The first utilitarian treatment of taxation is in Edgeworth (1897).

[10] Arrow changes his mind in his later work (Arrow, 1973). See also Harsanyi (1975) and Vickrey (1945).

(1971, chapter 1). There may be as many different opinions about what society to choose as there are individuals in the society, and so Harsanyi has the unenviable task of aggregating these opinions in a rational way.

The standard view of attitudes to risk is that they are a subjective, personal quirk of the individual decision maker, and are, therefore, not open to criticism. If a decision maker likes taking risks, nobody can argue that he is wrong, nor can his decisions be defended by anything but his own personal tastes for risk taking. This means that anyone's estimation of social welfare using Harsanyi's method, depending as it does on his particular attitudes to risk, will be arbitrary. Harsanyi, therefore, fails to provide a rational, objective way in which individual utilities may be weighted to arrive at social welfare. A somewhat desperate escape has been suggested by Mueller (Mueller, 1973; Mueller *et al.*, 1974; see also Vickrey, 1960). It is claimed that an objective observer should not employ his own attitude to risk in making a choice of society, but should assume that he has an equal probability of having the risk attitude of each person within the society. Just as the veil of ignorance hides what utility the observer will have, it hides what attitude to risk he will have. Unfortunately, Mueller later realised that deciding in this way not only calls for a quite unrealistic quantity of information, as attitudes to risk need to be determined as well as utility levels, but also generates an infinite regress (Mueller, 1979).

(v) The fifth objection to Harsanyi is, in many ways, the most fundamental. The central problem for Harsanyi is why it is that an agent should act in accordance with social values even where this means going against his own selfish desires and interests. Since the agent is motivated only by his own selfish interests, social values must be seen as in some way serving these interests. Thus, when contemplating a number of societies in a state of ignorance about his own social position, Harsanyi argues that it is in the *selfish interest of the agent* to value each society as the arithmetic mean of the utility enjoyed by each member of the society. In choosing the best society, valued in this way, the agent maximizes his own expected utility. In this way, social values can be seen as based upon selfish ones, and so the binding, or motivating, nature of social values may be explained. Agreement about social values is also explained in this way.

To base social values upon selfish ones is, however, ultimately self-defeating. Imagine the same agent as before, facing the same choice, but now endowed with full knowledge of his own place in each society. If he is motivated only by his own selfish interests, his evaluation of the societies before him will be very different, and he will obviously favour those where he is lucky enough to receive a high personal utility. What reason can the agent have for thwarting his private interests by retaining the evaluations made when he was ignorant of his position within the societies? Once it is admitted that private interests alone motivate, no answer can be given to this question. It in no way serves these interests to stick to the evaluations made under ignorance.

A possible answer to this line of criticism exploits the idea of fairness. It might be held that, just as ignorance about what slice ends up in what mouth ensures a fair division of the cake, ignorance about one's place within society ensures its fair appraisal. The value placed on a society is then not dependent upon the urge to exploit one's own special talents to further selfish ends. But this really gives us no answer to the problem. If this is what a fair appraisal of a set of societies amounts to, why should an agent who knows his position in the societies retain the fair appraisal? What selfish interest can possibly motivate such conservatism? If a veil of ignorance conceals from me which slice of cake I will receive, it is in my selfish interests to cut the cake in equal slices. But if I do know that I will be able to choose my own portion it serves my private interests to slice the cake very differently; I may not cut it at all but devour the whole confection myself. What reason is there for persisting in cutting the cake into equal slices when the veil of ignorance is lifted? If the term 'fair' is appended to this division, the question remains unanswered, for what reason have I for favouring the fair allocation of cake now that the ignorance that made this in my selfish interest has been lifted?

Harsanyi's attempt to explain the binding nature of social values therefore fails. As we shall see in chapter 9, the failure is one which is well known to students of philosophical ethics. Harsanyi's theory is an objectivist one – it seeks to find objective reasons for the holding of social values, reasons which transcend the agent's selfish, private motivations and interests. This he finds in the evaluation of societies under a veil of ignorance, where agents with all kinds of private values can come to agreement on a set of objective social values. The great difficulty for all objectivist accounts of value is to forge a link between the objective values which they postulate and human action. The problem is to see how objective values, which transcend the agent's subjective interests, can possibly guide the agent's actions, all of which are expressions of these private interests. Without this, the authority that these objective values must have over the agent's behaviour cannot be explained. In Harsanyi's case, the reason for valuing societies by the average utility enjoyed by their members is that this is in everyone's selfish, private interests when a society has to be chosen under a veil of ignorance. Granted the cogency of his argument, Harsanyi undoubtedly explains the link between the objective evaluation of societies and the private interests of those making the evaluation, but only as long as the veil of ignorance hides from them knowledge which some of them could exploit to obtain a better social position. When the veil is lifted, it no longer serves their private interests to value societies by the average utility rule, and Harsanyi can given no reason why they should not pursue their private interests by valuing societies quite differently.

Social Contract Theory

There has always been a deep rivalry between utilitarianism and social contract theories according to which social welfare is founded in some original contract between society's members — for an historical survey see Gough (1957) and Gierke (1934). If utilitarianism fails to show how the justificationist model of decision making can be developed to explain social decisions by representing the choice of society as a veiled decision under risk, it is therefore natural to ask if social contract theories might have more success. Rawls has presented a modern version of a social contract theory which clearly exploits the justificationist model to explain social values and social decision making. Like Harsanyi, Rawls exploits the idea of a choice of society behind a veil of ignorance, but where Harsanyi considered one person making such a choice, Rawls thinks of a group of agents who must agree among themselves on what society to adopt (Rawls, 1972). The function of the assumption is, however, exactly the same in both cases. Social arrangements are unfair because people can exploit inequalities in the society, so that a hypothetical fair society can be constructed by hiding such inequalities behind an imagined veil. In any society principles of social justice are required to determine the division of wealth and position, and so to resolve the unavoidable conflicts of interest that arise under this head. Rawls, therefore, tries to imagine what principles of social justice would be agreed upon by a group unable to exploit personal inequalities because these are hidden behind the veil of ignorance. Such principles will lay down a fair structure for society, covering its major institutions and the distribution of rights and duties which they govern.

In Rawls' 'original position' a group of rational, and mutually disinterested agents must choose principles of social justice to govern a society in which they will live, although they are all in ignorance of the place they will finally occupy in the society, and of their own natural assets, abilities and disabilities, and those of their fellows. Rawls argues that they will choose two principles of social justice. The first of these is relatively straightforward, and states that each person has an equal right to basic liberties compatible with the same right to others. The second principle requires the concept of primary social goods. There are some things which a person needs in order to satisfy whatever wants he may have, and these are primary social goods; the powers and prerogatives of authority, income and wealth. In the original position, Rawls argues, it is rational to adopt the maximin principle to govern the distribution of primary social goods within the group. This leads directly to the second principle of social justice (the difference or maximin principle); social and economic inequalities are to be arranged so that they are both:

(a) to the greatest benefit of the least advantaged; and
(b) attached to offices and positions open to all under conditions of fair equality of opportunity.

Assuming that the first principle of social justice and part (b) of the second principle is met, Rawls tells us that social welfare increases when the least advantaged in the society is made better off, whatever happens to those enjoying a greater advantage. In measuring changes in social welfare, therefore, provided that the above conditions are satisfied, the utility of everyone except the least advantaged is to be weighted zero. The actual weight given to the utility of the least advantaged individual is, of course, of no significance, merely affecting the scale by which social welfare is judged. This is in marked contrast to Harsanyi's utilitarian principle according to which all are to be weighted equally.[11]

Harsanyi's theory was criticized earlier under five heads and we may now ask whether or not Rawls' falls to the same comments. Whereas Harsanyi requires to know the utility of all the individuals in each social state before deciding which state is best, Rawls needs only to know to what extent the lot of the least advantaged has been changed. This requires no interpersonal comparisons of utility, and the utility of the least advantaged individual may be measured purely ordinally. Thus Rawls escapes the first two criticisms which were made of Harsanyi's account.[12] The remaining criticisms are, however, just as pressing as before.

We saw that Harsanyi seems to think, mistakenly, that his account is applicable to relatively micro-problems of social choice. Rawls, on the other hand, denies this and sees his theory as providing a rational structure for society in which micro-problems may be resolved. But even this modest claim is to be seriously doubted. Taxation is part of society's structure, according to Rawls, but despite a few starts, no suggestion about types and rates of tax derivable from Rawls' theory comes anywhere near being practically applicable (Rawls, 1972, pp. 277-84; see also Itsumi, 1974; Phelps, 1973). Like Harsanyi, Rawls seems to offer an account of social decision making, which for all its theoretical niceties and subtleties, is impotent in the fact of the complexities of the real world.

The second criticism of Rawls is theoretical and concerns attitude to risk. Someone who employs a maximin criterion in making a decision under risk is taking the least possible risk. Whatever the potential gains, they will choose so as to maximize the benefit received from the worst outcome of each option. In discussing Harsanyi, it was observed that the attitude to risk of the chooser will influence the weighting of individual utilities in the summation which produces social welfare. If he is prepared to take risks he will favour a society where some enjoy a utility higher than others, and so he will weight the utility of such an advantaged person more than that of someone not so advantaged.

[11] The literature on Rawls' theory is now very large and cannot be reviewed here. Of particular interest, however, is the debate between Rawls and Harsanyi in Rawls (1972, pp 25-34. 90-2 and 150-75; 1974) and Harsanyi (1975a, 1975b). Sen's weak equity axiom in his (1973), 18-23, may provide a sort of half way house.
[12] Though things may not be quite so simple — see Arrow (1973), Harsanyi (1975b) and Klevovrick (1974).

If, on the other hand, he is averse to risk taking, he will seek to protect himself by adjusting the weights of individual utilities in the opposite direction. We can now see a greater similarity between Harsanyi and Rawls than at first appears. As we have seen, Harsanyi assumes his single chooser to be neutral towards risk, so that the utility of all is weighted equally; but Rawls assumes each of his choosers to be infinitely averse to risk, so that they will employ the maximin principle for the distribution of primary social goods.[13]

This point was used to attack Harsanyi's suggestion, and the same criticism applies to Rawls. Rawls' individuals in the original position must come to an agreement about what principles of social justice to employ, but agreement is only possible if all of the individuals are infinitely averse to risk and so willing to employ maximin in their choice. Thus, Rawls requires unanimity in attitude to risk just as much as Harsanyi. If some of Rawls' original choosers are not infinitely risk averse, but are willing to take a gamble on getting a larger share of unequally distributed primary social goods, then there can be no agreement about principles of social justice. Moreover, on standard accounts of decision making, attitude to risk is a matter of subjective taste, and there can be no rational argument capable of showing that someone's attitude is wrong. If attitudes to risk in Rawls' original position vary, therefore, this is a conflict for which there is no rational solution, and so no rational principles of justice can emerge. Both Harsanyi and Rawls attempt to overcome this problem by elevating some chosen risk attitude — neutrality and infinite aversion respectively — but this will not do. Different attitudes to risk are possible and cannot, at least on traditional accounts of decision making, be stigmatized irrational or unreasonable. We might even imagine a group of choosers in the original position who are infinitely risk seeking so that they employ the maximax rule, the value of a society being determined solely by the utility of the best off member.

Unless Rawls can offer cogent reasons for the adoption of the maximin rule in deciding the distribution of primary social goods, his account would seem to founder, so let us look at what he has to say. Rawls offers three reasons:

the situation is one in which a knowledge of likelihoods is impossible, or at best extremely insecure. In this case it is unreasonable not to be skeptical of probabilistic calculations unless there is no other way out, particularly if the decision is a fundamental one that needs to be justified to others.
The second feature that suggests the maximin rule is the following: the person choosing has a conception of the good such that he cares very little, if anything, for what he might gain above the minimum stipend that he can, in fact, be sure of by following the maximin rule. It is not worthwhile for him to take a chance for the sake of a further advantage, especially when it may turn out that he loses much that is important to him. This last provision brings in the third feature, namely, that the rejected alternatives have outcomes that one can hardly accept. The situation involves grave risks (Rawls, 1972, pp. 154-5)

[13] For a very neat formalization of this point see Arrow (1973). The close proximity of the two views is also revealed by their reformulation in terms of grading principles. See Suppes (1966) and Sen (1970a, pp. 146-51) and chapter 9*).

This will hardly do. Ignorance of probabilities in no way entails that the maximin rule should be employed, any more than maximax. Neither rule requires estimates of probability, so either may be used for decisions where these cannot be given, as may a number of other rules. But this is not to say that ignorance of probabilities requires the use of any one of these rules. The second reason seems merely to assume what is to be shown. Assuming that the chooser 'cares very little, if anything, for what he might gain above the minimum stipend that he can be sure of by following the maximin rule' obviously gives the desired conclusion, for why risk losing the minimum stipend for such slight gain, but the magnitude of the assumption is just a little too great for palatability. The choosers in the original position might be imagined with radically different attitudes to additional primary social goods, in which case maximin would be quite inappropriate. Rawls has simply cooked the books to favour the decision rule his theoretical apparatus requires. Matters do not improve when Rawls' third reason is considered. This seems to collapse into the second reason because what consequences of adopting a given decision rule are or are not acceptable is to be judged by the rule's users and so will depend upon their attitudes to risk. The existence of 'grave risks' may frighten some into using the maximin rule, but bolder spirits may pay more attention to the great benefits that come from the possession of a privileged social position. Thus Rawls fails to give an adequate defence of the maximin rule and the principle of social justice that follows from its use – see Arrow (1973); Hare (1973); Nagel (1973); Mueller *et al.* (1974); Harsanyi (1975*a*) and Sen (1970*a*, pp. 135–41).

Having seen how the rival views of Rawls and Harsanyi stem from a very similar approach, it should be no surprise that the fifth criticism against Harsanyi also counts against Rawls' version of the social contract. Rawls tries to base social values upon selfish ones in essentially the same way as Harsanyi. He seems to accept that only selfish values can motivate, so that the problem is to find some way of showing how the adoption of some social values serve an agent's selfish ends. This is, as before achieved by a veil of ignorance. Having no knowledge about his own and his fellow's abilities and disabilities, it is in the *selfish interests* of any agent to secure himself against misfortune by adopting the maximin principle, according to which a society is valued by the utility enjoyed by its worst-off member. The agent might find himself to be in this unhappy position, and so it is wise to favour societies where even the worst off enjoys a relatively high utility. Since any agent should protect his own interests in this way, agreement about social values is also explained. But what is to prevent an agent's evaluation of a society altering as he acquires knowledge about his own place in the society, and those of his fellows? If he finds himself in a privileged position, it will serve his selfish interests to maintain his position by valuing the society more than he might have done under the veil of ignorance. On the other hand, if he is in a poor position, his selfish desires will lead him to value the society as worse than he might have done before knowledge of his social position was granted him. If selfish interests alone can motivate, why should the agent maintain the valuations which he made under the veil of ignorance? What can motivate him to this? Again, it will not serve to say that the evaluations made under the veil are fair, because this merely leads to a restatement of the question. If this is what fairness is, then we can ask what selfish interests of the agent are served by retaining evaluations which are fair, rather than adopting new, unfair, ones.

In conclusion, it can be said that the same fundamental pair of problems beset Harsanyi's and Rawls' account of the origin of social values, and, perhaps, beset any version of utilitarianism and social contract theory. In both, a special set of circumstances is described, and it is shown, given these circumstances, that certain social values are in the selfish interests of every agent. In this way it is hoped to explain how there can be a consensus over social values, despite differences in selfish values, and why social values are binding. The explanation of consensus fails, however, when it is realised that different attitudes to risk are possible and that argument over such attitudes is impossible, at least on conventional accounts of decision making. The explanation of the authority of social values fails when the very special circumstances described are replaced with more realistic ones. It can then be seen that although selfish interests might lead to the acceptance of one set of social values in the special circumstances, quite different social values would serve these interests in more ordinary circumstances.

Arrow's Theorem

Throughout this chapter we have discussed the problems that beset attempts to base social values upon the values held by the individuals who make up the society. The transition from private to public values calls for some value judgements, and the traditional aim has been to find some set of such judgements which are weak enough to be acceptable by everybody. Hence, of course, Pareto, Harsanyi and Rawls. The possibility of finding a set of value judgements that are sufficiently strong to allow the transition from private to public values, sufficiently weak to be generally acceptable, and consistent has been investigated by Arrow (1963). He makes the following assumptions about a group of individuals:

(a) No interpersonal comparison of utility is possible.
(b) No individual receives enjoyment from the decision process *per se*.
(c) There is no strategic misrepresentation of individual values.
(d) The method of social choice does not influence individual values.
(e) All individuals are rational.
(f) All individuals have a complete knowledge of all possible social states.
(g) Each individual can order these social states rationally.

By the term 'rational' used in assumptions (e) and (g), above Arrow means that an individual's preference judgements about social states x, y etc. are logically consistent, in accordance with the following axioms, where R is the relation 'prefered or indifferent':

Axiom A

For all x and y, either xRy or yRx (connectivity)

(It follows that for all x, xRx (reflexivity))

Axiom B

For all x, y and z, xRy and yRz imply xRz (transitivity)

If these axioms are met, all individuals will be able to place all possible social states in order of preference. Arrow then defines a social welfare function as follows:

A social welfare function is a rule which, for every set of individual orderings of social states (one for each individual), states a corresponding social ordering of social states.

Arrow then considers what value judgements are likely to govern the choice of a social welfare function. He suggests a number of perfectly reasonable necessary conditions and then shows that they are inconsistent, and cannot be met together. Any attempt to derive a social order of social states from the orderings of social states made by individuals therefore breaks at least one of the conditions, despite their weakness and intuitive appeal. Many forms of the argument exist; that given here follows the rather neat version of Mueller (1979, pp. 185-8).

Axiom 1
Unanimity (the Pareto postulate). If an individual preference is unopposed by any contrary preference of any other individual, this preference is preserved in the social ordering.

Axiom 2
Non-dictatorship. No individual enjoys a position such that whenever he expresses a preference between any two alternatives and all other individuals express the opposite preference, his preference is always preserved in the social ordering.

Axiom 3
Transitivity. The social welfare function gives a consistent ordering of all feasible alternatives. That is, $(aPbPc) \rightarrow (aPC)$ and $(aIbIc) \rightarrow (aIc)$.[14]

[14] P denotes 'strongly preferred' and I 'indifferent'.

Axiom 4
Range (unrestricted domain). There is some 'universal' alternative u such that for every pair of other alternatives x and y and for every individual, each of the six possible strict orderings of u, x and y is contained in some admissible ranking of all alternatives for the individual.

Axiom 5
Independence of irrelevant alternatives. The social choice between any two alternatives must depend on the orderings of individuals over only these two alternatives, and not on their orderings over other alternatives.

Axiom 4 perhaps requires an additional word of explanation. The notion of a universal alternative is not crucial here. What is implied by the range axiom is that the social choice process presumes that any ordering of the three alternatives x, y and u is possible. The process is not established in such a way as to rule out possible orderings.

The theorem states that no social welfare function satisfies these five postulates. To understand the significance of the theorem it is useful to run through the proof. We first define a decisive set D.

Definition of decisive set
A set of individuals D is decisive, for alternatives x and y in a given social welfare function, if the function yields a social preference for x over y, whenever all individuals in D prefer x to y and all others prefer y to x.

Proof

Step		Justification
1	Let D be a set of individuals decisive for x and y	Assumption
2	Assume for all members of D $xPyPu$, and for all others (those in C) $yPuPx$	Range
3	For society xPy	Definition of D
4	For society yPu	Unanimity
5	For society xPu	Transitivity
6	But for only members of D is xPu	Assumption
7	Society must prefer x to u regardless of changes in rankings of y or any other alternatives	Independence
8	D is decisive for x and u	Definition
9	D is decisive for all pairs of alternatives	Repetition of steps 2–8
10	D must contain two or more persons	Non-dictatorship

Proof *cont.*

Step		Justification
11	Divide D into two non-empty sub-sets A and B	Assumption
12	Assume: for A $xPyPu$: for B $yPuPx$; for C $uPxPy$	Range
13	Since for all members of A and B, yPu, for society yPu	Definition of D
14	If for society yPx, B is decisive for y and x	Definition of D
15	If for society xPy, then for society xPu	Transitivity
16	But then A is decisive for x and u	Definition of D

In either case one of the proper sub-sets of D is decisive for a pair of issues, and therefore by step 9 for all issues. Steps 10–16 can be repeated for this new decisive set, and then continued until the decisive set contains but one member, thus contradicting the non-dictatorship postulate.

The force of the proof is that any transition from a set of individual rankings of social states to a social order of these states must be in breach of at least one of the five conditions. The problem, however, is that each condition seems perfectly reasonable and innocuous by itself, so that all five of them make a very weak set of postulates. It is very hard to see how the transition from individual to social ordering can be made if one of the conditions is not met. It would seem to follow that the liberal ideal of making social choices that reflect the preferences of society's members is an impossibility. Needless to say, Arrow's result is very disturbing and has generated a whole cottage industry directed towards a remedy. The literature is now immense, and cannot possibly be reviewed here, except to note that after a quarter of a century of effort no acceptable solution has been found – for reviews see Sen (1970*a*, 1977), Pattanaik (1971), Fishburn (1973) and Mueller (1979, chapter 10).

Conclusion

The chapter has surveyed the main attempts that have been made, within the justificationist model of decision making, to show how the social values that are required for social decision making can be based upon the preferences that individuals within the society have. The enterprise has more nobility than achievement. At every turn problems are encountered, and if this is true of any intellectual pursuit, what impresses here is the profundity of the problems which arise. It is not that there is inadequate data to compute changes in gross consumption, or some technical issue about how much knowledge is allowed in the original position, or that measurement of interpersonal utilities has yet to be perfected, or that methods of constructing social welfare functions are still a little primitive, all of which could be allowed; rather it is that every attempt to found social values upon individual values in conformity with the justificationist model of decision making is rotten at its very core. The problems encountered are not peripheral, technical, formal niceties, but each time concern the fundamentals of the attempt which is being made.

Surveying the depressing landscape at the end of a recent review Mueller strikes a note of desperate optimism when he tells us that all these difficulties:

should be neither surprising nor particularly discouraging. Indeed, it is precisely because it deals with some of the oldest and toughest questions a community faces, that public choice attracts so many fine scholars. And for this reason, one can remain optimistic about the field's future growth and development. (Mueller, 1979, p. 270)

When does optimism become pig-headedness? If one asks how to get to a realistic and robust theory of social values from the position briefly considered in this chapter, the only answer is the one from the Irish philosopher, 'If I were you I wouldn't start here'.

References

Armstrong, W. (1951) 'Utility and the theory of welfare', *Oxford Economic Papers*, 3, 259–71.
Arrow, K. (1963) *Social Choice and Individual Values*, New York, John Wiley (2nd edn).
Arrow, K. (1973) 'Some ordinalist – utilitarian notes on Rawls', *Journal of Philosophy*, 70, 245–75.
Bentham, J. (1789) *The Principles of Morals and Legislation*.
Dobb, M. (1969) *Welfare Economics and The Economics of Socialism*, Cambridge University Press.
Edgeworth, F. (1888) *Mathematical Psychics*.
Edgeworth, F. (1897) 'The pure theory of taxation', *Economic Journal*, reprinted in *Papers Relating to Political Economy*, Vol. 2, London, Macmillan (1925), partially reprinted in Phelps, S. (ed.) (1973) *Economic Justice*, Harmondsworth, Penguin.
Ellsberg, D. (1954) 'Classical and current notions of measurable utility', *Economic Journal*, 64, 528–56.
Fine, B. (1978) 'Individual liberalism in a Paretian Society', *Journal of Political Economy*, 86.
Fishburn, P. (1973) *The Theory of Social Choice*, Cambridge, Mass., Princeton University Press.
Fleming, M. (1952) 'A cardinal concept of welfare', *Quarterly Journal of Economics*, 66, reprinted in Phelps, S. (ed.) (1973) *Economic Justice*, Harmondsworth Pengiuin, pp. 245–65.
Gierke, O. (1934) *Natural Law and the Theory of Society*, Cambridge University Press.
Goodman, L. and Markowitz, M. (1952) 'Social welfare functions based on individual rankings', *American Journal of Sociology*, 58, 257–62.
Gough, J. (1957) *The Social Contract*, Oxford University Press, (2nd edn.).

Hare, R. (1973) 'Rawls' theory of Justice', *Philosophical Quarterly*, 23, 144–55; reprinted in Daniels, N. (ed.) (1974) *Reading Rawls*, New York, Basic Books, pp. 81–107.
Harsanyi, J. (1953) 'Cardinal utility in welfare economics and in the theory of risk taking', *Journal of Political Economy*, 61, 434–5.
Harsanyi, J. (1955) 'Cardinal welfare, individualistic ethics and interpersonal comparison of utility', *Journal of Political Economy*, 63, reprinted in Phelps, S. (ed.) (1973) *Economic Justice*, Harmondsworth, Penguin, pp. 266–85.
Harsanyi, J. (1975a) 'Non-linear social welfare functions', *Theory and Decision*, 6, 311–30.
Harsanyi, J. (1975b) 'Critique of Rawls' theory of justice', *American Political Science Review*, 69, 594–606.
Hicks, J. (1939) 'The foundations of welfare economics', *Economic Journal*, 49, 696–712.
Hildreth, C. (1953) 'Alternative conditions for social orderings', *Econometrica*, 21, 81–94.
Itsumi, Y. (1974) 'Distributional effects of income tax schedules', *Review of Economic Studies*, 41, 371–81.
Kaldor, N. (1939) 'Welfare propositions and interpersonal comparisons of utility', *Economic Journal*, 49, 549–52, reprinted in 1960 in *Essays in Value and Distribution*, pp. 143–46, London, Duckworth.
Kemp, M. and Asimakopulos, A. (1952) 'Social welfare functions and cardinal utility, *Canadian Journal of Economics and Political Science*, 18, 195–200.
Klevorick, A. (1974) 'Discussion', *American Economic Review*, 64, 158–61.
Leibenstein, H. (1965) 'Long run welfare criteria', in Margolis, J. (ed.) *Public Economy of Urban Communities, Proceedings of the 2nd Conference on Urban Public Expenditure*, Resources for the Future.
Lerner, A. (1944) *The Economics of Control*, London, Macmillan.
Little, I. (1957) *Critique of Welfare Economics*, Oxford University Press (2nd edn).
Lyons, D. (1965) *Forms and Limits of Utilitarianism*, Oxford University Press.
Mill, J. S. (1863) *Utilitarianism*.
Mueller, D. (1973) 'Constitutional democracy and social welfare', *Quarterly Journal of Economics*, 87, 60–80.
Mueller, D. et al. (1974) 'The utilitarian contract', *Theory and Decision*, 4, 345–67.
Mueller, D. (1979) *Public Choice*, Cambridge University Press.
Nagel. T. (1973) 'Rawls on justice', *Philosophical Review*, 82, 220–34, reprinted Daniels, N. (ed.) (1974) *Reading Rawls*, New York, Basic Books, pp. 1–15.
Nath, S. (1973) *A Perspective on Welfare Economics*, Basingstoke, Macmillan.
Ng, Y. (1975) 'Bentham or Bergson? Finite sensibility, utility functions and social welfare functions', *Review of Economic Studies*, 42, 545–69.
Pareto, V. (1909), *Manuel d'économie politique*, Paris. For selected translation see Page, A. *Utility Theory: A Book of Readings*, New York, Wiley (1968), pp. 38 ff.
Pattanaik, P. (1968) 'Risk, impersonality and the social welfare function', *Journal of Political Economy*, 76, reprinted Phelps, S. (ed.) (1973) *Economic Justice*, Harmondsworth, Penguin, pp. 298–318.
Pattanaik, P. (1971) *Voting and Collective Choice*, Cambridge University Press.
Phelps, S. (1973) 'Taxation of wage income for economic justice', *Quarterly Journal of Economics*, 87, 1973; reprinted in Phelps, S. (ed.) (1973) *Economic Justice*, Harmondsworth, Penguin, pp. 417–38.

Rawls, J. (1972) *A Theory of Justice*, Oxford University Press.
Rawls, J. (1974) 'Some reasons for the maximin criterion', *American Economic Review*, **64**, (Papers and Proceedings), 141–6.
Rothenberg, J. (1953) 'Marginal preference and the theory of welfare', *Oxford Economic Papers*, **5**, 248–63.
Rothenberg, J. (1954) 'Reconsideration of a group welfare index', *Oxford Economic Papers*, **6**, 164–80.
Samuelson, P. (1950) 'The evaluation of real national income', *Oxford Economic Papers*, **2**, 1–29, reprinted in Phelps, S. (ed.) (1973) *Economic Justice*, Harmondsworth, Penguin, pp. 65–91.
Samuelson, P. (1964) 'A. P. Learner at 60', *Review of Economic Studies*, **31**.
Scitovsky, T. (1941) 'A note on welfare propositions in economics', *Review of Economic Studies*, **9**, 77–88.
Sen, A. (1969) 'Planner's preferences; Optimality, distribution and social welfare', in Margolis, J. and Guitton, H. (eds), *Public Economics*, London, St. Martins Press.
Sen, A. (1970a) *Collective Choice and Social Welfare*, New York, Holden Day.
Sen, A. (1970b) 'The impossibility of a Paretian liberal', *Journal of Political Economy*, **78**, 152–7.
Sen, A. (1970c) 'Interpersonal aggregation and partial comparability', *Econometrica*, **38**, 393–409.
Sen, A. (1973) *On Economic Inequality*, Oxford University Press.
Sen, A. (1972) 'Correction', *Econometrica*, **40**, 959.
Sen, A. (1977) 'Social choice theory: A re-examination', *Econometrica*, **45**, 53–89.
Shaftesbury (1711) *An Inquiry Concerning Virtue and Merit*.
Sidgwick, H. (1893) *The Method of Ethics*, London, Macmillan.
Sidgwick, H. (1902) *Outlines of the History of Ethics*, London (5th edn.).
Smart, J. (1961) *An Outline of a System of Utilitarian Ethics*, Cambridge University Press.
Suppes, P. (1966) 'Some formal models of grading principles', *Synthese*, **6**, 149–58.
Vickrey, W. (1945) 'Measuring marginal utility by reactions to risk', *Econometrica*, **13**, 319–33.
Vickrey, W. (1960) 'Utility, strategy and social decision rules', *Quarterly Journal of Economics*, **74**, 507–35.

PART II

THE CRITICAL MODEL

5 The Critical Turn — Popper's View of Science

So far we have arrived at the sceptical conclusion that no preference judgement can be justified. This is a disturbing result for it seems to indicate that any judgement of preference is as good as any other, and that reason can have no part to play in evaluation. This is, however, a mistaken conclusion as I hope to show in this part of the work. What I hope to show is that there is a way between the impossible optimism of justificationist accounts of preference and the darkness of total scepticism, which relies upon the possibility of subjecting the preference judgements we make to criticism. I hope to develop a theory of preference that admits the first sceptical claim below, but denies the second:

1. No preference claim can be justified.
2. No reason can be given for favouring one preference claim over another.

In developing such an account of preference, reference to the theory of scientific inquiry proposed by Karl Popper will be very rewarding, for the problem which Popper addresses bears a close analogy to our present problem. Popper is convinced that traditional views about the certainty of observation statements are wrong and that induction cannot be shown to be a legitimate form of argument. It follows from this that no scientific claim can be justified. Popper does not, however, surrender to complete scepticism about the external world. Instead, he develops a theory of science which admits the first, but denies the second sceptical claim below:

1. No scientific claim can be justified.
2. No reasons can be given for preferring one scientific claim to another.

Popper's view is that scientific claims may be tested and compared by being submitted to criticism, or, in other words, by being exposed to falsification and rejection. The theory of preference to be proposed in chapter 6 will follow him in this; maintaining that preference judgements, although impossible to justify, may be assessed by exposure to criticism. The present chapter lays the foundation for chapter 6 by considering Popper's theory of science. What is offered is not, however, a bland description of Popper's views, but an account that highlights those features of his views that are particularly relevant to the development of an analogous theory of value. For this reason, deep and detailed discussion has generally been avoided, as have comments on Popper's numerous critics.

The Rationality of Popper's Methodology

Popper proposes a methodology for the testing and assessment of scientific claims that provides substance to the basic idea that such claims may be tested by being subjected to falsification and rejection. Before discussing the details of his methodology, however, the first question is why this methodology is appropriate to the assessment of scientific claims. What reasons are there, in other words, for adopting the methodological rules proposed by Popper rather than some rival set of rules?

Popper's first reply to this question is that the methodological rules he proposes be regarded as comprising a definition of empirical science, so that 'they might be described as the rules of the game of empirical science' (Popper, 1959, section 11). The definition is not arbitrary, however:

It is only from the consequences of my definition of empirical science, and from the methodological decisions which depend upon this definition, that the scientist will be able to see how far it conforms to his intuitive idea of the goal of his endeavours.

The philosopher too will accept my definition as useful only if he can accept its consequences. We must staisfy him that these consequences enable us to detect inconsistencies and inadequacies in older theories of knowledge, and to trace these back to the fundamental assumptions and conventions from which they spring. But we must also satisfy him that our own proposals are not threatened by the same kind of difficulties. This method of detecting and resolving contradictions is applied also within science itself, but it is of particular importance in the theory of knowledge. It is by this method, if by any, that methodological conventions might be justified, and might prove their value.

The problem with Popper's original suggestion is that no link is forged between the proposed methodology and truth. The search for a scientific method is the search for ways of assessing our ideas about the world if we are interested in the truth, and any adequate methodology must connect with this interest in truth. Popper sought to frame his methodological proposals without reference to truth because at the time he regarded it and related concepts as thoroughly contaminated with bogus metaphysics. Tarski was, however, able to dispel Popper's suspicions about the propriety of these concepts with his semantic theory of truth (Popper, 1969, pp. 231-3). Having appreciated the need to link his methodology with truth, Popper attempted to do this through his notion of verisimilitude. The verisimilitude of a scientific theory is a measure of the difference between its truth content (the set of true sentences it entails) and falsity content (the set of false sentences it entails). Popper sees the aim of science as being the development of theories which get closer to the truth in the sense of having ever larger verisimilitude.

If T_2 has a greater logical and empirical content than T_1 (e.g., if T_2 entails T_1), then the truth content of T_2 is at least as great as the truth content of T_1. Hence, the verisimilitude of T_2 will be at least as great as that of T_1 unless the falsity content of T_2 is greater than the falsity content of T_1. The search for high verisimilitude, therefore, reduces to the investigation of T_2's falsity content (i.e., the search becomes an attempt to falsify T_2). This, Popper tells us, 'forms the logical basis of the method of science' (Popper, 1974).

There are two problems with this attempt to connect methodology and truth. The first is that the concept of verisimilitude is far more difficult to formalize than Popper originally suggested. Indeed, a whole cottage industry devoted to the concept's elucidation seems to have grown up and to be prospering.[1] Given the present state of confusion, it would seem unwise to base a whole methodology upon considerations of verisimilitude.

The second objection is even more fundamental. Even if the concept of verisimilitude is eventually clarified, the search for high verisimilitude cannot possibly constitute the 'logical basis of the method of science'. If science aims at high verisimilitude, then it may be appropriate to construct bold theories of high logical content and then attempt to falsify them in order to assess their falsity content, but what is to count as falsification? A theory may always be saved from falsification by employing one of a whole number of conventionalist stratagems (see below), or else the falsification may be taken as proper criticism of the theory. According to Popper, the latter is always needed. To assess a theory's falsity content, for Popper, involves searching for experimental evidence against the theory, and taking this, if found, as criticism of the theory, conventionalist stratagems being prohibited. Indeed, these prohibitions form the backbone of Popper's methodology. But why, in assessing a theory's falsity content should such stratagems be outlawed? (Popper, 1969, p. 246.) An answer is desperately called for, but simply appealing once again to the search for theories of high verisimilitude cannot settle the issue. Assessing verisimilitude involves probing a theory's falsity content, and for Popper, this requires the prohibition of conventionalist stratagems. Why conventionalist stratagems are prohibited cannot, therefore, be explained by the need to assess the verisimilitude of theories. Verisimilitude cannot, therefore, provide the connection between truth and methodology which Popper so urgently requires.

A third suggestion about the reasons for adopting Popper's rules of method is due to Lakatos. Like Popper, he is aware of the need to connect methodology and truth and so sees Popper's methodology as requiring the inductive principle that its application produces theories of ever-larger verisimilitude. Popper claims to explain why one theory should be preferred to another, but:

Preference is only a pragmatic concept within the context of this game [of science]. This preference can only assume epistemological significance with the help of an additional . . . , *inductive* . . . *principle* which would somehow assert the superiority of science over pseudoscience. Such an inductive principle must be based on some sort of correlation between 'degree of corroboration' and 'degree of verisimilitude'. (Lakatos, 1974, p. 257)

[1] For recent discussions see the various contributions to *Synthese*, 38 (1978).

Popper has, however, exposed the fatuousness of this suggestion (Popper, 1974, pp. 999–1011) and no words of mine are required.

Before considering a positive suggestion about the reasons for adopting Popper's methodology of science, a final suggestion must be considered. According to Popper, the central problem for rationalism, the thesis that problems can be solved by critical discussion, is that no arguments can be given for it. Before an argument can be taken seriously, a rationalist attitude must already have been adopted. The choice between rationalism and its antithesis – irrationalism – is, therefore, seen by Popper as a moral one (Popper, 1945, chapter 24). Although admitting that arguments cannot decide moral issues, Popper nevertheless thinks that the choice between rationalism and irrationalism can be helped by argument, and he therefore presents arguments pointing to the beneficial consequences of the former. Since Popper's methodology of science is part of an overall rationalist scheme, the decision to adopt it also appears as a moral issue. How scientific claims are to be assessed, in other words, will depend on what moral commitments are made.

Popper's case is not, however, acceptable. To give arguments in favour of rationalism, as he does, be they determining or merely persuasive, presupposes that a commitment to rationalism has already been made.[2] Rationalism, therefore, can only be based upon an ethical commitment in the way suggested by Popper at the cost of denying the possibility of *any* kind of reason for this commitment, and so for rationalism itself (see the discussion of ethical commitment in chapter 3). If Popper's methodology of science is seen as part of a rationalist scheme, then – since there can be no reason for adopting such a scheme – there can, in the final analysis, be no reasons for adopting Popper's methodology.

We may now turn to what I think is a happier way of connecting Popper's methodology with truth. In making this suggestion I am fully aware that Popper has not explicitly propounded it, nor has anyone else, and I have no wish to attribute implicit views to anyone. What I claim is that the following view connects Popper's methodology with truth in the way required, and that it fits naturally with the rest of Popper's thinking, whether or not he or anyone else would agree with the view. I wish to suggest that Popper's methodology may be derived from two claims, both of which are made by Popper, although he does not seem to have explicitly noted the connection. These are that scientific statements have a truth value in a perfectly straightforward way, and that no scientific statement can be justified. The first claim may seem trivial at first until the long history of views of science that deny it, such as instrumentalism, phenomenalism and conventionalism with their many variants, is remembered. Against such views, Popper is a realist:

... I am a realist in holding that the question whether our man-made theories are true or not depends upon the real facts; real facts which are, with very few

---

[2] For this reason Bartley has proposed his theory of comprehensively critical rationalism in his (Bartley, 1962).

exceptions, emphatically not man-made. Our man-made *theories* may clash with these real *facts*, and so, in our search for truth, we may have to adjust our theories or to give them up. (Popper, 1972, pp. 328-9.)

Popper also discussed this point in Popper (1969, pp. 114-19) and Popper (1972, pp. 317-29 and 38-45).

In support of his second claim, Popper has several arguments. All scientific claims must be theory laden because they must contain some universal term that cannot be correlated with any finite body of sensory data. The claim 'Here is a glass of water', for example, contains the universals 'glass' and 'water', both of which denote bodies which behave in certain law-like ways (Popper, 1959, section 25 and Appendix *v; see also Popper, 1969, pp. 118-19 and 387-8). In addition, any attempt to justify a particular scientific claim must lead to an endless proliferation of tests (Popper, 1969, pp. 21-4). Finally, any attempt to justify a scientific theory from observational reports founders on Hume's problem of induction (Popper, 1959, section 1 and Appendix *i; Popper, 1972, pp. 1-13 and 85-101).

If we are interested in the truth then we must attempt to resolve any contradition between statements which we wish to hold, for the contradiction means that not all of the statements are true. Scientific statements have a truth value and so, if we are interested in the truth, contradictions between scientific statements need to be resolved. If a set of scientific statements is contradictory then at least one of them must eventually be abandoned. Since none of the statements is justified there can be no reason for regarding any one of them as sacrosanct. Any one of the statements may be abandoned; all are open to rejection. This is Popper's 'supreme rules of methodology', which states that all other rules of methodology are to be designed to ensure that no scientific claim is immune from criticism and rejection. This simple consideration also generates his criterion of demarcation, which states that a statement is scientific only if it is possible to falsify it empirically (Popper, 1959, p. 54 and section 6). To put it another way: any scientific statement, having a truth value and being beyond justification, may be false. It follows that any such statement must be open to criticism and rejection, an openness to be ensured by Popper's rules of methodology. If we seek truth, then our scientific conjectures must be submitted to assessment by a methodology which ensures that all can receive criticism and that any may finally be rejected. In Popper's own words:

I saw that what has to be given up is the *quest for justification*. . . . All theories are hypotheses; all *may* be overthrown
On the other hand, I was very far from suggesting that we give up the search for truth: our critical discussions of theories are dominated by the idea of finding a true (and powerful) explanatory theory; and *we do justify our preferences by an appeal to the idea of truth*: truth plays the role of a regulative idea. (Popper, 1972, pp. 29-30.)

The connection between the methodology and truth is here extraordinarily simple, especially when compared with the complex nature of verisimilitude. If we are interested in the truth, contradictions between statements must be resolved, and since none of the statements is justified, it is possible to abandon any one of them. For all its simplicity I suggest that this provides an adequate basis for Popper's methodology. We may speak of the two claims that generate this methodology, that scientific statements have a truth value and that they cannot be justified, as constituting a metatheory. This simple metatheory is all that is required for Popper's methodology.

Test Sentences

According to Popper all claims within science are to be exposed to criticism and rejection. Principal among these claims are scientific theories, expressed in universal sentences. It is important, therefore, to find a type of sentence that can be used to falsify universal sentences. Popper calls such sentences 'basic statements', but I prefer the term '(scientific) test sentences'. These test sentences must be of the form 'there is such and such a thing at place p and time t'. There is a further condition that test sentences must fulfil. Since their function is to test scientific theories there must be some way in which the acceptance of test sentences can be agreed upon. Without such agreement (which may, however, only be provisional) science would resemble the tower of Babel. Observation provides a way of achieving agreement about test sentences, as almost universal agreement can often be reached by different observers, for example, about sentences like 'This pen now on my desk is yellow', 'The duck now on the bridge is quacking' and so on. We can say, therefore, that scientific test sentences must be of the above form and must refer to some observable state of affairs (Popper, 1959, sections 27-30; Popper, 1969, pp. 365-8). Science has, however, no interest in stray, unreproducible effects, so that a scientific test sentence should be accepted only if it describes a reproducible effect (Popper, 1959, pp. 86-8).

For Popper, test sentences are just as uncertain as the theories that they test. There must, therefore, be some way of testing test sentences by exposing them to criticism. This can be done in two ways. In the first, test sentences are tested in exactly the same way as theories are tested. If a test sentence falls into question, then deductive consequences may be drawn from it and these consequences exposed to falsification by accepted test sentences. Suppose, for example, a piece of litmus paper is seen in bad light, so that there is some doubt about the test sentence 'There is blue litmus paper at p, t'. The test sentence entails 'If the litmus paper is observed in daylight then it will appear blue'. This sentence, and hence the original test sentence, will be falsified if observation leads to the acceptance of the test sentence 'There is daylight at p, t and the litmus paper appears pink at p, t'.[3]

[3] Remembering that a conjunction of test sentences is a test sentence.

THE CRITICAL TURN – POPPER'S VIEW OF SCIENCE

The second way in which a test sentence is criticizable is through falsification of the theory it depends upon. Once it is agreed that all sentences are theory laden to some degree, we can accept a sentence such as 'There is a star at p, t' as a test sentence, because we have instruments for observing the heavens which lead to agreement about this sentence. Astronomers observing with their telescopes will generally reach agreement about a sentence such as 'There is a star at p, t', just as laymen, observing with their eyes, will reach agreement about 'There is a cat at p, t'. If, now, the theory of the telescope is falsified, then all grounds for accepting 'There is a star at p, t' may be destroyed (Lakatos, 1970, pp. 127–31).

Popper's views of the nature of observation must be distinguished from traditional justificationist views. These hold that some sentences referring to observation are justified by the observation, without need for evidential support from further sentences, so that they provide a foundation for all knowledge. We have seen that Popper rejects this view and maintains that knowledge has no foundations. Experience can motivate an observer to accept a sentence, but in no way can it justify a sentence. Test sentences, for Popper, are special only in that agreement about them can be reached by observation. This agreement, however, is only provisional and tentative, for an accepted test sentence may at any time be faced with falsification. Thus:

The empirical base of objective science has thus nothing 'absolute' about it. Science does not rest upon solid bedrock. The bold structure of its theories rises, as it were, above a swamp. It is like a building erected on piles. The piles are driven down from above into the swamp, but not down to any natural or 'given' base; and if we stop driving the piles deeper, it is not because we have reached firm ground. We simply stop when we are satisfied that the piles are firm enough to carry the structure, at least for the time being. (Popper, 1959, section 11.)

This problem is also discussed in Popper (1959, section 8).

It is usual to view the attempted falsification of a scientific theory T in the following way. T is conjoined with some set of initial conditions I and an auxiliary hypothesis A (though not every test will involve such a hypothesis), to yield the negation of some test sentence O. If observation leads to the acceptance of O, then T is falsified, whilst if not-O is accepted, T is corroborated. For example, let:

T = For all metallic conductors, the current flowing is directly proportional to the potential difference across the conductor.

A = In the circuit C, meter X reads the potential difference across the metallic conductor M and Y reads the current through M.

I = When the reading on X is 2 and 4 V, the reading on Y is 1 and 2 A respectively.

O = The reading on X is 6 V and the reading on Y is not 3 A.

$T \cdot A \cdot I$ entails not-O. Hence, if observation of the two meters leads to the acceptance of O, T is regarded as falsified, whilst T is corroborated to some extent if observation leads to the acceptance of not-O.

The logic of such a test can be put in other ways, which we will find useful later on in chapter 6. For example:

$$T \cdot A \rightarrow \text{not } (I \cdot O)$$

Here, the theory-plus-auxiliary-hypothesis forbids the conjunction of I and O, which can sometimes itself be regarded as a test sentence. In our example, this is the case, as observation can lead to a verdict about both I and O.

A third way of viewing any test is given by observing that since:

$$T \cdot A \rightarrow \text{not } (I \cdot O)$$

then

$$I \cdot O \rightarrow \text{not } (T \cdot A)$$

$T \cdot A$ and $I \cdot O$ can, therefore, be seen as mutual counter arguments. This will be particularly useful later on.

Empirical Content

The requirement that scientific claims be submitted to criticism naturally leads to a criterion for good scientific theories. A good theory is one which is easily tested (i.e., one which may be falsified by many test sentences whose negation it entails). The class of test sentences contradicted by a theory, Popper calls the empirical content of the theory. A good theory, therefore, has a high empirical content. But such a theory also says more about the world than one of low empirical content. Good theories are, therefore, powerful and bold (Popper, 1959, chapter 6).

The simplest way of comparing the empirical content of two theories is by the entailment relations between them. Let us denote the empirical content of a theory T by $C_E(T)$. If theory T_2 entails theory T_1 then:

$$C_E(T_2) \geqslant C_E(T_1)$$

If T_1 also entails T_2

$$C_E(T_1) = C_E(T_2)$$

If T_2 neither entails nor is entailed by T_1, then the empirical content of the two theories is not comparable by entailment relations. Another measure, using the so-called method of dimensions, may be possible for two such theories, but this has little value for our purposes.

It is easy to show that, once conventionalist stratagems have been banned (see below) empirical content follows logical content, $C_L(\ )$, the set of sentences entailed by a theory.

$$C_E(T_2) \geqslant C_E(T_1) \quad \text{if} \quad C_L(T_2) \geqslant C_L(T_1)$$

This suggests that the upper limit of empirical content, which we can assign the number 1, be ascribed to a contradiction, and that the lower limit, to which we may allot 0, be attributed to a tautology. Logical content is the complement of probability. Whilst a contradiction and a tautology provide the upper and lower limit of logical content respectively, they respectively provide the lower and upper limit for probability. Thus, if $p(T)$ is the (absolute logical) probability of T, we may measure empirical content by

$$C_E(T) = 1 - p(T)$$

There are two ways in which one theory T_2 may entail another T_1. It may be because T_2 has a greater universality than T_1, as in (a) and (b) below, or because T_2 is more precise than T_1, as in (b) and (c). Hence, Popper's demand for theories of high empirical content leads to the demand for theories of high universality and precision, two features that scientists intuitively favour. Popper also claims that theories of high empirical content are simpler than those of low content, so that his account can also explain the need that scientists often express for simple theories (Popper, 1959, chapter 7):

(a) All heavenly bodies move in circular orbits.
(b) All planets move in circular orbits.
(c) All planets move in elliptical orbits.

Corroboration

In evaluating a theory we need to know how it has stood up to the tests that have been made of it. It is not enough to know what and how many tests it has passed or failed, for we also need to know how severe these tests have been. A test is severe if we can expect the theory to fail it. A theory is, therefore, only severely testable if it has some novel, unexpected consequence, normally a prediction but occasionally a retrodiction, and the more unlikely the consequence, the more testable the theory. A theory is successful if it passes some test, and the more severe the test, the greater the success which accrues to the theory. When a theory passes a test Popper talks of it as being corroborated by the test, and a theory's degree of corroboration is a measure of how successful it has been in withstanding falsification. A theory that makes novel predictions can acquire a higher degree of corroboration than one that does not. This is perfectly reasonable, for the first theory has risked its neck whilst the second has risked virtually nothing. Compare, for example, the predictions made by Einstein's theory of relativity with the predictions made by today's horoscope, which are so vague and imprecise that they can hardly help but come true. Obviously relativity should acquire a greater success in having its predictions confirmed than that acquired by astrology through the confirmation of its predictions (Popper, 1959, sections 82 and 83; Popper, 1969, pp. 33–9 and 220–1).

In talking in this way of success and corroboration, it must not be thought that some inductive principle has been smuggled in by Popper. Nothing can be further from the truth. For Popper degree of corroboration is:

> . . . nothing but a measure of the degree to which a hypothesis h has been tested, and of the degree to which it has stood up to tests. It must not be interpreted, therefore, as a degree of the rationality of our belief in the *truth* of h. . . . Rather, it is a measure of the rationality of accepting, tentatively, a problematic guess, knowing that it is a guess — but one that has undergone searching examinations. (Popper, 1959, p. 145)

Any critical discussion must assume a background of sentences which are accepted — though perhaps provisionally and undogmatically — as being true. Such sentences may be said to form 'background knowledge' and exist far from the centre of critical debate. They provide something against which more controversial claims may be tested. Examples might be, 'Grass is green', the theories underlying the use of ordinary measuring devices such as the galvonometer and manometer and 'Wheat contains protein'. An item of background knowledge may at any time fall under suspicion during a debate, when it will have to leave the periphery for the debate's centre.

For Popper a test of a theory is severe if the theory can be expected to fail the test on the basis of our background knowledge. A theory can be tested severely only if it yields predictions which, on the basis of present background knowledge, must be regarded as highly unlikely. If a theory T is to be tested through its prediction of E, then the severity of the test for the theory given background B, $S(E,B)$ is measured by:

$$S(E,B) = 1 - p(E,B)$$

The more unlikely E, given B, the more severe the test. This may be normalized to:

$$S(E,B) = \frac{1 - p(E,B)}{1 + p(E,B)}$$

The requirement that T entails E may be weakened, noting that the severity of the test must fall as $p(E,T \cdot B)$. The more general formula, in its normalized form is:

$$S(E,T,B) = \frac{p(E,T \cdot B) - p(E,B)}{p(E,T \cdot B) + p(E,B)}$$

The explanatory power of T for E given B may be defined thus:

$$E(T,E,B) = S(E,T,B)$$

THE CRITICAL TURN – POPPER'S VIEW OF SCIENCE

The degree of corroboration of a theory T by a test E is a measure of the success which T has in surviving the criticism offered by E. It will, of course, be relative to background knowledge. Popper lists a number of requirements for a satisfactory measure of degree of corroboration, and suggests a number of possible measures. What is more important than the selection of a particular measure, however, is the fact that all of Popper's requirements can be satisfied together. Perhaps the simplest measure is given by:

$$C(T,E,B) = \frac{p(E,T \cdot B) - p(E,B)}{p(E,T \cdot B) - p(T \cdot E,B) + p(E,B)}$$

(see Popper, 1959, Appendix *ix).

Protection from Falsification

Popper is aware that it is all too easy to protect some cherished theory from falsification and that 'any nice adaptation of conditions will make any hypothesis agree with the phenomena' (Joseph Black, quoted in Popper, 1959, p. 82). A strategy for avoiding falsification, Popper calls a conventionalist (or immunizing) stratagem. If our aim is to expose all scientific claims to falsification, according to the supreme rule of methodology, then these conventionalist stratagems must be banned from science. These prohibitions form lower order rules of methodology. When a theory is protected from falsification, it no longer belongs to science, but to pseudo-science (or 'metaphysics' as Popper calls it). This is, of course, Popper's famous criterion of demarcation (Popper, 1959, section 6). This states that the defining characteristic of a scientific claim is the possibility of its clash with experience, or, more formally, with test sentences accepted through observation. If this clash is rendered impossible by conventionalist stratagems, then science is deserted for pseudo-science.

To give just one example, in 1936 Eddington proposed a theory which entailed that the ratio of the masses of the proton and electron is 1847.6, which was, unfortunately, outside the experimentally determined range of 1836.56 ± 0.56. Ten years later Eddington amended his theory, incorporating a mysterious factor of $(137/136)^{\frac{5}{6}}$ in order to obtain a value for the mass ratio which was within the experimental range. His amended theory fits the experimental facts, but this cannot count as success for the theory. Success can only be achieved at the risk of failure, and in this case Eddington's theory has not been exposed to possible failure. The fact that the theory gives the correct answer for the mass ratio of the proton and electron in no way corroborates the theory. We can see this from the measure for degree of corroboration given in the previous section. Since the value of the mass ratio is already experimentally determined, it forms part of the background knowledge, B, so that the probability of the ratio having this value, given B, is 1. In this event the degree of corroboration afforded to Eddington's theory is 0. Such *ad hoc* devices for getting theories to agree with known facts must, therefore, be outlawed from science by suitable methodological rules.

When is One Theory Better than Another?

We have already seen that preference should be given to bold theories because they are easily tested, but it would be more useful to have a criterion for one theory being better than another. Popper provides just such a criterion. It is not enough to say that theory T_2 is better than theory T_1 if T_2 has a higher empirical content than T_1, for we could then produce an endless sequence of better and better theories simply by conjoining them with some sentence so as to increase their empirical content. Nor is it enough to insist that T_2 has a greater empirical content than T_1 and that T_2 has some novel consequence not shared by T_1, through which it may be highly corroborated. This would allow us to make any theory better than another simply by conjoining it with some novel sentences such as 'All kettles freeze when heated on Tuesdays'. These difficulties can all be overcome if we insist that T_2 is better than T_1 only if T_2 has some novel consequence not shared with T_1 which is corroborated. The final criterion for T_2 being a better theory than T_1 is, therefore, threefold. Firstly, T_2 must ensure the redundancy of T_1 by explaining all that T_1 can explain. Secondly, T_2 must make some novel prediction(s) not made by T_1, and, thirdly, some of these novel predictions must be corroborated by experiment (Popper, 1969, pp. 240-8). Hence, special relativity is a better theory than Newtonian mechanics. It explains all that the earlier theory can explain and has corroborated novel predictions not shared by Newton's theory, such as the gravitational bending of light. Newton's theory was, in its turn, a better one than Kepler's theory of the planets, because it could explain all that Kepler's theory could explain and because it predicted many new phenomena whose existence was confirmed by experiment (Popper, 1972, chapter 5).

The passage from Kepler's theory to Newton's and from there to Einstein's illustrates what Popper regards as a central feature of science, its growth. Growth is achieved, not by the assembly of ever more facts and observations, but by the replacement of old theories by new ones which are even more testable, and so even more bold. The falsification of a theory by an experiment is not a sufficient reason for the rejection of the theory. The theory should be rejected only when a better theory is ready to replace it (Popper, 1959, section 85; Popper, 1969, pp. 240-8; Popper, 1972, p. 30).

References

Bartley III, W. (1962) *The Retreat to Commitment*, La Salle, Ill., Open Court.
Lakatos, I. (1970) 'Falsification and the methodology of scientific research

programmes', in Lakatos, I. and Musgrove, A. (eds) *Criticism and the Growth of Knowledge,* Cambridge University Press, pp. 91–195.

Lakatos, I. (1974) 'Popper on demarcation and induction', in Schillp, P. (ed.) *The Philosophy of Karl Popper,* La Salle, Ill., Open Court.

Popper, K. (1945) *The Open Society and Its Enemies,* London, Routledge and Kegan Paul.

Popper, K. (1959) *The Logic of Scientific Discovery,* London, Hutchinson.

Popper, K. (1969) *Conjectures and Refutations,* London, Routledge and Kegan Paul.

Popper K. (1972) *Objective Knowledge,* Oxford University Press.

Popper, K. (1974) 'Reply to my critics', in Schillp, P. (ed.) *The Philosophy of Karl Popper,* La Salle, Ill., Open Court.

6 A Critical Theory of Preference

The aim of this work is to produce a critical theory of decision making in the fallibilist tradition to which Popper has contributed so much. All attempts at justifying decisions will be abandoned, but this does not mean that reason has no part to play in decision making and that all choices are arbitrary, for although the justification of choice is impossible, plans of action may be criticized and revised in the light of criticism.

This chapter will lay down the foundations for such a critical theory of decision making, and if its results are accepted the theory follows simply and without any fuss as will be shown in the following chapters. Making a decision, like believing in something, is a psychological event, and just as it is often useful to characterize a belief as the acceptance of some sentence, so that logical rules may be applied to it, so it will benefit the present discussion to have a sentential characterization of decisions. If a decision maker faces a choice sufficiently important to call for rational assessment, and favours option Q, we may say that he accepts the *decision maxim* 'no option which is open is preferable to Q', and where he actually chooses Q we may speak of him as acting on this decision maxim. To talk of a decision as rational, irrational, intelligent, stupid, neutral or biased is then to apply these epithets to the decision's maxim. The advantage of this device is that maxims, unlike decisions themselves, have logical relationships which can be exploited in assessing them.

The introduction of maxims also reminds us of the obvious, that to make any kind of decision is to express a preference for the chosen action over any others that may have been available. To decide something is to express a judgement of preference, but the conclusion of chapter 3 was that no preference judgement can be justified. Attempting justification leads to a regress, which must terminate somewhere if the attempt is to be successful, but drawing a non-arbitrary halt to the regress seems to be impossible. In the second place, conjunctions of preference judgements may have factual consequences. If it is possible for these consequences to be discovered to be false, then the conjunction of preference judgements may prove to be falsified so that at least one of the conjuncts must be rejected. The possibility of such rejection means that the preference judgements cannot be regarded as justified. If preference judgements in general cannot be justified, then the special variety of those preference judgements constituting decisions cannot be justified. This is an even stronger conclusion than that of Part I which established that traditional attempts to show how decisions might be justified were a failure. This leaves open the possibility of some other view of decision making being developed which can remedy this scepticism by showing how decisions are, after all, capable of justification. The argument of the above paragraph closes this possibility. So long as decisions are regarded as expressions of preference and the conclusions of chapter 3 accepted, then no choice may be justified, whatever detailed view is taken of decision making.

If chapter 3 is sufficient to ensure scepticism about the justification of decisions, it also suggests a way in which scepticism may be alleviated. Even if no preference claims can be justified, as that chapter concludes, perhaps some claims may be rationally assessed by being submitted to criticism. It may, therefore, be possible to construct a critical theory of preference which accepts the first sceptical claim below but vigorously denies the second:

1 No preference claim can be justified.
2 No reasons can be given for favouring one preference claim rather than another.

Since, as we have seen, to decide is to express a preference, formally to adopt a decision maxim that is a preference claim of a particular form, then decisions will be covered by such a critical theory of preference. Though no decision may be justifiable, it may be possible to show how decisions may be criticized, and reasons given for favouring one option over another on the basis of this criticism. This is how our account will proceed. This chapter develops a critical theory of preference, which is then applied to the special case of decision maxims in the chapter which follows.

The theory to be developed here will be closely modelled on Popper's account of science, which was discussed in chapter 5. In their attempt to show how scientific claims can be justified, justificationist philosophers of science have endowed science with special features such as inductive logic and protocol sentences or sense data reports. The great power of Popper's view is that science does not need such special apparatus; instead it employs the *critical method* — the method of conjecture and criticism — and this method underlies all our attempts to apply reason to the problems which we have. On Popper's view scientific method can be seen as a particularly precise application of critical method, and one which can, therefore, serve as a model for the development of methodologies in other areas, such as ethics and decision theory.[1]

---

[1] For some attempts to base a theory of ethics upon science see Ackoff (1949), Baylis (1952), Caws (1967, pp. 50-8), Edel (1955, 1961, 1963), Gerwith (1960), Lackey (1976), Margenau and Oscanyon (1969/70), Mesthene (1947), Monro (1967), Schoeman (1974), Walter (1974). Among others who have proposed, or come close to proposing a critical theory of value are Brown (1976), Edel (1963, p. 318), Hare (1963, pp. 87-8, 92 and 136), Humphrey (1969/70), Mesthene (1947) and especially Watkins (1963, 1967).

Metatheory

The first step in the construction of a critical theory of preference is the statement of a metatheory upon which a methodology for the assessment of preference judgements may be based. Popper's metatheory, discussed in chapter 5, consists of two claims; that scientific statements have a truth value in a perfectly straightforward way and that no scientific statement can be justified. These two claims entail Popper's supreme rule of methodology, that all scientific claims are to be kept open to criticism. The metatheory for the corresponding theory of value consists of two analogous claims:

1 A statement of preference (X pref Y) is a sentence having a truth value.
2 No statement of preference can be justified.

The first claim may appear trivial until it is put into context. Many philosophers have wished to deny it. Logical positivists, for example, thought that 'X pref Y' could not be a sentence since it has no empirical consequences (see, for example, Ayer, 1964, pp. 107-8). At best the utterance of 'X pref Y' might serve to evince certain feelings. Claim 1 is a denial of all such views and cannot, therefore, be accused of triviality. It will be remembered that the analogous claim of Popper's seems trifling until its many historical denials are brought to mind. Claim 2 has been defended in chapter 3. The view of preference proposed here is undoubtedly counter to the 'commonsense' view. According to 'commonsense', an agent has privileged access to his own preferences — if he says that he prefers a to b, then he does prefer a to b (at least if he cannot be shown to be lying, to be linguistically confused etc.), just as when he says that his big toe hurts, then his big toe hurts. This is a plausible view, although a mistaken one, when a and b are taken to be such things as colours, tastes, smells, sounds etc. It is not outrageous to say that if a man prefers celery to cabbage, then he prefers celery to cabbage and this is the end of the matter. To argue with him is to forget that he knows about his preferences in much the same way as he knows about his pains. Error about his own preferences is impossible. But even commonsense admits that mistakes are possible in more complex situations. In choosing between motor cars, for example, a person may very well be mistaken about his own preferences. If he lists say, ten cars in order of preference and then makes a pair-wise comparison between the cars, an interesting experiment may be performed. An order of preference for the ten cars may be calculated from the list of pair-wise preferences, and it generally happens that this conflicts with the orginal ordering. Since the person's original set of preferences is thus shown to be inconsistent, he must have been in error about his own preferences.

It is interesting to see why this is so common. In choosing a motor car there are a great many factors to be considered. The first source of error is that one or more factors may be overlooked. For example, a person may select one car as the best, but revise his decision when it is pointed out that his employer will pay him a lower mileage allowance because of the car's small engine, a factor quite overlooked in the original decision. A second cause of error is that no one car will generally be the best on all counts. It will, therefore, be necessary to 'trade-off' preferences. The person's chosen car may, for example, have the best upholstery but not the lowest fuel consumption, the extra fuel consumption being more than compensated for by the quality of the upholstery. In such complex decisions errors about the trading between different factors is almost unavoidable.

Commonsense is wrong to think that the same possibilities of error do not infect mundane decisions, such as preferring celery to cabbage. It is thought that in such a judgement there is only one factor to be considered – in this case taste – so that factors cannot be overlooked, and trading between different factors is not called for. The simplifications involved here are, however, quite unrealistic. Many, many factors are involved even in this simple choice; the nutrition to be obtained from celery and from cabbage, possible health risks from eating them, the need to teach children how delightful cabbage is, the effects of demand for the vegetables on celery and on cabbage growers, the digestibility of the vegetables, and so on. Mistakes about preferences are, therefore, possible even here. The eater may have an incomplete knowledge of the factors involved; he may, for instance, be quite ignorant about nutrition, and he may miscalculate the trading he does between the various factors, just as in choosing a motor car. There is nothing revolutionary about this view, for it is a fact of everyday experience that a person's preference for even such things as food can be altered by the acquisition of knowledge, about nutrition and the ability of his own digestive system, for example, or the influence his choice has over his children. Similarly, the same experiment mentioned above, concerning the choice of a motor car, can show a person that he is wrong in how he trades between factors when choosing food.

Here it might be objected that even if 'I prefer celery to cabbage' is corrigible, then something as weak as 'I prefer the taste of celery to the taste of cabbage' is not. The judgement may be weak, but it nevertheless involves many factors, and is therefore open to the kind of errors we have been discussing. For example, suppose that the taste of celery leads to an uncontrollable urge to eat more celery with disastrous consequences to the intestines, or that the taste itself drives people insane. It is a contingent fact that these are not consequences of tasting celery, but there may be as yet unknown facts of the same sort which would make us reverse our preferences once disclosed to us. There can, of course, be no certainty that such facts will not be discovered. How facts may influence preferences has, of course, been explored in chapter 3.

My claim that statements of preference are corrigible may run counter to ordinary language. It does sound odd to say that a person prefers one thing to another, but is mistaken about it, but this locution is unavoidable on my view of value. To some extent it would appear that the doctrine that an agent has privileged access to his own preferences is built into our everyday language, but I can see no harm in challenging the doctrine and exposing a common error. In the same way that an extension of our knowledge of the physical world has led, quite naturally and correctly, to changes in our employment of terms like 'magic', 'witch', 'supernatural' and so on, advances in the philosophy of value should lead to revision in how we speak of preferences. This may seem shocking to those philosophers who see ethics as the unearthing of the rules of everyday discourse about values, but I reject their approach to the subject. Such exploration seems to me vacuous and trifling, but I cannot go into this here for reasons of length. All I shall say is that I see the prime function of the philosophy of value or ethics as producing a methodology by which evaluative claims may be assessed, and such a methodology cannot be achieved by any kind of linguistic analysis (Collingridge, 1975).

The two claims of the metatheory together yield a very different picture of the making of preference judgements than that given by traditional theories. For one reason or another an agent may be led to accept the judgement 'I prefer a to b', and this will be, by 1, a genuine sentence. By 2, however, the agent can never be sure of the truth of the sentence, (i.e., he can never be sure that he really does prefer a to b). If he genuinely wishes to search for the truth of the matter he must, therefore, hold his preference claim open to criticism. He must search for factors that are relevant to the judgement but which he has overlooked, and he must look critically at the trading between the various factors which he has recognised. Since none of his preference claims can be justified, all of them should be open to criticism. This is the supreme rule of methodology for the assessment of preference judgements and it is entailed by the metatheory consisting of 1 and 2, just as Popper's metatheory entails his supreme rule.

Test Sentences

Chapter 3 shows that factual sentences have three properties which enable them to be considered as test sentences for judgements of preference:

1 Factual sentences may contradict preference sentences.
2 There are ways of coming to agreement about the acceptance or rejection of factual sentences.
3 Factual sentences are testable.

Not all factual sentences have all three properties, but some do. All test sentences for preference judgements will be factual, but not all factual sentences will be test sentences. Examples of the first property have been given of the form $F \to$ not $(N_1$ and $N_2)$ where F is a factual sentence and N_1 and N_2 value judgements. Since no example of form $F \to$ not-N is known, as far as I am aware, no single preference sentence will be falsifiable by a factual sentence, although some conjunctions of preference sentences will be so falsifiable. Exactly the same is true in science. No single scientific test sentence can falsify a scientific theory, but only a conjunction of a theory and some initial conditions.

We saw in chapter 5 that an attempt to falsify a scientific theory can be seen in two ways; as involving the deduction of the negation of a test sentence from the theory plus auxiliary hypothesis and initial conditions or the development of a counter argument to the theory from an auxiliary hypothesis and initial conditions. It may help to refresh the memory by considering an example. Let the theory be

$$T = \text{All samples of urine are acid}$$

the auxiliary hypothesis be

$$A = \text{All acid samples turn litmus paper red}$$

the initial conditions be

$$I = \text{there is a litmus paper in a urine sample at } p, t$$

the observation be

$$O = \text{the litmus paper at } p, t \text{ is not red.}$$

Therefore

$$T \cdot I \rightarrow \text{There is an acid at } p, t$$

$$A \cdot O \rightarrow \text{not-(There is an acid at } p, t)$$

Here we can see $A \cdot O$ as providing a counterargument to $T \cdot I$, and thence to T itself. We can also view the situation as:

$$T \cdot A \rightarrow \text{not-}(I \cdot O)$$

Here the theory plus auxiliary hypothesis entails the negation of the test sentence $I \cdot O$ (remember that a conjunction of test sentences is a test sentence). If I is accepted by observation and if O is similarly accepted, then $T \cdot A$ must be regarded as falsified, which may be taken as a criticism of T, because A forms part of the critical background, being a long way from the centre of debate and not expected to require revision.

Exactly the same is true of the falsification of a universal preference sentence by a factual sentence. These are of particular interest because decision maxims are universal and additional reasons for paying particular regard to universal sentences will be given in the next section. Imagine an individual who is greatly impressed by the need for man to live in harmony and balance with his environment and thinks, therefore, that any action which retains the balance of nature is prefereable to an action which alters the balance of nature. In other words, he adopts the preference judgement U below — where 'pref' denotes strong preference; a pref b meaning that a is better than b, which exlcudes a being equally as good as b. We may also suppose the individual to believe B below, which together with U entails that tolerating smallpox is preferable to eliminating the disease. The preference judgement V we may also attribute to the agent. Someone wishing to persuade the agent to alter his preferences may point out that tolerating smallpox will lead to more deaths than eliminating smallpox (C), so that eliminating the disease is, after all, preferable to tolerating it:

$U = (x)(y)$ (x does not alter the balance of nature and y alters the balance of nature $\supset x$ pref y).

$B = $ Eliminating smallpox alters the balance of nature and tolerating smallpox does not alter the balance of nature.

$V = (x)(y)$ (x leads to fewer deaths than $y \supset x$ pref y)

$C = $ Eliminating smallpox leads to fewer deaths than tolerating smallpox.

Formally, $V \cdot C$ provides a counterargument to $B \cdot U$ since:

$B \cdot U \rightarrow$ Tolerating smallpox pref eliminating smallpox.

$C \cdot V \rightarrow$ Eliminating smallpox pref tolerating smallpox.

Faced with such a counterargument, the agent has no choice but to revise his values, giving up either V or U. If he gives up U and retains V, his opponent has convinced him that his original views on the eradication of smallpox are wrong.

The logic of the situation may be viewed in another way by noting that

$$U \cdot V \rightarrow \text{not-}(B \cdot C)$$

Here the conjunction of two preference sentences entails the negation of a factual sentence ($B \cdot C$) which we may, therefore, take as a test sentence. If $B \cdot C$ is accepted, by whatever rules are appropriate for the acceptance of factual sentences, then $U \cdot V$ must be regarded as false. This may be taken as a criticism of V when, as in the present case, V is a preference sentence which is not, at the moment, in question — though it may come to be so later (i.e., when V is a background sentence). Any testing of preference sentences by factual ones can be seen in either way.

To reinforce this conclusion let us consider another, more mundane, example. A person is offered a bowl of fruit containing apples and oranges after a good meal and immediately chooses an apple. He then remembers that eating apples after large meals always makes him sick, whereas he can happily digest oranges. The realisation of this fact makes him reverse his preferences and select an orange. Let:

$W =$ Eating apple A pref eating orange O.

$X = (x)(y)$ (x does not make me sick and y makes me sick $\supset$ x pref y).

$D =$ Eating apple A will make me sick and eating orange O will not make me sick.

One way to view the logic here is that $X \cdot D$ is a counter-argument to W since

$$X \cdot D \rightarrow \text{Eating orange } O \text{ pref eating apple } A$$

Alternatively, we may observe that

$$W \cdot X \rightarrow \text{not-}D$$

Here the conjunction of two preference sentences entails the negation of a factual test sentence, which, if accepted, must lead to a rejection of either W or X. If W is rejected and X retained, then the agent has reversed his original preference for the apple over the orange. What I wish to stress by considering such a lowly example is that our preferences are altered by our awareness of facts very many times a day. How this can be explained if it is denied that facts can falsify preference sentences in the way described, I fail to see. If facts lead us to alter our preferences, then facts must reveal our original preferences to be in error.

A test of a preference sentence N_1 will be of the form $N_1 \cdot N_2 \rightarrow \text{not } F$ where N_2 is another preference sentence and F a factual sentence. If F is discovered to be true, then one of N_1 and N_2 must be rejected. If N_1 is under test it therefore makes sense to ensure, in constructing a test, that N_2 is a preference sentence which is not itself in the centre of any debate and which has not been criticized in the past. N_2 may then be said to be a *background* preference sentence, since it forms the setting in which more suspect claims are to be assessed. If N_2 is a background sentence then the arrow of falsification points, prima facie, to N_1, which is as it should be since this is the claim under test. Belonging to the background is not, however, justification for N_2 and it may later come into question and have to be ejected from the critical background. Such a move must not, of course, be done in an *ad hoc* way just to protect N_1 from criticism (see below), but requires reasons. All this should become much clearer from the case studies to be presented in the chapter which follows.

Factual Content

So far we have seen that an individual trying to decide what his preferences are cannot justify any preference claim that he finally adopts; all he can do if he is serious about trying to discover his own preferences is hold whatever preference judgements he ventures open to criticism. This is the supreme methodological rule, from which lower order rules of method may be drawn.

Criticism of preference claims is, as we have seen, to be by factual test sentences. In adopting a preference judgement, an agent is not committing himself to the judgement come what may, as some justificationists have thought; rather, he is accepting the judgement provisionally to see how it stands up to being tested. What kind of preference claim, then, should be adopted for testing? If the agent is seriously interested in investigating his preferences, then obviously he should adopt preference sentences which are easy to test in favour of ones which are difficult to test. In other words, he should favour highly testable (or highly falsifiable) preference sentences.

A preference sentence is to be tested by drawing from it the negation of some factual test sentence, so we may measure a preference sentence's testability by what I shall call its *factual content* — the set of factual test sentences which it forbids. Absolute values for factual content are impossible, since the number of factual test sentences contradicted by a given preference sentence is either zero or infinity, but relative values may still be given. If, for example, one preference sentence P_2 entails another, P_1, then any factual test sentence contradicted by P_1 will also be contradicted by P_2, so that the factual content, or testability, of P_2 is at least as great as that of P_1 (once immunizing stratagems are prohibited — see below). The logical content of a sentence is the set of sentences which the sentence entails, so that the logical content of P_2 is at least as great as that of P_1. This suggests that logical content may also be used as a measure of factual content and of testability (again, once immunizing stratagems are prohibited). Consider the preference sentences below:

1   Any £5 win   pref   any £4 win
2   A £5 win today pref   any £4 win
3   Any £5 win   pref   a £4 win tomorrow
4   A £5 win today pref   a £4 win tomorrow

The entailment relations between the four preference sentences may be represented by Fig. 6.1

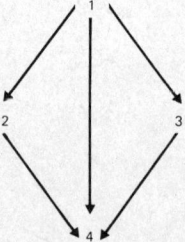

Fig. 6.1. Logical relationships between the preference sentences

It follows that the logical content of 1 is greater than that of 2 and 3, which are both greater than that of 4. Preferences 2 and 3 cannot be compared for logical content. From this we may say that 1 is at least as testable (has at least as high a factual content) as 2 and 3 which are, in turn, at least as testable as 4. The testability of 2 and 3 cannot be compared, at least by logical content. It follows that an agent seriously investigating his own preferences should, all things being equal, prefer to adopt 1 to 2 or 3 and 2 or 3 to 4, since this is the order of the ease with which the sentences can be tested.

The favour that should be shown for the adoption of highly testable preference sentences gives special place to universal preference sentences of the form 'All - - pref all . . . .', or, better, $(x)(y)$ $(--x$ and $\ldots y \supset x$ pref $y)$. Preference 1 above is of this form, since it may be phrased $(x)(y)(x$ is a £5 win and y is a £4 win $\supset x$ pref $y)$. Such universal sentences are highly testable, as the discussion above illustrates.

Corroboration

Our picture is of an agent who has provisionally adopted some preference sentence for testing, favouring high testability in his choice, and who is trying to test his adopted sentence as strenuously as he can against factual test sentences. If his sentence is falsified in such a test, he must look for a better one, but if it passes a test he should regard it as successful. The problem for this section is to see *how* successful the sentence is in passing tests. When a preference sentence passes a test, we may say that it is corroborated by the factual test sentences involved, and we may use the term 'degree of corroboration' to measure the cumulative success which accrues to the sentence. Success for a preference sentence is the passing of a test, and the more severe the test, the greater the success of the sentence in passing it. A test is, of course, an attempt to falsify the preference sentence and a severe test is one that we expect the preference sentence to fail. A severe test is, therefore, one that we expect to falsify the preference sentence under test. If a preference sentence manages to pass such a test, then it is highly corroborated. If, on the other hand, the preference sentence passes only tests that we already expect it to pass, its success must be counted as small, and it is only weakly corroborated, though the tests be as numerous as we please. Success goes only to guesses which risk failure, and the greater the risk of failure, the greater their success in surviving. It must always be remembered, however, that a preference sentence's degree of corroboration is in no way a measure of its probability or the likelihood of its being true, and in no sense is it predictive of future performance. Degree of corroboration is a measure of a preference sentence's success in passing tests. As such it says nothing about how future tests will turn out. A highly corroborated preference sentence may very well fail the very next test that is applied to it, and its degree of corroboration tells nothing about the likelihood of such failure.

A measure for the degree of corroboration of preference sentences may be based on Popper's measure for the degree of corroboration of scientific sentences. It will be remembered that Popper's measure for the corroboration of a theory T by a scientific test sentence E, $C(T,E)$ is:

$$C(T,E) = \frac{p(E,T) - p(E)}{p(E,T) + p(E) - p(T \cdot E)}$$

It is undoubtedly odd to talk of the probability of a preference sentence, though this is perfectly permissible on the views being developed here. The oddity stems from the view, which is to some extent embedded in ordinary language, that an agent has privileged access to his own preferences. If this is so, he knows what his preferences are immediately and it is otiose to ascribe probabilities to preference judgements. On the view being developed here, these judgements are as fallible as any other and the agent may well be mistaken in accepting a preference claim, so that ascribing probabilities is perfectly in order. Having said this, if a is a preference sentence and b the negation of a factual sentence entailed by a, then the corroboration of a by b is measured by:

$$C(a,b) = \frac{p(b,a) - p(b)}{p(b,a) + p(b) - p(a \cdot b)}$$

This may be relativized to some background preference sentence c:

$$C(a,b,c) = \frac{p(b,a \cdot c) - p(b,c)}{p(b,a \cdot c) + p(b,c) - p(a \cdot b,c)}$$

There are three requirements for a high corroboration, all of which are embodied in the above measure for degree of corroboration. The preference sentence under test, a, must be 'logically close' to the test sentence, b; the limiting case being where $a \cdot c$ entails b so that $p(b, a \cdot c)$ is unity. The test sentence, b, must have a low probability. This means that high corroboration is only achieved where a forbids a test sentence which is expected to be true. In testing a we must be concerned with its novel consequences, for the more unexpected they are, the greater corroboration a can achieve. This fits with the idea of severity of test, for a severe test of a is one that it is expected to fail. Great success is acquired by a, therefore if, contrary to expectations, it manages to pass the test. The third condition for high corroboration is that a itself has a low probability. This means that preference sentences of high factual content should be favoured, for these will be of low probability and so able to achieve a high degree of corroboration.

The measure of degree of corroboration is of no use in giving absolute values for corroboration, but serves for a comparison of the corroboration of two or more preference sentences. It is of some use in practical decision making, where it often concentrates the mind on the logical structure of the problem, but its primary value is in proving that the intuitive *desiderata* for high corroboration, logical closeness, novel consequences and a bold preference sentence, can be simultaneously satisfied and are not contradictory.

The concept of corroboration and its measurement may be illustrated by returning to the smallpox example discussed in an earlier section. An agent was imagined to hold the preference sentence U, which is to be submitted to test. V is a preference sentence, which the agent regards as innocent and far from the centre of any evaluative debate, so that it may serve as a background sentence in the testing of U:

$U = (x)(y)$ (x does not alter the balance of nature and y alters the balance of nature $\supset x$ pref y)

$V = (x)(y)$ (x leads to fewer deaths than $y \supset x$ pref y)

The test involves the deduction of the negation of a factual sentence from $U \cdot V$. That is:

$$U \cdot V \to \text{not } B \cdot C$$

where

B = Eliminating smallpox alters the balance of nature and tolerating smallpox does not alter the balance of nature

and

C = Eliminating smallpox leads to fewer deaths than tolerating smallpox

If B and C are both accepted as true, U must be regarded as falsified. If, on the other hand, one of them is shown to be false, this will corroborate U. Applying the measure above yields:

$$C(U, \text{not }(B \cdot C), V) = \frac{p(\text{not }(B \cdot C), U \cdot V) - p(\text{not }(B \cdot C), V)}{p(\text{not }(B \cdot C), U \cdot V) + p(\text{not }(B \cdot C), V) - p(U \cdot \text{not}(B \cdot C), V)}$$

In this case a high corroboration should be conferred. U and not $(B \cdot C)$ are logically close; indeed they are a limited case of closeness because $U \cdot V \to$ not $(B \cdot C)$ so that $p(\text{not }(B \cdot C), U \cdot V)$ is unity. In addition B and C are both expected to be true, so that $P(\text{not }(B \cdot C), V)$ is low. In other words, not $(B \cdot C)$ is a novel consequence of U, given the background sentence V. U is a universal preference sentence and, as such, has a high factual content and low probability which elevates the degree of corroboration.

Protection from Falsification

Popper has pointed out how it is possible to protect a cherished theory from falsification by making a whole series of what he calls *ad hoc* manœuvres or immunizing (conventionalist) stratagems. A theory protected in this way never finds itself in disagreement with observation, since all disagreement is discretely avoided, so that it may appear extremely successful. This success is, however, wholly illusory for it is achieved without risk of failure. According to Popper's supreme rule of methodology, all scientific theories are to be held open to falsification. It is necessary, therefore, to banish such protected theories from science, and they may be labelled 'pseudo-scientific'. The stratagems that produce these theories must also be prohibited, and these prohibitions form some of the lower order rules of Popper's methodology of science.

Exactly the same is true of preference sentences. The supreme rule of the methodology derived above states that all preference sentences should be open to falsification, and we know that such falsification can come from factual test sentences. It is possible, however, to protect any chosen preference sentence from falsification by factual sentences, and so we need rules to ensure that this does not happen. It is best to show this by means of an example.

In his defence of the utilitarian principle, Smart states boldly that whenever the principle comes into conflict with any value judgement, he is going to retain the principle and reject the recalcitrant judgement (Smart, 1961). Let us consider how this can work. Smart accepts the utilitarian principle which we may briefly paraphrase as:

$$S = (x)(y) \ (x \text{ produces more happiness than } y \supset x \text{ pref } y)$$

Imagine now a possible criticism of S; that there are some acts which produce the greatest amount of happiness but which are not preferable to other actions because they cause avoidable deaths. Let:

$$E = a \text{ produces more happiness than } b$$

$$F = b \text{ leads to fewer deaths than } a$$

$$V = (x)(y) \ (x \text{ leads to fewer deaths than } y \supset x \text{ pref } y)$$

Now:

$$S \cdot V \rightarrow \text{not } (E \cdot F)$$

$E \cdot F$ may be regarded as a factual test sentence for $S \cdot V$. If E and F are both accepted as true, then at least one of S and V must be regarded as falsified. Smart would, of course, always insist that V be rejected, since he is committed to the defence of S. Obviously if this policy were to be consistently followed, there would be no chance of falsifying S. S is always protected from criticism. The conformity of S to the facts cannot, however, be regarded as corroborating S since success can only be achieved at the cost of risking failure, and S has risked nothing. Returning to the measure of corroboration discussed in the previous section, it will be seen that this is indeed the case. If values like V are always adjusted to make S fit factual sentences known or expected to be true, then the probability of these factual sentences is extremely high, so that they confer very little corroboration on S. Employing Popper's notion of corroboration, therefore, effectively prevents Smart from claiming any success for his protected utilitarian principle.

This discussion obviously raises the question of when it is legitimate to save a principle like S from falsification by rejecting some other preference sentence, such as V, which figures in the test. Briefly, we may say that this is only allowable when the falsified preference sentence can be replaced by one which is *better*. What, then, are the conditions which make one preference sentence better than another?

When Is One Preference Sentence Better Than Another?

Consider an agent who is seriously investigating his own preferences by submitting them to possible falsification from factual test sentences. Suppose that one particular preference sentence is falsified by such a test, when should a falsified sentence be *rejected* by the agent? In science, Popper points to the need for a certain degree of toleration towards falsified theories, recognising that nearly all theories are falsified, at least at their inception, so that rejecting a theory as soon as it fails a test would mean that science would be empty. The problem posed by the falsification may be solved without changing the theory; the falsification may, for example, be attributed to an erroneous auxiliary hypothesis, or false initial conditions. It will, of course, take time and effort to explore these possibilities, so that immediately rejecting the theory on falsification would be premature. What Popper suggests, as we have seen, is that the theory should be rejected only if it can be replaced by a better theory, and he gives us criteria for one theory being better than another.

The same problem arises in the testing of preference sentences. Any test of a preference sentence will involve other preference sentences and factual assertions, so that any falsification may be directed at these and not the preference sentence under test. As before, adopting the rule that a preference sentence is to be rejected as soon as falsified means that it is impossible to explore these possibilities. As in science, toleration towards falsified preference sentences is essential. My suggestion is that a preference sentence should only be rejected if it can be replaced by a better one, and that preference sentence P_2 is better than preference sentence P_1 if:

1 All factual test sentences forbidden by P_1 are also forbidden by P_2.
2 P_2 forbids some factual test sentences which are expected to be true and which are not forbidden by P_1.
3 Some of the factual test sentences of 2 are shown to be false (thus corroborating P_2).[2]

[2] The satisfaction of 1-3 is a sufficient, but not a necessary condition for P_2 being better than P_1. Condition 1 may be generalized to cover instances where the two preference sentences do not forbid the same factual sentences, along the lines suggested in Popper (1969, pp. 215-50).

The reasoning behind this criterion is exactly the same as Popper's for the corresponding criterion for scientific theories. 1 ensures that P_1 and P_2 are rivals and that nothing is lost if P_2 replaces P_1, while 2 and 3 are needed to ensure that the testability of P_2 exceeds that of P_1 and that this is not the consequence of *ad hoc* stratagems.

This concludes the development of the critical theory of preference. The next step in building the critical theory of decision making which is desired is the application of the methodology of the present chapter to the special case of decision maxims.

References

Ackoff, R. (1949) 'On a science of ethics', *Philosophy and Phenomenological Research*, **9**, 663-72.
Ayer, A. (1964), *Language Truth and Logic*, London, Gollancz (2nd edn).
Baylis, C. (1952) 'The confirmation of value judgements', *Philosophical Review*, **61**, 50-8.
Brown, J. (1976) 'The appraisal of value judgements', *Ratio*, **18**, 56-72.
Caws, P. (1967) *Science and the Theory of Value*, New York, Random House.
Collingridge, D. (1975) 'The failure of language in ethics', *Journal of Value Inquiry*, **9**, 81-94.
Edel, A. (1955) *Ethical Judgement: The Use of Science in Ethics*, New York, Free Press.
Edel, A. (1961) *Science and the Structure of Ethics*, University of Chicago Press.
Edel, A. (1963) *Method in Ethical Theory*, London, Routledge and Kegan Paul.
Gerwith, A. (1960) 'Positive ethics and normative science', *Philosophical Review*, **69**, 311-30.
Hare, R. (1963) *Freedom and Reason*, Oxford University Press.
Humphrey, C. (1969/70) 'The testability of value claims', *Journal of Value Inquiry*, **3**, 221-7.
Lackey, D. (1976) 'Empirical disconfirmation and ethical counterexample', *Journal of Value Inquiry*, **10**, 30-5.
Margenau, H. and Oscanyon, F. (1969/70) 'A scientific approach to the theory of values', *Journal of Value Inquiry*, **3**, 163-72.
Mesthene, E. (1947) 'On the need for a scientific ethic', *Philosophy of Science*, **14**, 96-101.
Monro, D. (1967) *Empiricism and Ethics*, Cambridge University Press.
Popper, K. (1969) *Conjectures and Refutations*, London, Routledge and Kegan Paul.
Schoeman, F. (1974) 'A rational approach to the foundations of ethics', *Journal of Value Inquiry*, **8**, 241-51.
Smart, J. (1961) *Outline of a System of Utilitarian Ethics*, Melbourne University Press.
Walter, E. (1974) 'Reasoning in science and ethics', *Journal of Value Inquiry*, **8**, 252-65.
Watkins, J. (1963) 'Negative utilitarianism', *Proceedings of the Aristotelian Society, Suppl. Vol. 37*, pp. 95-114.
Watkins, J. (1967) *Decisions and Belief*, London, BBC, pp. 9-26.

7 The Criticism of Decision Maxims

After the excursion of the previous chapter into philosophical ethics and the theory of value, it is now time to return to the problems of decision making and decision theory. We have seen that one way to obtain a formal grip on decisions is to regard a decision as the adoption of a decision maxim, so that to chose Q is to adopt the maxim 'no option is preferable to Q'. This may be formally expressed as (x) (x is an option other than $Q \supset$ not (x pref Q)), remembering that 'pref' denotes strong preference; not (x pref Q) stating that x is not better than Q, although it may be equally good, in which case Q and x are joint best options. Since decision maxims are a variety of preference sentence, the theoretical apparatus of the previous chapter may be applied to them in order to test them. This is the theme of the present chapter, where a brief introduction is followed by a number of case studies which highlight the principal features of the criticism of decision maxims by the methodology generated in chapter 6.

If a decision is reckoned to be of sufficient importance to warrant rational scrutiny then the corresponding decision maxim may be submitted to the methodology of the critical theory of preference. The first principle of that theory's metatheory entails that the decision maxim, being an assertion of preference, is a genuine sentence with a truth value. It is not just a sophisticated expression of emotion, or a disguised order or an attempt to evince feelings. The second principle of the metatheory entails that the decision maxim cannot be justified; there is no way of being sure about its truth. This, of course, conforms with the results of Part I of the book, and especially of chapter 3 where scepticism about the possibility of justifying any kind of preference claim was defended. If decision maxims have a truth value, and if none can be established as true, it follows that any maxim may be false, so that none should be protected from attempts to criticize them by revealing their falsity. This, of course, is the supreme rule of methodology of the critical theory of preference as it applies to the special case of decision maxims. If you please, it may be thought of as the supreme rule of methodology of the critical theory of decision making.

Criticism of maxims is possible because maxims may be conjoined with background preference sentences, ones not under suspicion at the moment and expected to remain unsullied by criticism, to forbid some matters of fact. Formally, the conjunction of maxim and background preference sentence entails the negation of some factual sentences. If these forbidden matters of fact actually occur, if the factual sentences are found to be true, then the conjunction is falsified. Either the decision maxim or the background preference sentence must be abandoned, the prima facie candidate being the maxim, because of the expected innocence of the background sentence. Returning to the smallpox example of the previous chapter, an agent was there faced with determining his preference between tolerating smallpox and eliminating the disease. Suppose now that he has resolved this, and gone further to adopt the option of tolerating smallpox. This may be seen as the acceptance of the decision maxim M.

$M = (x)$ (x is an option other than tolerating smallpox $\supset$ not (x pref tolerating smallpox))

Assume too that the agent accepts V as a background value

$V = (x)(y)$ (x leads to fewer deaths than $y \supset x$ pref y)

Now

$$M \cdot V \to \text{not } C$$

where

$C =$ Eliminating smallpox leads to fewer deaths than tolerating smallpox

If C is found to be true, M should be regarded as falsified, although as we shall see, this does not mean that it should be immediately abandoned. If C is found to be false, however, the maxim M has been corroborated and has successfully passed a test. How much success should be granted to M depends upon how severe this test was. If M was expected to fail the test (i.e., if C was expected to be true), then the test is a severe one and M has achieved considerable success in surviving it. If, on the other hand, C is expected to be false, then M may be expected to pass the test, and so achieves little credit in actually doing so. In the limit, where C is known to be false, M gains no corroboration by passing the 'test' for a test that cannot be failed is no test at all. Success therefore calls for M to have novel unexpected factual consequences, so that it is bold and risky. The cumulative success of a decision maxim may be measured by its degree of corroboration. In the example above, the degree of corroboration of M by not C given the background preference sentence V is:

$$C(M, \text{not } C, V) = \frac{p(\text{not } C, M \cdot V) - p(\text{not } C, V)}{p(\text{not } C, M \cdot V) + p(\text{not } C, V) - p(M \cdot \text{not } C, V)}$$

The general formula shows that three conditions are required for a high degree of corroboration: logical closeness between the maxim and forbidden test sentence, in the limit the former entailing the latter as in the example;

a low probability for the forbidden test sentence, which is another way of saying that the consequence under test should be novel; and a low probability for the maxim itself. Maxims which are of a low probability are bold — they forbid a very great deal and so say a great deal, or, to put it another way, they have a large logical content. If a number of maxims may be selected for testing, it makes sense to choose the one which is most easily tested. This will be the one which forbids the most factual test sentences or has the greatest factual content. Once immunizing stratagems have been forbidden by lower-order rules of method, the demand for high factual content becomes equivalent to the demand for low probability or high logical content. This is the justification for the third condition for a high degree of corroboration.

Consider the decision maxims below:

1 No option is preferable to removing all harmful substances from vehicle exhausts now.
2 No option is preferable to removing harmful lead from vehicle exhausts now.
3 No option is preferable to removing all harmful substances from vehicle exhausts now or in the future.
4 No option is preferable to removing harmful lead from vehicle exhausts now or in the future.

The logical relationships between the maxims are shown in Fig. 7.1.

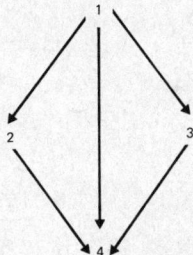

Fig. 7.1 Logical relationships between the maxims

Here, 1 is more universal than 2, and 3 more universal than 4, while 1 is more precise than 3 and 2 more precise than 4. If immunizing stratagems which protect some favoured decision maxim from falsification are prohibited in the spirit of the supreme rule of methodology, then the factual content of the four maxims is measurable by their logical content, and the diagram above also reveals the ordering of factual content, or testability of the maxims.

It should be noted here that no amount of corroboration can ever amount to a proof of a decision maxim. Background preference sentences that may be used in corroboration are ones that are of such lowly content that they are likely to come under no significant challenge. A decision maxim, however, has the form (x) (x is an option other than $Q \supset$ not (x pref Q)), which — being universal — has a high logical content, so that no sentence of this form can be reckoned as a background preference sentence. Background sentences may be thought of as simple expressions of preference, a pref b, thus excluding the high content and contentiousness which comes from universal preference sentences. No number of singular sentences of form a pref b can ever entail a decision maxim, for this makes the universal claim that Q is preferable to *all* other options. Background preference sentences may yield conclusions that Q is preferable to option 1, to option 2, to option 3 and so on; but this can never be enough to ensure that Q is preferable to all other options. Background sentences cannot, therefore, entail any decision maxim. Anyone making a choice is inevitably taking the risky course of expressing a preference, which (because of its content) transcends any set of unproblematic unsuspected, uncriticized background preference sentences. Making decisions is inherently risky.

The falsification of a decision maxim will employ background preference sentences and factual test sentences, and the immediate conclusion is not that the maxim is false, but that the conjunction of maxim, background sentence and accepted test sentence is contradictory. At least one of the trio must be false, but the test itself gives no information as to which. Toleration towards falsified maxims is, therefore, essential, because falsification does not entail their falsity. The falsified maxim may be true the fault lying with one or both of the other elements in the test. These possibilities may be explored before a too hasty conclusion is reached. This makes it easy for a favoured decision maxim to be protected against criticism. Each time it is falsified, the failure is placed at the door of the background preference sentence or the factual test sentence being used in the test. The arrow of falsification is never allowed to point at the maxim (see Collingridge, 1980, chapter 8). Consider, first, an example where the factual test sentence was blamed for the falsification of a highly favoured decision maxim, which maintained that the best option was the building of an experimental fast breeder reactor at Dounreay. Let Lord Hinton tell the story:

Argument about safety went on for many months; Lord Cherwell laughed at the idea that a minor nuclear explosion was possible but we decided that in view of all the uncertainties that existed, we would put the whole assembly inside a steel sphere.

Because of the unknowns we had, from the outset, planned to build the reactor on a remote site. Kendal, Owen and I had examined the Galloway and South Ayrshire coasts without finding anything that was suitable. We decided that we had to go further afield and surveyed the coasts of Sutherland and Caithness and there we found what we knew to be the best site at Dounreay. But why, if we were giving the reactor containment, were we putting it on a remote site? This could only be logical if we assumed that the sphere was not absolutely' free from leaks. So we assumed, generously, that there would be 1% leakage from the sphere and, dividing the country around the sites into sectors, we counted the number of houses in each sector and calculated the number of inhabitants. To our dismay this showed that the site did not comply with the safety distances specified by the health physicists. That was easily put right; with the assumption of a 99% containment the site was unsatisfactory so we assumed, more realistically, a 99.9% containment and by doing this we established the fact that the site was perfect. (Hinton, 1977, p. 11)

The maxim may be stated as:

$M_1 = (x)$ (x is an option other than siting the reactor at Dounreay $\supset$ not (x pref siting the reactor at Dounreay))

The background preference sentence, B_1, was laid down by the health physicists to protect the health of the population near the reactor.

$B_1 = (x)$ (x exposes a population of more than N to more than a radiation level of $R \supset$ not doing x pref x)

Clearly $$M_1 \cdot B_1 \rightarrow \text{not } F_1$$

where

$F_1 =$ Siting the reactor at Dounreay exposes a population of more than N to more than a radiation level of R.

F_1 and B_1 entail that not siting the reactor at Dounreay is preferable to siting it at Dounreay, so that siting it there cannot be the best option, contrary to M_1. Assuming a 1 per cent leakage from the reactor means that F_1 is accepted, and M_1 consequently falsified. Rather than allow this, a 0.1 per cent leakage was assumed, from which not F_1 followed, with 'corroboration' of M_1.

In the second example the arrow of falsification is directed at the background preference sentence. In the spring of 1940 Rudolf Peirls and Otto Frisch, refugee scientists working in Birmingham, warned the British Government that it might be possible to build a superbomb with an explosive power equal to several thousand tons of TNT from suitably processed uranium, and that Germany might have plans for such a weapon. The Maud Committee was set up in Britain to develop the uranium weapon as a counter to the threat of Germany proving to be working in the same direction. When America entered the war, the work of the Maud Committee was transferred to the USA, under the name of the Manhattan Project. This was well underway by early 1943, by which time British intelligence experts were becoming more and more convinced that the Germans had no programme for a super-bomb, conclusions which were strengthened as time went on. The pace of the Manhattan Project did not, however, falter. Instead a new reason for it gradually replaced the original one. The Allied bomb was not needed to counter a German threat, but it was required as an offensive weapon in the war against Japan. I have examined this change of objective in some detail elsewhere (Collingridge, 1980, chapter 8), where I argued that it is best seen, not as a well thought out exploitation of options that the Project's progress opened up, but as a hasty, uncritical manœuvre to preserve the Project once its original justification had evaporated.

The decision maxim may be expressed:

$M_2 = (x)$ (x is an option other than making an Allied atom bomb $\supset$ not (x pref making an Allied atom bomb))

The original background value, B_2, stated the need for the Allies to possess an atomic bomb if one of their enemies was going to have one, and that this was the only ground for the bomb; building the bomb just as a very large offensive weapon was agreed by all to be a serious waste of resources which could be better invested in the development of more conventional weapons.

$B_2 = $ An Allied bomb programme pref no allied bomb programme if and only if one enemy of the Allies has a bomb programme

Clearly

$$M_2 \cdot B_2 \rightarrow \text{not } F_2$$

where

$F_2 = $ No enemy of the Allies has a bomb programme

$F_2 \cdot B_2$ entails that no allied bomb programme is preferable to a bomb programme, contrary to M_2 which claims that the programme is the best option that is open. The discovery, in early 1943, that the German threat was unreal and that no enemy had a bomb programme falsified M_2. But by this time the momentum of the Manhattan Project was not stoppable and this criticism of the Project was turned aside by the abandonment of B_2. Reasons apart from the need to respond to an enemy atomic bomb programme were hastily assembled to justify the Project's continuation. Formally, the background preference sentence B_2 was rejected. The bomb, it was now argued, was needed to kill Japanese.

It should be clear that such *ad hoc* manœuvres to protect a cherished decision are quite against the spirit of the supreme rule of methodology, which states that all decision maxims are to be open to criticism and abandonment. This is achieved by the measure for degree of corroboration. Where a maxim is protected in the way we have seen in the two examples, it cannot possibly fail any test, so it should receive no credit (i.e., no corroboration) from managing to pass a test. In examining real decisions from the viewpoint of the critical theory of decision making it is very important to be on guard against *ad hoc* stratagems for the protection of choices, for their presence blunts the operation of reason in decision making.

The logical feature of testing maxims from which the danger of these *ad hoc* moves springs (namely that a test tells us only that a maxim, a background preference sentence and an accepted factual test sentence are contradictory without indicating which members of the trio are false) also demands tolerance towards a falsified maxim, as we have seen. Falsification of a maxim cannot be taken as the sign for its immediate rejection, because one of the other elements in the test may be false and the maxim quite innocent. I suggest, therefore, that a maxim M_i be rejected only when it can be replaced with a maxim M_j which is better according to the triple criterion below:

1. All factual test sentences forbidden by M_i are also forbidden by M_j.
2. M_j forbids some novel factual test sentences not forbidden by M_i.
3. Some of the factual test sentences of 2, above, are shown to be false (thus corroborating M_j).

When these conditions are met M_j may replace M_i and any corroboration of M_i may be transferred to the better maxim. The first condition ensures that the two maxims are rivals and that there is no loss of factual content upon replacement of M_i by M_j. The other conditions are needed to ensure that the testability of M_j exceeds that of M_i, so that M_j is to be favoured on this score, and that this relationship has not been specially constructed in an *ad hoc* move to ensure the acceptance of M_j.

It may be illuminating to apply the triple criterion to the everyday problem of eliminating options from a shortlist until only one, the best option, remains. Consider the very simple question of when it is appropriate to drop an option from a shortlist. Take a simple case where the shortlist consists of three options, a, b and c, one of which is reckoned to be the best option. Under what circumstances should this be thinned down to two options, a and b? Formally, this is a question of when one decision maxim M_4 should replace another, M_3, where:

$$M_3 = (x) \quad (x \text{ is an option not } a, b \text{ or } c \supset \text{not } (x \text{ pref } a, b \text{ or } c))$$

$$M_4 = (x) \quad (x \text{ is an option not } a \text{ or } b \supset \text{not } (x \text{ pref } a \text{ or } b))$$

First of all notice that M_4 entails M_3, so that condition 1 is satisfied. This can hardly justify the replacement of M_3 by M_4, however, because we could then replace M_4 by the maxim that option a is the best, or equally by the maxim that b is the best option. Something more than additional content is needed if M_4 is to replace M_3. Notice that the second condition may also be satisfied without making the replacement a reasonable move. Suppose that there is a background preference sentence B_3 and a factual test sentence F_3 such that

$$B_3 \cdot F_3 \rightarrow \text{option } c \text{ pref option } a \text{ or option } b$$

Then

$$M_4 \cdot B_3 \rightarrow \text{not } F_3$$

whereas $M_3 \cdot B_3$ is quite silent about the truth value of F_3. In this case M_4 forbids at least one factual test sentence not forbidden by M_3, so that it has a higher testability. This does not mean that M_4 can replace M_3 however, because a whole series of maxims with even greater content than M_4 could be constructed in *ad hoc* ways and these would have to replace M_4. Clearly, what is needed are reasons for thinking that c is not the best option. When these are known, the shift from M_3, which says the best option is either a, b or c, to M_4, which says the best option is either a or b, is straightforward. What will such reasons look like? Consider B_3 and F_3 above.

$$B_3 \cdot \text{ option } a \text{ or } b \text{ pref option } c \rightarrow \text{not } F_3$$

Finding not F_3 therefore provides a reason for accepting that option a or b is preferable to option c, because it corroborates this preference claim. In other words not F_3 provides a reason for thinking that c is not the best option and for substituting M_4 for M_3. But it will be remembered that

$$M_4 \cdot B_3 \rightarrow \text{not } F_3$$

so that the acceptance of not F_3 corroborates some of M_4's excess content over M_3, in accordance with the third condition above. Narrowing a short list is therefore an example of moving to better and better decision maxims; better according to the triple criterion.

Consider an example where a firm is choosing a computer and after much research has narrowed the field to a short list of three, A, B and C. Suppose that it is objected that C, unlike its rivals, has no software and so should be eliminated from the shortlist. The reduced shortlist would, of course, consist just of A and B. How does this simple example fit into the theory of critical choice, and in particular how does it illustrate the substitution of one decision maxim by another which is better according to the triple criterion? Formally, the firm's first decision maxim is M_5 and its second M_6 where

$M_5 = (x)$ (x is an option other than buying one of A, B or C $\supset$ not (x pref buying one of A, B or C))

$M_6 = (x)$ (x is an option other than buying one of A or B $\supset$ not (x pref buying one of A or B))

The argument against C employs the background preference sentence B_4 and the factual test sentence F_4.

$B_4 = (x)(y)$ (x is a computer with software and y is a computer with no software $\supset x$ pref y)

$F_4 = A$ is a computer with software and C is a computer with no software.

Clearly

$$B_4 \cdot C \text{ pref } A \rightarrow \text{not } F_4$$

The factual F_4, therefore, falsifies the claim C pref A, assuming the continued acceptance of B_4. This means, of course, that buying C cannot be the best option, so that it can be eliminated from the firm's shortlist. This is pretty obvious, the real problem being to see how this fits in with the substitution of one maxim for an inferior one. The little story above is enough to ensure that the decision maxim M_6 is better than M_5. The first condition is met because

$$M_6 \rightarrow M_5$$

so nothing will be lost by the substition of M_6 for M_5. The second condition is also met because

$$B_4 \cdot M_6 \rightarrow \text{not } F_5$$

whereas there is no equivalent entailment for M_5.

$F_5 =$ C is a computer with software and A is a computer with no software

This means that M_6 forbids some factual test sentence not forbidden by M_5; it has excess factual content, so that condition 2 is met. The third condition is also met because F_4 and F_5 are contraries. The acceptance of F_4 used in the falsification of C pref A therefore entails that not F_5 also be accepted. But, as we have seen, not F_5 corroborates some of the excess factual content of M_6, showing that the final condition of the triple criterion is met.

This illustrates a point of no little importance. In real decision making the options which are available are scrutinized, examined, criticized and altered in the light of this process, but the movement always tends to be towards narrowing down the options that are open. The closure of an option after critical scrutiny is always an achievement in the process of decision making. If the aim is to make decisions that can be justified this commonplace observation is paradoxical. In moving towards decision maxims of greater precision and universality (i.e., greater factual content), the decision maker is making it harder and harder to justify his adopted maxim. If justification is sought, it would seem appropriate to move in quite the opposite direction, towards maxims of lower content, with less precision and universality of scope. On the other hand, if justification is seen to be the impossible dream that it is and if openness to criticism is the real method of the decision maker, then this shift towards precision and universality is easily explained as I hope I have made clear.

A final issue remains. When, during the process of critical appraisal, should one decision maxim be settled on and a decision taken? For preferences other than decision maxims this is no problem because revision is costless. A particular preference sentence may, therefore, be appraised quite differently as the process of debate goes on. At one point, for example, it may be falsified only to be rescued later when the background values employed in the test come under suspicion, only to be falsified by a new test later still, and so on. It is enough to adopt whatever preference sentences seem most highly corroborated at the time, because if later tests alter the relative degrees of corroboration to favour some other preference sentence, then this may be adopted in the place of the first at no cost, save that of mental effort. It is notoriously otherwise in making a decision, however. Any decision involves the investment of resources of some kind, whether material or not, and it is very rare that all of these resources can be recovered if the first decision is later seen as wrong and some other option substituted for the original.

This is a very serious problem. If a decision is made on the basis of the degree of corroboration of some maxim relative to that of its rivals, coming to recognise the decision as mistaken later on when further tests have been conducted may be beside the point because the resources the decision has caused to be invested may be irrecoverable. If such changes in appraisal are to be the norm as the critical process proceeds, then it seems arbitrary to halt the process at some point by making a decision, after which further debate is just ornament. The solution to this problem must await the next chapter for a full development, but essentially it consists in realising that not all decisions call for an irreversible investment of resources. Some decisions are totally reversible, all the resources being recoverable, some are quite impossible to reverse, but the vast majority are somewhere in the spectrum between these extremes. A critical approach to decision making calls for favour to be given to an option whose corresponding decision maxim is highly corroborated *and* that is easy to reverse. Since it is easy to reverse, the critical debate about the maxim may proceed after the option has been implemented. If later tests show that some other option has a higher degree of corroboration, then the original choice may be easily revised, with only a little loss of resources, and the newly favoured one implemented again, provided that it too is easily reversed should it prove necessary.

The case studies that follow have been chosen to illustrate the points made in this chapter so that considerations of reversibility do not arise. This gap will be remedied later.

Case Studies

The case studies that follow illustrate that part of the critical theory of decision making that has so far been constructed, the apparatus for criticizing decision maxims. This is not such a straightforward affair as it might seem, because the theory is normative — it states how decisions ought to be made — so it may be asked how descriptions of actual decisions and debates about what to do can be relevant. The truth is that all normative theories have a double aspect. Consider, for example, Popper's theory of science, which lays down methodological rules that ought to be followed in the pursuit of truth. Now science appears to be extremely successful in furthering our understanding of the Universe and in providing answers to the more mundane practical questions which we pose to it. If a firm finds that a batch of the glue it sells fails to stick whatever it is supposed to stick, it may wish to discover why and what can be done to prevent its recurrence, in which case the problem is passed to the laboratory where answers are sought from those initiated into the mysteries of chemistry, physics and so on. The answers obtained in such a way tend to be superior to those that might be offered by sheer guesswork, navel gazing, consulting oracles and so on, and there is a hard-nosed test for their superiority, the stickiness of future batches of the firm's glue. So science seems to be successful in ways little and big a thousand times a day. This needs to be explained in some way — why is science more successful at solving a particular class of problems than all the other ways which might be taken?

One explanation is that the secret of success is that science actually follows the methodological rules laid down by Popper, and so represents a rational pursuit of truth. Scientists are successful in tackling problems because the methods they use are ones appropriate to the pursuit of truth. This explanation of the success of science must be strongly favoured by Popperians. Any other explanation would have to view the success of science as an illusion or as a huge accident. If science does not use Popperian methodology, it cannot be seen as a rational pursuit of truth, and any success it may have must either be merely apparent, perhaps because other systems of problem solving have not been explored in sufficient detail, or purely coincidental. To avoid such embarrassment, Popperian philosophers have attempted to see the actual practice of science as a reflection of Popperian methodology in action.

The same is true in decision theory. Bayesian theory is normative, in that it prescribes rules that ought to be followed by a rational agent, but it also claims that something approaching these rules is actually used in practical decision making, so that we can explain why decision making tends to be successful. This we must believe, or else we would never bother to make any decisions at all, but merely decide arbitrarily what to do, becoming passive objects tossed haphazardly by whatever happens around us. If we want something, it certainly seems better to strive towards it, thinking what might be done to achieve it, than to wait helplessly in the hope of its delivery. Bayesian theorists would claim that this is because we make decisions in a way they have managed to formalize, so that their normative theory also explains whatever success we have had in our attempts to get what we want. The theory proposed by Lindblom and known as disjointed incrementalism, which will be considered in more detail in chapter 10, similarly presents a double aspect. It is claimed that decision makers ought to operate in various ways and that they actually do this. The success of organizations in operating, often in very difficult environments, is therefore explicable. Their success is due to them using, in a rough and ready, intuitive manner, the rules they ought to use to achieve their plans.

Critical decision theory is in exactly the same position. It is first of all claimed that decisions ought to be made in a particular way, following various methodological rules, but it is also held that this is, in fact, something like how real decision makers operate, so that the success of their operations is explicable. There may, of course, be rival explanations, for example the ones offered by Lindblom or Bayesian theory, but then the explanations offered may be compared and judged between, as will be done in chapters 9 and 10. It is, therefore, highly relevant to consider the extent to which actual decision making practices follow the methodological rules laid down in the previous section and how much illumination the real world can throw upon these normative rules

The main points to be highlighted by the case studies are listed below:

1 The applicability of critical decision theory to cases where no version of the justificationist model of decision making can be applied.
2 The public nature of the criticism of decision maxims.
3 The relationship between factual and evaluative elements in debates about what to do.
4 The distinction between motivation and argument.
5 The interpretation of data and the role of expert opinion in decision making.
6 The use of degree of corroboration in decision making.
7 The possibility of exploiting *ad hoc* immunizing stratagems to protect an option once chosen.
8 Boundary problems in justifying and criticizing decision maxims.

The first three of these deserve a discussion before the details of the case studies are encountered.

Decisions under ignorance

In chapter 2 conditions for the application of Bayesian decision methods were listed and found to be extremely restrictive. Where these conditions are not met, it was agreed to refer to the decision in question as one under ignorance. This highlights the crucial distinction between decision making under (restricted) uncertainty where Bayesian methods may be applied, and those under ignorance where no benefit from such methods can be hoped for; a distinction traditionally blurred by the blanket application of the term 'uncertainty'. All the decision problems to be considered in the following case studies are under ignorance. Consider the final case study where the issue is whether to lower lead levels in petrol in the USA to prevent injury to the health of the population from lead exposure (Collingridge, 1980, chapter 2).

Lead is a well-known poison of the nervous system and yet a typical city dweller is in contact with the metal through the air he breathes (where it originates largely from motor car exhausts), from the food he eats (most of which is the result of contamination during processing, for example, in canning) and in the water he drinks (from lead piping). Lead is excreted from the body fairly rapidly so the metal does not accumulate indefinitely, but reaches an equilibrium concentration throughout the body that is far below the levels required to produce the symptoms of classical lead poisoning.

Nevertheless, recent experimental and epidemiological work has pointed to the possibility that even these low levels may have subtle health effects, particularly on the central nervous system. The group particularly at risk here are pre-school children whose nervous systems are developing rapidly and are sensitive to any toxin. It is possible that a proportion of children of this age with quite normal exposure to lead in the environment have impaired central nervous function which reveals itself in lower IQ scores, difficulty in learning and behavioural problems. The evidence on this point can hardly be reviewed here, but suffice it to say that — despite a considerable research effort — there is at the moment no consensus in the scientific community about the existence of these effects.[1]

Exposure to lead may be lowered in a number of ways: by reducing the amount of lead added to petrol as an anti-knock agent; reducing lead in food (by, for example, replacing lead solder in canning); and reducing the levels of the metal found in domestic water by water treatment or the removal of lead piping. However, none of these options are cheap. The decision must be made, in the light of the scientific evidence mentioned above and the various control costs, whether to lower environmental lead levels by invoking one of these controls now, or to delay the decision until the scientific community eventually reaches a consensus about the health effects of lead. This is a very common decision problem and it yields to Bayesian optimization only if a number of conditions can be met. The problem can be represented in the customary form of a decision tree shown in Fig. 7.2. For a Bayesian solution to be possible the following must be known:

(a) the reduction in damage to health per year that would be achieved by the control, measured in the same units as the cost of the control, which must also be known;
(b) the time t needed for a consensus to be reached about the health effects of lead in the environment and;
(c) the probability that lead will be found to be harmful by time t.

If these are known, it is easy to identify which course of action — 'apply control now' or 'delay decisions' — yields the greatest expected pay-off.

None of these vital factors is known. If lead proves to be a hazard to health, it will still not be possible to measure the improvement in health brought about by the control in money terms so that it is comparable to the cost of control; there is simply no method by which this can be done. Secondly, there is no way of knowing how long a scientific consensus will take to emerge, and no way of rationally assigning a probability to the consensus being that lead is or is not a health hazard. The Bayesian approach therefore fails in this case, which provides us with an example of a decision which must be taken under ignorance.

Before leaving this example, let it be noted that there is nothing peculiar about

---

[1] An excellent review is provided in Lawther (1980).

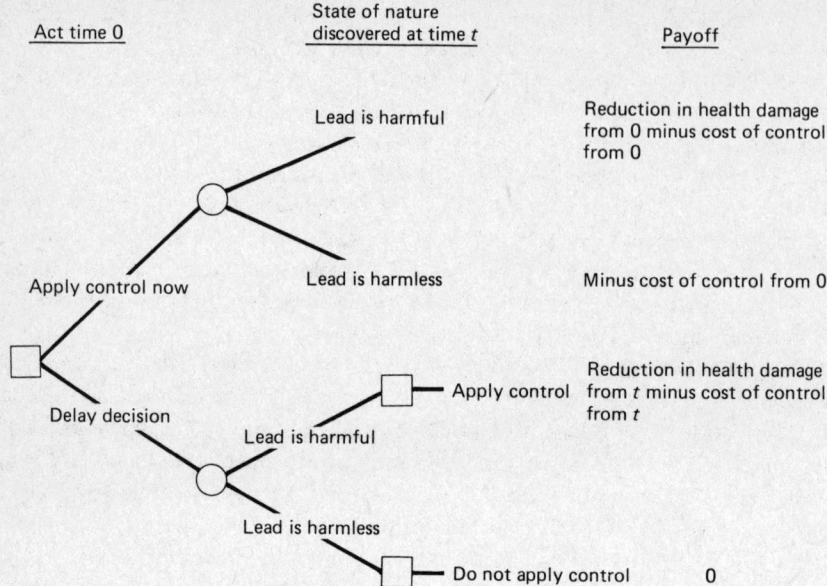

Fig. 7.2 Decision tree for the removal of lead from petrol. From Collingridge (1980), p. 27.

it — rather it is typical of decisions about the imposition of controls on environmental hazards, and indeed, typical of decisions dependent on research findings. Research is generally slow at reaching a consensus. Occasionally one remarkable breakthrough will settle the matter at issue once and for all, but a more general picture is that of a slowly emerging consensus in the community of experts that the growing body of data can only be interpreted in one way. In such a case the decision maker inevitably faces the same sort of problem about the control of lead. Should he act before a final consensus is reached, or should he delay his decision until it can be settled on the basis of the consensus? For the same reasons as before, such a decision will be one under ignorance.

The public nature of debates about decisions

We have seen in chapters 3 and 4 how the justificationist model of decision making is forced to adopt a subjective view of decision making. Making a decision requires knowledge of the agent's preferences, to which the agent himself has privileged access. Nobody can deny that his preferences are as he asserts (unless they accuse the agent of drunkenness, linguistic aberration etc.), just as nobody can deny that he has a headache if he so claims. An agent can therefore receive no advice, nor any criticism of his preferences, provided only that they are consistent, so that the determination of preference is as private a matter as the suffering of pain.

On the theory of preference proposed here, however, a very different view has to be taken. Private commitment to values has no part to play in such a theory. Commitment is supposed to justify the agent's acceptance of a preference judgement, but such justification is altogether impossible. Instead, the agent must realise that none of his preference judgements is justifiable, so that all should be open to criticism and possible falsification and rejection. This criticism proceeds through trying to find factual sentences that falsify the value claim in question and for which there are reasons for accepting. This is a public matter. Nobody has privileged access to the facts that can test a particular evaluative claim. The agent himself may be aware of facts that falsify or corroborate one of his preference judgements, or someone else may point to the existence of this set of facts. Whether the fact falsifies, or the extent to which it corroborates the value judgement is an objective, public issue. Thus, the critical theory of preference emphasises the public dimension of evaluation denied by justificationist views of preference.

This may be illuminated by Popper's three worlds. Popper's world 1 is the world of physical objects; the second is the world of private mental states and world 3 is the world of intelligibles, or of ideas in the objective sense:

. . . it is the world of possible objects of thought: the world of theories in themselves, and their logical relations; of arguments in themselves; and of problem situations in themselves. (Popper, 1968)

Traditional theories of knowledge place great emphasis on the second world, the world containing the scientists' perceptions and experiences, because it is upon these that the whole structure of science is supposed to rest. Popper rejects this psychologistic approach, arguing that justification for scientific claims is not possible, but that they can nevertheless be subject to critical appraisal, Popper (1972). Criticism does not rest upon receiving special privileged information about one's own mental state. Instead it is a public enterprise conducted in the third world. An individual scientist must make up his own mind about, say, the rejection of some physical theory, and in doing so he will of necessity employ only what relevant knowledge he has himself managed to acquire during his professional career, but whilst this is a statement of great profundity on justificationist epistemologies, for Popper it is a banality. If the individual scientist has been unaware of information relevant to the fate of the theory, then this shortcoming may be remedied by his colleagues. If his judgement about the relationship between fact and theory is shaky, his colleagues may criticize him on this score. The fate of the theory is something which is to be settled, not by private introspection, but by public debate – or debate in the third world.

Exactly the same is true of the appraisal of a judgement of preference according to the critical theory of preference. In deciding, for example, that some preference judgement of his is falsified, an agent must conduct his own logical deductions and can only use knowledge that he has managed to acquire for himself in the past. But, as before, there is nothing profound in any of this. If his logic is faulty, this can be pointed out; if he is unaware of relevant facts, these may be made known to him. In other words, the appraisal is best seen, not as an essentially private affair of mysterious commitments, but as a public, third-world matter involving, at least potentially, many people. Logic was de-psychologized in the early part of this century, and Popper has continued the process to epistemology. It is now time to de-psychologize ethics and the theory of value. For this reason, all of the case studies given below concern highly public evaluative debates. Things are much clearer here, of course, than in purely 'private debates' between an agent and his conscience.

Fact and value in debates about action

On the traditional view of value, any disagreement about a particular evaluation either rests upon a confusion over facts or is irreconcilable. If all disagreements about factual matters are resolved between the two parties, and if they still differ over some evaluation, there is nothing that can be done to settle this dispute, assuming that both parties use language properly and are logically consistent. Evaluation is essentially private and subjective, so if one agent values an object differently from another agent, there is really no more dispute between them than if one were to say he has a pain in his foot, and the other to say that his own foot is free from pain. On this view, we would expect debates about values to progress so far, when disagreements over factual matters are gradually cleared up, and then to halt stubbornly and finally, when the different values of the two parties meet head on.

Inspection of real debates over evaluative questions, like the ones which follow, show this to be a very mistaken view. Debates about values do not need to end with an irreconcilable clash of opinions; indeed the progress of such a debate can usefully be seen as the avoidance of such clashes. A second feature of debates about values, which is very surprising on traditional views, is that they can be very protracted and extended, and yet contain no explicit discussion of values whatever. This is, however, understandable on the critical view of preference, as I now hope to show.

Consider two parties A and B, the first wishing to defend a decision maxim M, the second hoping to argue against M. Assume that both parties have the preference sentences $V_1 \ldots V_N$ in common, so that these may be counted as background preferences. A can assert M and B can assert not-M, but this simply produces a head-on clash between them and the end of all debate. The clash may be avoided, however, if the parties employ only preference sentences on which they agree (i.e., $V_1 \ldots V_N$). A may seek a factual sentence F_1, which is supported by evidence and which couples with a background preference sentence, V_i, to corroborate M, because $M \cdot V_i \to F_1$. B, on the other hand, may attempt to falsify M by discovering a factual sentence F_2, which has evidence in its favour and which couples with a background preference sentence, V_j, to falsify M, since $M \cdot V_j \to$ not F_2. The key element in the debate is now the acceptability of the two factual sentences, F_1 and F_2. If A can persuade B to give up F_2 and adopt F_1, he has succeeded in showing that M is indeed, corroborated, while if A can be convinced by B to give up F_1 and adopt F_2, B has shown M to be falsified. The debate can now, of course, proceed because it concerns what factual sentences are acceptable. These factual issues are only relevant to the debate because of the background preference sentences $V_1 \ldots V_N$, but because these are shared and not expected to require alteration, these values usually receive no explicit mention in the debate. Thus inspection of debates about what course of action ought to be adopted nearly always reveals a paradox. The issue is obviously a normative one, but the arguments of the antagonists are exclusively concerned with facts. The critical theory of decision making can, as I hope I have indicated and as will become clearer later on, explain this paradox. What explanation might be forthcoming from rival models of decision making I have no idea.

Just as criticism of A's maxim M centres on factual issues, so does the criticism of any background preference sentence which may fall into doubt as the debate proceeds. Suppose that B has convinced A to adopt F_2, so that M is put in jeopardy. A might save the day by showing that V_j is, after all, false. It must be remembered, of course, that V_j's belonging to the background of the debate is no justification of V_j. A background preference sentence is as beyond justification as any other preference sentence, all that distinguishes it is its provisional acceptance by both parties. If A can bring V_j into question, it can no longer be reckoned a background preference, and it must leave the periphery for the centre of debate. A can question V_j by appealing to some factual sentence F_3, which has evidence to support it and which, when coupled with background preference sentence V_k falsifies V_j since $V_j \cdot V_k \to$ not F_3. No doubt B will wish to counter by denying F_3, and so the debate may continue, but only by revolving, once again, around factual issues.

At this point it may be useful to return to the question of the publicity or privacy of decision making according to different theoretical views. What *motivates* A and B to defend or attack the decision maxim M is, indeed, private, covert, hidden and a question for psychologists to answer. The cogency of the case they make out for or against the maxim is, on the other hand, an objective, public matter. If A uses immunizing stratagems to protect M from falsification, this may be reckoned a weakness in his case, for whatever psychological reason A has behaved in this way. If B claims that some factual sentence falsifies M, this is not a matter for his own private determination, but a public question which may be discussed by anyone, and discussion requires no knowledge of B's motivation.

The debate between A and B is, as we have seen, dominated by factual issues, and in many important debates in the real world these issues resolve into what is the best interpretation of an agreed body of data. Both parties accept a body of evidence but differ in its interpretation, one side favouring an interpretation which allows corroboration of the maxim it seeks to defend, the other side upholding a rival interpretation which shows the maxim to be falsified. The debate is then an extremely common one within pure science, which is the better of the rival interpretations — and this may proceed in exactly the same way as normal scientific debates, notwithstanding its origin in a question of action. As we shall see in the final case study, this leads to a quite different and much richer view of expert opinion in decision making than that offered by upholders of the justificationist model.

Case Study 1: The Corporal Punishment Bill

Parliamentary debates are a rich source of material to which the theory of value developed earlier may be applied. Rather than consider the grand debates on urgent political issues of the day, I have chosen for our present purpose a Private Member's Bill receiving its second reading in the House of Commons on a sleepy Friday afternoon. Such debates often contain more real attempts at dialogue and less party bickering than grander ones. The Bill is the Corporal Punishment Bill, moved by Mr Graham Page on Friday 29 April 1977 (*Hansard*, 29 April 1977, pp. 1736-98; see also Collingridge, 1982). The long title tells us that the Bill aims to:

Permit a sentence of corporal punishment upon a person convicted of an offence involving bodily harm to another or malicious damage to property.

The chief point I wish to bring out is that although the question whether or not to re-establish corporal punishment is clearly an evaluative one, the debate contains hardly any mention of values, all the important issues being factual. I hope to show how the theory developed here can accommodate what, on conventional views of value, must be a highly surprising feature of the debate.

The Bill would enable corporal punishment by birch, cane or strap, under circumstances and for crimes laid down in affirmative orders of the Secretary of State. To expedite punishment the Secretary of State may also lay before the House affirmative orders enabling a convicted person:

to waive an appeal against conviction or sentence, sufficient to allow the sentence of corporal punishment to be inflicted before the expiration of the time allowed for appeal. (Clause 3(e)).

The Bill's mover, Mr Page, saw the operation of this clause in this way. If a Magistrate wishes to impose a sentence of corporal punishment on a convicted person, then he may ask whether the offender would appeal against such a sentence. If he does not wish to appeal, then the sentence would be passed and would be carried out as quickly as possible. If the offender wishes to appeal, however, corporal punishment is likely to be ineffective due to the great delay between offence and punishment, and so some other sentence would probably be favoured by the Magistrate. For juvenile offenders, the choice would lie with the offender's parents. The Bill sets no upper or lower age limit for corporal punishment, nor would it exclude women from receiving such punishment, although Mr Page saw both issues as open to debate.

The debate opened, of course, with Mr Page making out his case for the Bill. He claimed that public opinion favoured corporal punishment over conventional forms of punishment; that the great increase in crimes against the person and vandalism showed existing punishments to be ineffective; that corporal punishment would be especially effective against juvenile crime, which had increased alarmingly and would be a good deterrent to other offenders. Notice that all of these arguments are entirely factual. As is perfectly normal, the Bill's proposer has not made explicit the evaluative claims involved in his argument. It is not hard to see why this was so, because — as will emerge below — the value claims are all very mundane.

Before considering the force and logic of the arguments above, it may be best to look first at some of the criticisms made of the Bill. The Bill's defenders support the decision maxim C, (x) (x is an option other than passing the Bill $\supset$ not (x pref passing the Bill)), and it may now be asked how this maxim was attacked by those members opposed to the Bill. The principal claim of the opposers was:

$F_1 = $ conventional punishments are a better deterrent than any form of corporal punishment

In support of F_1 it was argued that physical punishment can only be effective when administered immediately after the offence, so that the inevitable delays of the judicial process made any form of institutional corporal punishment a very weak deterrent. F_1 was also defended by appealing to the statistical analyses of two earlier committees, under Cadogan in 1938 and Barry in 1960, which showed that among convicted prisoners those birched were more likely to return to crime than those punished in other ways. This is further supported by the experiences of Magistrates who refrained from passing sentences of corporal punishment, even when empowered to impose it, because they had concluded that it was ineffective.

How can F_1 constitute criticism of C? Obviously, the factual claims need to be supplemented by evaluative ones if they are to falsify the preference sentence C. The evaluative part of the case against the Bill is captured by the preference sentence V_1:

$V_1 = (x)(y)$ (If punishment x deters more than punishment y then x pref y)

This is a very mundane preference claim, accepted by both sides in the debate and not expected to come under critical suspicion. It is, therefore, a background value and, typically, is not made explicit in the arguments of those who employ it.

There are two ways of looking at the logic here:

$$C \rightarrow V_x$$

where

$V_x =$ Corporal punishment administered as laid down in the Bill pref conventional punishments

But

$F_1 \cdot V_1 \rightarrow$ Conventional punishments pref any form of corporal punishment

so that

$$F_1 \cdot V_1 \rightarrow \text{not } V_x$$

$F_1 \cdot V_1$ can, therefore, be seen as a counterargument to C. C entails V_x, but $F_1 \cdot V_1$ entails not V_x. This is a serious challenge to C, because F_1 has been defended by a considerable body of past experience and V_1 is a background preference sentence. Since something has to go, it looks like C.

Another way of viewing the criticism is that it provides a factual falsification of C because:

$$C \cdot V_1 \rightarrow \text{not } F_1$$

but F_1 appears to be true. As before, this must place C under a considerable critical cloud.

Having considered the main arguments against the Bill, the case made out by its supporters can be seen in more detail. They argued that, despite appearances, F_1 was false. The statistical results of Cadogan and Barry were dismissed as irrelevant because they principally concerned gang violence, and the great growth in crime since then showed that conventional punishments are much less effective deterrents than previously thought. Growth in juvenile crime also made the reports outdated, because corporal punishment is especially effective with young offenders. Experience of corporal punishment in the Isle of Man has shown that it can provide a deterrent superior to that provided by conventional punishments. Against the argument that the inevitable delay between the offence and the punishment would make any form of corporal punishment a poor deterrent, it was held that such delay is not inevitable and that the Bill allowed for swift punishment by allowing the offender to waive his right of appeal.

The force of these arguments is that F_1 is false and F_2, its contrary, true:

$F_2 =$ Corporal punishment administered under existing circumstances and in accordance with the Bill is a better deterrent than conventional punishments

The substitution of F_2 for F_1 is not an *ad hoc* device for the protection of

C from criticism, because, as we have seen, the move is closely argued. The substitution means success for C. As falsification can be seen in two ways, so can success:

$$C \rightarrow V_x$$

and

$$V_1 \cdot F_2 \rightarrow V_x$$

so that $V_1 \cdot F_2$ supports C by offering an independent argument for a logical consequence of C. Notice that there is no hope of finding a background preference V_i which is sufficiently strong to entail C itself when coupled with factual sentences. C has the form 'No option is preferable to Q' so that V_i would have to be of this form as well. V_i would, therefore, be much stronger than any background preference sentence like V_1, which has the form 'R is preferable to S'. Indeed V_i would be so strong as to be unable to be regarded as part of the background. This is an important point: decision maxims can be falsified or corroborated by background preference sentences, but cannot be deduced from them.

A second way of viewing the success of C is to note that

$$C \cdot V_1 \rightarrow \text{not } F_1$$

and not F_1 is found to be true since F_2 is true. The obvious question at this point is what degree of success ought to be conferred on C by this transformation of falsification into corroboration? If the arguments for F_2 are accepted, C has a high degree of corroboration because its supporters have successfully challenged a large body of evidence and conventional thinking. F_1 is expected to be true, which falsifies C, but C's defenders respond to this challenge by showing F_1 to be false and its contrary F_2 true, which corroborates C. The Bill's opponents were, of course, very keen to deny this corroboration of C. To this end they argued against the facts adduced in support of F_2. The debate, therefore, came to centre on purely factual issues.

It was argued that if corporal punishment is a deterrent then behaviour in British schools, the only ones in Europe retaining such punishment, should be better than in European schools — something for which there is no evidence. In reply to this criticism it was stated that behaviour in British schools would be even worse if corporal punishment were abolished there.

Several critics of the Bill argued that corporal punishment would be chosen by an offender as the lesser of two evils, so that it could hardly be reckoned a deterrent. In reply, it was argued that it would still be a deterrent, even though a somewhat weakened one.

It was also argued that corporal punishment might well increase the level of violence in society, by adding to the glamour and status of an offender so punished, especially a juvenile. One objection to this was that it ought to apply to all forms of punishment, so that imprisonment and fines would also lead to a higher crime rate. A second objection was that even if corporal punishment leads to more violence by some sections of the community, it might reduce the total level of violence by its deterrent effect.

A slightly different point was made by one objector to the Bill who argued that corporal punishment, although quite possibly a deterrent, was not the best deterrent. A better one would be the full use of existing powers to impose stern penalties of imprisonment or fines. In reply to this, it was pointed out that these powers were not used for some reason, and that other punishments should, therefore, be attempted.

It can be seen that this part of the debate concerned entirely factual issues. Why this should be so when what is under question is the evaluative issue of what to do, can be explained in the way I have indicated. What sort of explanation it might receive from justificationist accounts of decision making cannot even be guessed.

Explicit mention of values occurred three times in the debate, and there is something different to be learned from each. One argument in defence of the Bill, as before, made without explicit mention of values was:

F_3 = Public opinion for corporal punishment is stronger than public opinion for conventional punishments.

The suppressed, background value here is something like V_2:

$V_2 = (x)(y)$ (If public support for measure x is stronger than public support for y then x pref y)

Since one option open to the House is to reject the Bill and continue with conventional punishments:

$$C \rightarrow V_y$$

V_y = Some form of corporal punishment pref conventional punishments

Now

$$F_3 \cdot V_2 \rightarrow V_y$$

so that $F_3 \cdot V_2$ provides an independent argument for a logical consequence of C, namely V_y, thus supporting C. Another way to formalize this point is to observe that:

$$V_2 \cdot C \rightarrow \text{not } F_4$$

F_4 = Public opinion for conventional punishments is stronger than public opinion for some form of corporal punishment

F_4 is the contrary of F_3, so establishing F_3 also means that not F_4 must be accepted, so corroborating C. When, however, the brevity of this argument in favour of C is contrasted with the complexities of the previous arguments about the acceptance of F_2, it seems intuitively clear that the new argument lends less support to C. This is borne out on analysis when it is realised that:

$$V_x \to V_y$$

V_x states that the punishment detailed in the Bill is preferable to conventional punishments, but V_y claims that some indefined form of corporal punishment is preferable to conventional ones. F_2 therefore corroborates C more than F_3; it establishes a greater part of C's factual content than that which follows from F_3.

Nevertheless, the Bill's opponents thought the second argument sufficiently important to counter. It was argued that:

$F_5 =$ Public opinion for castration of sexual offenders is stronger than public opinion for conventional punishment of sexual offenders

and that:

$$F_5 \cdot V_2 \to V_3$$

$V_3 =$ Castration of sexual offenders pref conventional punishment of sexual offenders

V_3, it was held, is something both sides to the debate would reject, so that not V_3 is a background preference sentence. This falsifies $F_5 \cdot V_2$, so that V_2 should be rejected. Thus V_2 begins the day by being a background value, tentatively accepted by both sides, but as the debate develops it is questioned and must therefore leave the periphery for the centre of debate and must lose its status of background value.

The second evaluative issue raised is slightly more complex. It was argued that corporal punishment is a degrading and inhuman punishment and so one that should not be used; indeed one that could not be used because of the European Convention on Human Rights (Article 3), signed by the UK. Whether corporal punishment is inhuman is clearly an evaluative question, but it is interesting to see how the debate's participants came to grips with it. This they did by considering various factual issues. The relevant factual questions were singled out by means of background value judgements. It was accepted by all that inhuman punishments should not be inflicted and that corporal punishment inflicted by a parent or teacher is not inhuman. The factual question then becomes whether the relationship between the state and the offender is similar to that between teacher or parent and offender. If it is, then corporal punishment by the state is no more inhuman than corporal punishment by a parent or teacher. If the relationship is significantly different, however, then corporal punishment by the state may well be considered inhuman. In this way what threatens to be a bald, intractable clash of values is converted into a factual question, which can be handled in debate.

Formally, we may view the Bill's supporters as advancing the following argument:

V_4 If corporal punishment by parent or teacher is not inhuman and if the relationship between parent or teacher and offender is similar to that between the state and offender, then corporal punishment by the state is not inhuman
V_5 Corporal punishment by parent or teacher is not inhuman
F_6 The relationship between parent or teacher and offender is similar to that between the state and offender

V_6 Corporal punishment by the state is not inhuman

V_4 and V_5 may be viewed as background value judgements, whilst F_6 is factual. Opponents of the Bill argued that F_6 is false, because the parent or teacher has a far greater knowledge of the likely effects of the punishment on the offender than has the state, and because the relationship between the punishing parent or teacher and the offender can still be one of affection, an emotion unknown to the state. This does nothing to show that corporal punishment by the state is inhuman but it effectively destroys the argument made out by the Bill's supporters.

The third evaluative issue to be raised was done so by an opponent of the Bill, Ms Maureen Colquhoun. She held that young people 'need to be left alone as much as possible by adults' and that they ought to be given rights as people. The Bill was wrong because it would lead to adults inflicting pain on children and would give adults too much power over young people. Ms Colquhoun's entry into the debate led to nothing. Nobody agreed with her and nobody thought it important to criticize her claims. This is hardly surprising because whatever Ms Colquhoun meant to say it obviously rests upon some value claim which is special to her and not common to the other participants in the debate. To engage in a debate about an evaluative question like the restoration of corporal punishment one must employ value judgements shared by one's opponents, or else the debate degenerates into a simple and totally intractable clash of rival value claims.

We cannot discover if anyone changed sides during the debate because of the arguments presented there. All we can record is that the Bill was lost by seventeen votes to six.

Case Study 2: Is Small Beautiful?

E. F. Schumacher's influential book *Small is Beautiful* does not consist of a closely reasoned, continuous argument, but is a collection of ideas around a central theme. Schumacher is a vociferous critic of modern technology and its handmaiden, economics, both of which he wishes to reform drastically. His writing is, therefore, an intimate mixture of factual and evaluative claims, which it may be rewarding to analyse from the point of view of the critical theory of preference. In particular, I shall look at the relationship between Schumacher's factual and evaluative claims.

Schumacher's criticism of conventional economics is that it regards consumption as the only good, and pays no regard to the burden that this consumption places on man's environment and on future generations who may have nothing left to consume because of our own greed. Despite its limited outlook, economics plays an overwhelmingly important part in our decision making:

Call a thing immoral or ugly, soul-destroying or a degradation of man, a peril to the peace of the world or to the well-being of future generations; as long as you have not shown it to be 'uneconomic' you have not really questioned its right to exist, grow and prosper. . . . [In] the market . . . there is no probing into the depths of things, into the natural or social facts that lie behind them. In a sense, the market is the institutionalisation of individualism and non-responsibility. Neither buyer nor seller is responsible for anything but himself. (Schumacher, 1973, pp. 38–40)

The dominance of economics amounts to:

. . . the religion of economics, the idol worship of material possessions, of consumption and the so-called standard of living, and the fateful propensity that rejoices in the fact that 'what were luxuries to our fathers have become necessities for us'. (Schumacher, 1973; p. 244)

This dependence on economics had led us to adopt technologies of ever-increasing size. Our consumption of the Earth's non-renewable resources is now on such a gargantuan scale that many vital resources, in particular fossil fuels, are likely to be exhausted very soon. The pollution produced by our ever-growing industries endangers the delicate mechanisms which make the Earth habitable. Work has become alienating and meaningless as more and more skills are sacrificed to machinery in the name of economic efficiency. In the developing world, production has been increased with scant regard to the distribution of the wealth so created, so that rich, sophisticated city dwellers form isolated islands in a sea of traditional poverty. For conventional economics:

The farmer is considered simply as a producer who must cut his costs and raise his efficiency by every possible device, even if he thereby destroys — for-man-as-consumer — the health of the soil and the beauty of the landscape, and even if the end effect is the depopulation of the land and the overcrowding of cities. (Schumacher, 1973, p. 97)

Schumacher sees as a solution to all these problems the adoption of what he calls Buddhist economics in place of conventional economics. The difference between these approaches is nowhere more marked than when they are applied to labour. In conventional economics, a man's labour is valuable if he can produce more saleable goods than he can by using his efforts elsewhere. The Buddhist point of view sees work as offering a man a chance to use his skills, and to develop them; as overcoming the worker's ego-centredness by his assisting other workers and as a means of producing the necessities of life:

To organize work in such a manner that it becomes meaningless, boring, stultifying, or nerve-racking for the worker would be little short of criminal; it would indicate a greater concern with goods than with people, an evil lack of compassion and a soul-destroying attachment to the most primitive side of this worldly existence. (Schumacher, 1973, p. 50)

Whereas conventional economics considers consumption as the sole good, Buddhist economics seeks an optimal pattern of consumption, one that produces a high degree of human satisfaction with a low rate of consumption. The modest use of local resources is favoured over a consumption so gross as to require imports from all parts of the world. In this, Buddhist economics is aware of the sharp difference between those resources which renew themselves and those that may be exhausted, a difference to which conventional economics is blind. Similarly, Buddhist economics would never countenance technologies that do violence to the long-term stability of the environment and the eco-system. Schumacher is somewhat despairing about the possibility of replacing conventional economics in the West, but sees a chance for developing countries to employ a more human, Buddhist economics to guide their progress.

Schumacher's thesis is that the best way to make decisions about resources is to employ Buddhist economics rather than any other variety of economics. This is, on the face of it, a very strong claim, for it says that Buddhist economics is the best way to make decisions in all circumstances and at all locations. Schumacher does not offer a neat, cut and dried definition of Buddhist economics; indeed he uses the term to denote a more human way of looking at decisions about resources than that provided by conventional economics rather than a well-structured theory. For this reason it might be expected that any particular decision about the use of resources will have several options which follow Buddhist economics. The account of this form of economics that Schumacher offers, is insufficiently precise for an option to be singled out as the only one that follows its prescriptions. Likewise, there may be a whole number of options that follow conventional economics. Schumacher can hardly claim that *every* option that follows Buddhist economics is preferable to *all* options that follow conventional economics. A much more realistic claim is that the best option will always be one that follows Buddhist economics, even though some options of this sort may be inferior to some options that follow conventional economics. With this in mind, Schumacher may be seen to be defending a decision maxim something like S:

$$S = (x)\exists y \ (x \text{ is an option not following Buddhist economics} \supset y \text{ is an option following Buddhist economics and not } (x \text{ pref } y))$$

The main arguments used in favour of S all have the same structure. Facts are adduced, which combine with background preference sentences to corroborate S by providing examples where Buddhist economics is superior to conventional economics. Such a form of argument can never hope to prove Schumacher's maxim, because this states that not only are the results of applying Buddhist economics *always* superior to those of applying conventional economics, but they are always superior to the results of applying *any other* form of economics which has been, or may in the future, be suggested. This should, I hope, come as no surprise at this point in the discussion; corroboration can never amount to proof. I propose to consider three arguments of Schumacher's which have this form.

The exhaustion of limited resources

Consider how Schumacher's maxim, S, might be falsified. A defender of conventional economics might argue that there are circumstances under which its application favours the consumption of more resources than that favoured by Buddhist economics. It is better to consume as much as possible because this consumption produces an increase in our standard of living, or at least that part of it which is measurable by GDP. Formally, the factual sentence F_1 and the preference sentence V_1, which is assumed to be a background sentence, are proposed. F_1 states that there is at least one decision where there is an option following conventional economics which consumes more than any option following Buddhist economics.

$V_1 = (x)(y)$ (x consumes more than $y \supset x$ pref y)

$F_1 = \exists x(y)$ (y follows Buddhist economics $\supset x$ follows conventional economics and x consumes more than y)

$F_1 \cdot V_1 \rightarrow \exists x(y)$ (y follows Buddhist economics $\supset x$ follows conventional economics and x pref y)

so that

$$F_1 \cdot V_1 \rightarrow \text{not } S$$

Schumacher attempts to turn this threatened falsification of S into a corroboration by arguing against V_1. He claims that far from consumption representing a good, the unrestricted exploitation of resources encouraged by conventional economics can only lead to their rapid and ruinous exhaustion:

Economics deals with goods in accordance with their market value and not in accordance of what they really are. The same rules and criteria are applied to primary goods, which man has to win from nature, and secondary goods, which . . . are manufactured from them. All goods are treated the same, because the point of view is fundamentally that of private profit-making, and this means that it is inherent in the methodology of economics *to ignore man's dependence on the natural world*. (Schumacher, 1973, p. 38)

What Schumacher needs to show is that in those cases where conventional economics favours a more rapid consumption of resources than Buddhist economics, following conventional economics leads to a more rapid exhaustion of the resources. The argument employs the background preference sentence V_2 and the factual sentence F_2:

$V_2 = (x)(y)$ (x exhausts resources more rapidly than $y \supset y$ pref x)

$F_2 = (x)(y)$ (x follows conventional economics and y follows Buddhist economics $\supset x$ consumes more than $y \supset x$ exhausts resources more rapidly than y)

$F_2 \cdot V_2 \rightarrow (x)(y)$ (x follows conventional economics and y follows Buddhist economics $\supset x$ consumes more than $y \supset y$ pref x)

so that

$$F_2 \cdot V_2 \rightarrow \text{not } V_1$$

Another way of looking at Schumacher's case is to see him as corroborating S through the rejection of the factual test sentence F_3. F_3 states that there is a decision with an option that follows conventional economics, which exhausts resources less rapidly than any option following Buddhist economics. As before, V_2 functions as a background preference sentence:

$F_3 = \exists x(y)$ (y follows Buddhist economics $\supset x$ follows conventional economics and y exhausts resources more rapidly than x)

F_3 is forbidden by S because

$$S \cdot V_2 \rightarrow \text{not } F_3$$

Schumacher's arguments for F_2 are equally arguments against F_3 since F_2 entails not F_3, so that these corroborate S. But we may ask by how much does Schumacher's not F_3 corroborate his decision maxim S? The degree of corroboration of a maxim x, by a factual test sentence y, given background preference sentences b is:

$$C(x, y, b) = \frac{p(y, x \cdot b) - p(y, b)}{p(y, x \cdot b) + p(y, b) - p(x \cdot y, b)}$$

In the present case:

$$C(S, \text{not } F_3, V_2) = \frac{1 - p(\text{not } F_3)}{1 + p(\text{not } F_3) - p(S, V_2)}$$

remembering that

$$S \cdot V_2 \rightarrow \text{not } F_3 \text{ and } p(\text{not } F_3, V_2) = p(\text{not } F_3)$$

There are two things to observe. First, nowhere does Schumacher give a detailed account of what exactly Buddhist economics consists of, although hints abound. Thus S is very imprecise and like any imprecise statement must be assigned a high probability, so making the degree of corroboration of S by not F_3 low. The second point concerns the probability of not F_3. To show F_3 is to find a decision where there is an option following conventional economics which exhausts resources at a certain rate, and where *all* options following Buddhist economics exhaust resources at a higher rate. This seems to be a highly improbable occurrence. The number of options that follow Buddhist economics is sure to be large, even if only because of the imprecise meaning Schumacher has attributed to the term, so there is a very high probability of finding one such option which exhausts resources less rapidly than the option that follows conventional economics. F_3 must, therefore, be assigned a low probability, and not F_3 a correspondingly high one. But this means that not F_3 confers only a poor degree of corroboration on S. It may be asked whether the results of applying the measure in this way are consistent with our intuitions about the degree of support an argument lends to a case about what to do. As far as I am concerned, this is the case, but others must judge for themselves.

Intermediate technology

Another argument against Schumacher's decision maxim S that might be proposed by defenders of conventional economics is that the use of this variety of the science produces more wealth in developing countries than would be achieved by using the Buddhist variety. This case couples V_3, presumed to be a background preference sentence, with the factual claim F_4, which states that there is a decision where an option following conventional economics produces more wealth than any option which follows Buddhist economics:

$V_3 = (x)(y)$ (x produces more wealth in a developing country than $y \supset x$ pref y)

$F_4 = \exists x(y)$ (y follows Buddhist economics $\supset x$ follows conventional economics and x produces more wealth in a developing country than y)

$F_4 \cdot V_3 \rightarrow \exists x(y)$ (y follows Buddhist economics $\supset x$ follows conventional economics and x pref y)

so that

$$F_4 \cdot V_3 \rightarrow \text{not } S$$

Schumacher's reply is that the argument ignores the distribution of the additional wealth produced by using conventional economics. According to Buddhist economics, the greatest benefit is from improving the lot of the poor, and this is to be favoured over larger absolute increases of wealth which benefit only those who already have. Instead of the large, capital intensive, centralized and highly productive technology favoured by conventional economics, Buddhist economics favours what Schumacher calls intermediate technology:

> If we define the level of technology in terms of 'equipment cost per workplace', we can call the indigenous technology of a typical developing country — symbolically speaking — a £1-technology, while that of the developed countries could be called a £1000-technology. The gap between these two technologies is so enormous that a transition from the one to the other is simply impossible. In fact, the current attempt of the developing countries to infiltrate the £1000-technology into their economies inevitably kills off the £1-technology at an alarming rate, destroying traditional workplaces much faster than modern workplaces can be created, and thus leaves the poor in a more desperate and helpless position than ever before. If effective help is to be brought to those who need it most, a technology is required which would range in some intermediate position between the £1-technology and the £1000-technology. Let us call it — again symbolically speaking — a £100-technology. Such an intermediate technology would be immensely more productive than the indigenous technology (which is often in a condition of decay), but it would also be immensely cheaper than the sophisticated, highly capital-intensive technology of modern industry. At such a level of capitalisation, very large numbers of workplaces could be created within a fairly short time; and the creation of such workplaces would be 'within reach' for the more enterprising minority within the district, not only in financial terms but also in terms of their education, aptitude, organising skill and so forth. (Schumacher, 1973, p. 167)

Such intermediate technology has the added advantage that it does not need to be sited in urban areas, so that its adoption may do something to stem the flow of people from the countryside to towns. Neither does it require foreign experts since its principles can easily be understood by the worker using the technology.

Schumacher's argument is that in all those cases where following conventional economics produces more wealth in a developing country than can be achieved by any option which follows Buddhist economics, following conventional economics produces a greater gap between rich and poor than would result from following Buddhist economics. His case depends on the background preference sentence V_4 and the factual claim F_5:

$V_4 = (x)(y)$ (x produces a greater gap between rich and poor in a developing country than $y \supset y$ pref x)

$F_5 = (x)(y)$ (x follows conventional economics and y follows Buddhist economics $\supset x$ produces more wealth in a developing country than $y \supset x$ produces a greater gap between rich and poor in a developing country than y)

$V_4 \cdot F_5 \rightarrow (x)(y)$ (x follows conventional economics and y follows Buddhist economics $\supset x$ produces more wealth in a developing country than $y \supset y$ pref x)

So that

$$V_4 \cdot F_5 \to \text{not } V_1$$

Schumacher can thus be seen as defending S by falsifying V_1, the background preference sentence used in the attack upon S. Another way of viewing the argument is that it is a corroboration of S by the rejection of the factual test sentence F_6, which states that there is a decision with an option that follows conventional economics and that produces a lower gap between rich and poor in a developing country than that produced by any option that follows Buddhist economics:

$F_6 = \exists x(y)$ (y follows Buddhist economics $\supset x$ follows conventional economics and y produces a greater gap between rich and poor in a developing country than x)

F_6 is forbidden by S since

$$V_4 \cdot S \to \text{not } F_6$$

Schumacher's arguments for F_5 are all arguments for not F_6 because F_5 entails not F_6, so that his earlier arguments corroborate S. As before, however, the degree of corroboration is weak. Buddhist economics is no more precisely stated than earlier and the probability of not F_6 is very high for the same reason as the probability of not F_3 is high. To establish F_6 is to find a decision where there is an option following conventional economics that produces a certain gap between rich and poor, and where *all* options following Buddhist economics produce a greater gap. Given the imprecision of Buddhist economics, there will be very many options following it and one of them is very likely to produce a lesser gap than any option favoured by conventional economics, so the probability of F_6 is low, and of not F_6 high. Thus not F_6 confers only a low degree of corroboration upon S.

Nuclear power

The third argument Schumacher uses in defence of his decision maxim S may be dealt with briefly since the logic of the argument is exactly the same as that of the earlier two. A possible argument against S is that following Buddhist economics would never permit the development of nuclear power which is, nevertheless, the cheapest form of electricity. The argument may be formalized as involving V_5, supposed to be a background preference sentence, and the factual sentence F_7 which states that since there is an option to develop nuclear power if conventional economics are followed, but not if Buddhist economics are accepted, following the former can produce cheaper energy than following the latter:

$V_5 = (x)(y)$ (x is a cheaper way of producing energy than $y \supset x$ pref y)

$F_7 = \exists x(y)$ (y follows Buddhist economics $\supset x$ follows conventional economics and x produces energy more cheaply than y)

$F_7 \cdot V_5 \rightarrow \exists x(y)$ (y follows Buddhist economics $\supset x$ follows conventional economics and x pref y)

so that

$$F_7 \cdot V_5 \rightarrow \text{not } S$$

Once again, Schumacher attempts to turn this threatened falsification into a corroboration of S by denying the offending background preference sentence V_5. This he does by arguing that although the nuclear route might be the cheapest way of producing energy, the environmental hazards of disposing of the long-lived wastes that nuclear reactors produce are quite unacceptable. What Schumacher must show is that following conventional economics allows cheaper energy than any option favoured by Buddhist economics, only at the cost of bearing a greater risk of damage to health and the environment, as expressed in F_8. His defence also requires the background preference sentence V_6:

$V_6 = (x)(y)$ (If x is more hazardous than $y \supset y$ pref x)

$F_8 = (x)(y)$ (x follows conventional economics and y follows Buddhist economics $\supset x$ produces energy more cheaply than $y \supset x$ is more hazardous than y)

$F_8 \cdot V_6 \rightarrow (x)(y)$ (x follows conventional economics and y follows Buddhist economics $\supset x$ produces energy more cheaply than $y \supset y$ pref x)

so that

$$F_8 \cdot V_6 \rightarrow \text{not } V_5$$

Another way of looking at Schumacher's defence of S is to see him as corroborating S by not F_9, using the background preference sentence V_6. S forbids F_9, which states that there is a decision with an option that follows conventional economics and that poses an environmental and health hazard of a certain size, and no option following Buddhist economics poses a smaller hazard.

$F_9 = \exists x(y)$ (y follows Buddhist economics $\supset x$ follows conventional economics and y is more hazardous than x)

$$S \cdot V_6 \rightarrow \text{not } F_9$$

so finding not F_9 corroborates S. Schumacher's arguments for F_8 are also arguments for not F_9 because F_8 entails not F_9. For the same reasons as before, however, the degree of corroboration of S by not F_9 must be counted as low, since the probability of the imprecise S and of not F_9 must both be reckoned as high. Schumacher's third argument is, therefore, no stronger than his first two.

I have examined the connection between the factual claims made by Schumacher and his evaluative claim that Buddhist economics ought to be used in making decisions about the use of resources, and I hope that the application of the critical apparatus developed earlier in the chapter has illuminated rather than obscured the case that Schumacher makes out. The case has been found to be a weak one, at least as far as the three examples considered go, and it must be asked whether this is in accord with our intuition. For myself this is certainly so, for Schumacher's vague and woolly characterization of his new economics is a weakness in itself. Then there is the lack of any factual novelty; things like exhaustion of resources, the gap between rich and poor in developing countries and the hazards of nuclear power were all well known long before Schumacher's comments on them, and he adds nothing to our understanding of any of these problems. Though undeniably a powerful polemic, the book does not seem to me to go much further. As to the judgement of others, I must wait their comments. A final point is that nowhere in the book does Schumacher make any of his background preferences explicit. Some kind of evaluative claims are obviously required because he is defending a normative claim about the superiority of his new economics whilst the page refers only to factual matters. This is extremely common. The background preferences are so mundane and ordinary and widely acceptable, that their explicit use would serve only to weary the reader.

Case Study 3: Ethyl Corporation vs. EPA

I have analysed the debate between the Ethyl Corporation and the United States Environmental Protection Agency (EPA) about the removal of lead from petrol elsewhere (Collingridge, 1980, chapter 11), but it is worth restating a few key points here. The Ethyl Corporation is a major USA manufacturer of lead additives for petrol and the debate concerns the claim by the EPA that lead from this source is a health hazard. The story begins with the enactment of a Federal Law requiring motor car exhausts to contain less of the noxious gases carbon monoxide and nitrogen oxides. In 1974 it seemed that the best way of achieving this would be to fit catalytic converters in the exhaust system of all new cars. One problem, however, was that the platinum catalyst in this device was poisoned by lead in the exhaust gases. The EPA therefore proposed that lead free fuel be available from July 1974 for use in those new cars fitted with catalytic converters. They also decided, however, to press for more than this and in 1972 proposed not only that a lead free petrol be available by July 1974, but that there should also be a phased reduction in the maximum levels of lead in other petrol to 1.25 g/gal in 1977. Their argument for the additional restriction on lead was that the metal from this source was a hazard to the health of the general public, a claim defended in their document EPA (1972).

The Ethyl Corporation, not unexpectedly, took great exception to the EPA's proposed regulations, arguing that catalytic converters might not prove to be the best way of reducing noxious gases from vehicle exhausts, and that, contrary to the EPA's claims, lead from vehicles was not a significant hazard to health. The bulk of their criticism of the proposed regulations was on this issue of the health effects of lead. The debate between the parties, although highly technical in many places, offers a useful example to which to apply the theory of preference developed here. It is very well documented and conducted by parties equipped with great resources, acumen and specialist knowledge. We might, therefore, expect to find in it examples of many of the points illuminated by the critical theory of decision making. Chief of these is the point that the debate, being about what course of action should be taken, is a debate about values, and yet values play no explicit part whatever in the debate. The debate between Ethyl and EPA concerns facts and facts alone.

The traditional view of value would see the present debate in something like the following way. Both EPA and Ethyl agree on the facts about the consequences of reducing lead in petrol and those of maintaining existing levels, or at worst there are a number of facts, which they have not yet agreed upon but which can be decided, one way or the other, without too much difficulty. What makes the argument between Ethyl and EPA so persistent is that each is committed to quite a different set of values. The EPA is charged with maintaining the health of the general public and a decent environment, and so places great value on clean and healthy air. Being a government agency it places little value on the profits of big business. Ethyl, on the other hand, is a private business and so must make money to survive. It is not surprising to find that it places a lower value on clean air than it does on its own profits. The conflict arises from the clash of these two, fundamentally irreconcilable, systems of value.

When we look at the details of the debate, however, this view of it appears a travesty. The debate between Ethyl and EPA concerns factual questions and factual questions alone. No discussion of values ever takes place in the whole debate. Values are needed to make any decision but they do not arise in the debate because the values employed by both sides are mundane background values shared by all.

There is no need to repeat the details of the long and complicated debate between the two parties, except to remedy an error, which may prove illuminating. In the earlier analysis I suggested that:

What EPA tries to show is that there are facts which, when coupled with some set of background values, entail that it is better to remove lead from petrol than maintain existing levels. Ethyl, on the other hand, tries to show that there are background values which, coupled with facts lead to the reverse conclusion. The debate then centres, not on the values used by the parties, because these are common, but on the facts elicited by each side in support of their case. (Collingridge, 1980, chapter 11)

This is perfectly true, as far as it goes, but it may suggest the possibility of the EPA establishing their case, that their regulations should be implemented, from background preference sentences. By now the impossibility of this should be quite clear. The EPA's claim is very much stronger than that the removal of lead from petrol is preferable to maintaining existing levels, for it is that the complex set of regulations governing the availability of lead free and low lead fuels should be enacted. Formally, we may attribute to the EPA the decision maxim E:

$E = (x)$ (x is an option other than the adoption of the EPA's proposed regulations $\supset$ not (x pref adopting the EPA's proposed regulations))

Since one option is maintaining existing levels of lead in petrol, E entails V_1:

$V_1 = $ Using low lead and lead free fuels pref maintaining existing lead levels

It is clear, however, that E is not entailed by V_1 and is much stronger. This said, it is true that EPA's arguments were all of the form indicated in the quotation above, they brought forward facts which when coupled with background preference sentences yielded V_1. V_1, however, is totally uninformative about what action to take; it merely says that one action is preferable to another. Action requires a maxim like E. The EPA's arguments can, therefore, be seen as attempts, not to deduce E from some set of factual and background preference sentences, but to corroborate E. Ethyl, on the other hand, sought to falsify E. The quotation above may give the impression that the argument was symmetrical, with both parties engaging in essentially the same logical operations. This is not so, however. Ethyl have to corroborate E, and do so by defending V_1, but Ethyl has to falsify E, chiefly by falsifying V_1, but is not concerned to defend any decision maxim of its own. The proposer of any action has a much more difficult task than the opposer who can be entirely negative, not suggesting any course of action and only criticizing what the proposer puts forward.

Without delving into too much detail, the following are some examples to illustrate the point. EPA argues that F_1 is true:

$F_1 = $ Leaded petrol is a fuel which poses a health hazard and low lead and lead free petrol is a fuel which does not pose a health hazard

This, by itself, tells us nothing; it needs to be supplemented by some value claim. As is usual, the factual support for F_1 received all the attention in EPA's arguments, which nowhere explicitly mention values. This is because the value is a background preference sentence, and mundane and not expected to be criticized. We may represent it by V_2:

$V_2 = (x)(y)$ (x is a fuel which poses a health hazard and y is a fuel which does not pose a health hazard $\supset$ using y pref using x)

$V_2 \cdot F_1 \rightarrow$ Using low lead and lead free fuel pref using leaded fuel

so that

$$V_2 \cdot F_1 \rightarrow V_1$$

$V_2 \cdot F_1$ may, therefore, be seen as offering an independent argument for a logical consequence of E, so that F_1 corroborates E. The Ethyl Corporation could respond to this by attacking V_2, but this seems extremely reasonable, or by criticizing F_1. Their attack concentrated entirely on F_1, so that the debate shows the usual pattern of being exclusively concerned with factual issues, the values employed receiving no explicit mention because they are accepted by both sides and are mundane enough to seem unlikely to fall under the cloud of criticism.

Ethyl amassed a considerable body of evidence against F_1, and were bold enough to suggest that its contrary, F_2, was true (Ethyl, 1972).

$F_2 = $ Lead free and low lead petrol is a fuel which poses a health hazard and leaded petrol is a fuel which does not pose a health hazard

They argued that not only is lead from exhausts harmless, but that changes in the chemical composition of petrol due to refining changes rendered necessary by the elimination of lead would pose a significant hazard. Clearly:

$$F_2 \cdot V_2 \rightarrow \text{not } V_1$$

and so

$$E \cdot V_2 \rightarrow \text{not } F_2$$

so that F_2 falsifies E. Again, the EPA made reply by attacking, not V_2, which they had already employed, but F_2, so the debate concerned facts and not values.

Another criticism made by Ethyl was that, on EPA's own admission, the removal of lead paint from delapidated, ageing housing would be considerably cheaper than the reduction of lead levels in gasoline. Such a programme of renovation would prevent the vast majority of existing cases of overt lead poisoning in children. We may formalize their case here in the following way:

V_3 If X improves the health of the population less than Y and if X is more expensive than Y then Y pref X

F_3 Removing lead from gasoline will improve the health of the population less than removing lead paint from old buildings

F_4 Removing lead from gasoline will be more expensive than removing lead paint from old buildings

V_4 Removing lead from old buildings pref removing lead from gasoline

so that

$$F_3 \cdot F_4 \cdot V_3 \to \text{not } E$$

Re-arranging this to the standard form, it can be seen that $F_3 \cdot F_4$ falsifies E using the background preference sentence V_3.

$$V_3 \cdot E \to \text{not } F_3 \cdot F_4$$

As before, EPA's response to Ethyl's argument concerned only the factual claims, F_3 and F_4. F_3 was held to be false, as petrol exhausts pose a hazard to the entire child population, unlike the localized hazards of lead in old paint. It is interesting to relate this argument to the discussion of the limits of Bayesian decision theory in chapter 2. It will be recalled that a necessary condition for the application of Bayesian decision procedures is that the set of options considered is complete, meaning that all options are considered whose pay-offs from any state of the world would be altered by the selection of another option. This is a severe restriction because in the real world we normally have only the very foggiest idea of how the choice of an option affects other decisions. In applying the methods of critical decision making, however, we are free from this problem. The decision maker may proceed by considering very few options, but only because he is open to the discovery, by some critics of his choice, of options which may be better than those he has considered. Justification calls for the identification of all relevant options, criticism can proceed without this.

A further move of some interest occurred in the second round of the debate when the EPA published a second version of their regulations, amended in the light of criticism from the Ethyl Corporation and others. This was supported by a new document, EPA (1973), in which it was claimed:

$V_5 =$ Presently recognised blood lead limits are too high to protect the public. Upper acceptable limits for expectant mothers (newborn babies, children, adults) are 30 (30, 40, 40) μg for 100 ml of blood

I take V_5 to be evaluative because it states that certain blood lead levels are the highest which ought to be accepted. EPA's argument for V_5 may be formalized as:

V_6 The upper acceptable limit for a toxin in the body is the lowest level at which the health of someone in the population is impaired

F_5 The lowest blood lead level at which the health of some expectant mother (newborn child, child, adult) is impaired is 30 (30, 40, 40) µg per 100 ml

V_5 The upper acceptable limit for lead for expectant mothers (newborn children, children, adults) is 30 (30, 40, 40) µg per 100 ml

V_5 forms the most important part of the EPA's case and so it is not surprising to find that it comes under severe fire from the Ethyl Corporation (Ethyl, 1973). As before, the criticism centres not on the evaluative issues but on factual claims. Ethyl apparently accepts V_6, which may, therefore, be regarded as a background value, but it seeks to deny F_5, a move which would, of course, destroy EPA's argument for V_5. Ethyl denied that there was any medical evidence supporting F_5. The only evidence cited by the EPA concerned a study of umbilical cord blood levels, but this found no urban–rural gradient and concluded that there was no evidence to implicate airborne lead as a contributor to high cord blood lead levels. Ethyl accused the EPA of making an *ad hoc* move in so redefining upper acceptable blood lead levels without supporting evidence. They also pointed out that the Surgeon General regarded children with a blood lead level of less than 50 µg per 100 ml as safe provided there is no evidence of continuing high lead exposure.

How is a debate like this to be analysed?[2] Deciding what to do requires facts and values. If two parties disagree about what is to be done, this may be because they accept different values or because they have different beliefs about the facts that are relevant to the decision. According to the analysis offered by what I shall call model 1, if both parties are advised by experts who have all the data open to them, they must both accept the same interpretation of the data so that a continuation of the disagreement about what to do can only come from the acceptance of different value judgements. The disagreement between the US Environmental Protection Agency and the Ethyl Corporation about whether lead should be removed from petrol cannot arise from differences over the facts which are relevant, since both sides have access to experts in all the required fields and these experts will come to the same opinion on each issue before them. The disagreement, instead, arises from the different values adopted by the two parties. Both agree that lead from this source is a danger to the health of children, but the Ethyl Corporation favours retaining lead in petrol because it considers its own profitable existence to be more valuable than the health of children. The EPA, on the other hand, operate with value judgements designed to protect the environment, so in this case they favour the removal of the health hazard from exhaust fumes over the continuation of the Ethyl Corporation. Figure 7.3 summarises the view which model 1 gives of the disagreement.

[2] The following discussion relies heavily upon Collingridge (1980, chapter 12).

THE CRITICISM OF DECISION MAXIMS

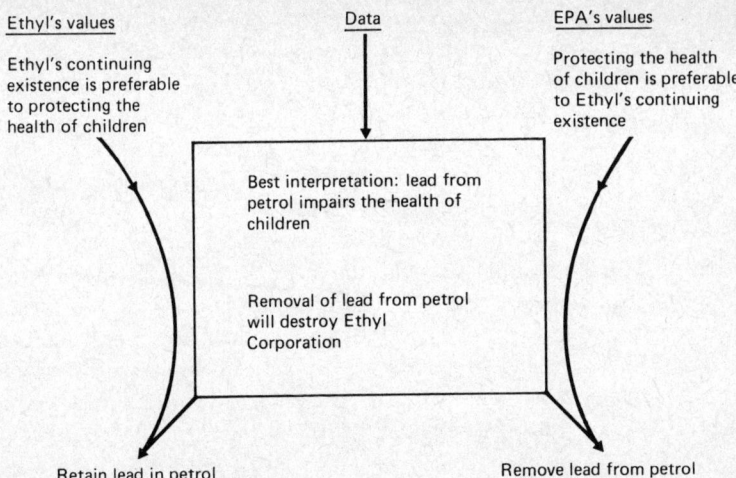

Fig. 7.3 Model 1 applied to the debate between EPA and Ethyl Corporation. From Collingridge (1980, p. 185)

I have criticized this model on a number of points. First of all, where the model is put against a real case, as above, it is immediately apparent that the mis-match is almost total. In the debate between Ethyl and EPA the values supposedly at the root of their disagreement were never discussed, or even mentioned, nor any values resembling them in the weakest respect. Values simply did not figure explicitly in any of the arguments between the parties. Nor, of course, did the rivals agree on the interpretation of the data concerning the effects of lead from vehicle exhausts on the health of children. EPA claimed that the best interpretation was that lead from this source impairs the health of children, but the Ethyl Corporation held that the best interpretation of the self-same body of data was that there is no effect on the health of children. The experts employed by each party failed to reach agreement in all important cases, totally counter to the view of expert opinion embodied in model 1. Real disagreements about what should be done are all like this; conflict concerns not values but what interpretation of the data is to be favoured. On model 1 the case of the EPA vs. Ethyl should be highly atypical, but it is not. Most important decisions are favoured by one interest group and heavily opposed by another, and the debate between them, when it happens, has the same form as the debate between Ethyl and the EPA.

Secondly, model 1 can only account for the failure to reach agreement about the best interpretation of the data in such cases as the one considered above, by attributing bias to one, or both of the parties to the debate. Either the EPA's experts are biased and interpret the data available to them in a distorted way to favour EPA's contention that lead from petrol is harmful, or else the experts employed by the Ethyl Corporation favour their master in the same way. The problem, however, is that there is no objective test for the presence or absence of bias. The model proposes a psychological, and so a covert and unexplorable view of bias. Bias is in the mind of the scientist. The data points to a uniquely favoured interpretation, and if this is not accepted by a scientist who is competent and acquainted with the data, the only cause can be bias. But what are the mechanisms by which an unbiased mind can be achieved, how can bias be eliminated if it is present, and what public tests are there for it?

The third criticism of model 1 concerns the relationship it supposes to hold between experts' advice on technical matters and their role in policy making. The expert, on model 1, is a mere provider of technical information and has no special role in the making of decisions. A scientist employed by the Ethyl Corporation in their fight against the EPA's plans to remove lead from petrol serves purely to provide his employer with data and to interpret data from other sources. That his professional opinions are relevant to the survival of the Ethyl Corporation and to the health of millions of children are of no concern to the expert. He may not share the values of either the Ethyl Corporation or the EPA, so that his expert opinions may point to no course of action at all as far as he is concerned. If he does share the values of one of the parties to the debate, then this is not because he is an expert, it is part of his non-professional existence. Thus the unbiased expert is, as professional expert, neutral between interested parties arguing what is to be done and disinterested in what decisions are made on the basis of his opinions. This, if you like, is model 1's *black box* view of expert advice. I have argued that this is an inadequate and oversimple view. Experts do not, and cannot exist in a vacuum; the decisions which rest upon their information have a profound effect on their behaviour and on the advice they offer.

A much superior analysis, which we may call model 2, may be developed from the critical theory of decision making. On this model the data of science, that is its collected observations and experimental results, is still recognised, but it is admitted that any set of data will be able to bear a number of conflicting interpretations. In a debate about what should be done both sides share a common fund of what may be called background values, and these are the ones to which they will appeal in making out their case. What each side tries to do is to find an interpretation of the agreed data that is scientifically respectable, and which leads — when coupled with background values — to the desired result. The debate between the parties over what should be done will, therefore, centre on which side offers the best interpretation of the data, and will not explicitly concern evaluative issues at all. This, of course, is the same sort of debate as goes on in science all the time, because one of the functions of science is the elaboration, testing and selection of rival interpretations of data. The debate about what to do therefore becomes like any similar debate in science, to be won or lost by the rules of scientific method.

THE CRITICISM OF DECISION MAXIMS

An example is given in Fig. 7.4, which outlines the analysis offered by model 2 of the debate about removing lead from petrol. The background values are such mundane things as 'lead should be removed from petrol only if it impairs the health of children' and 'if lead in petrol impairs the health of children then it should be removed'. Both of these are accepted by the Ethyl Corporation and the EPA who each then seek an interpretation of the scientific data which will couple with these background values to generate the result which is desired. The EPA tries to show that the best interpretation is that lead is hazardous, corroborating its decision maxim, and its rival defends the interpretation that lead is harmless, thus falsifying EPA's decision maxim. The two interpretations fight it out according to the general rules of scientific method.

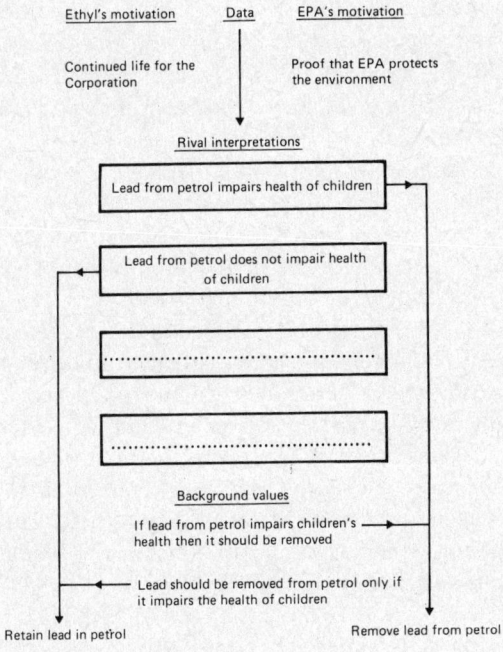

Fig. 7.4 Model 2 applied to the debate between EPA and Ethyl Corporation. From Collingridge (1980, p. 190)

The model makes a clear distinction between this *public argument* and the *motivation* behind it. The motivation for Ethyl's argument is obviously the Corporation's continued existence, but this is not an element in the public case which it makes out. Ethyl cannot argue that lead should remain in petrol so that it can continue to exist, because no other party to the debate has the slightest interest in the Corporation's future. No more can the EPA argue that lead should be removed as a way of showing how effectively the EPA protects the environment against big business, because nobody else in the debate cares a fig for EPA's image and status. If argument is to be more than the wasting of breath, it must appeal to values common to all parties (i.e, to background values). This, of course, is what happens in the public debate between Ethyl and the EPA, but there would be no reason for the debate at all if one side was not motivated in some way, so that it had no preferred option. Rival motivation ensures that the debate is carried out energetically and that the best case is made for each interpretation and that all suggested interpretations receive intense scrutiny. This, of course, is essential if the final decision is to be a good one, one based on a thoroughgoing scientific debate about the best interpretation of the data on the health effects of lead from vehicle exhausts on children.

The new model gives a much more satisfactory account of expert advice than that offered earlier. First of all it gives a much more realistic account of disagreements about what action to take. As observed in the previous case studies, debates of this kind have very little concern for evaluative issues, the key elements in the debate being factual and concerning the best interpretation of scientific data. This accords exactly with model 2. In addition, model 2 also explains why disagreement between experts is so common in the making of complex decisions. This does not reveal how common bias is within the community of experts, which is the only explanation open to a supporter of model 1. On model 2 data can be interpreted in a number of ways and different experts will favour different interpretations which they can then fight over. Disagreement and debate is not at all shocking, it is a sign of a healthy and exploring science, searching for the best way of seeing some set of data.

The problem with model 1's account of bias was that the existence of bias becomes a hidden, psychological feature of the individual expert. On model 2 it is possible for debates about what to do to be biased, but in a publicly discoverable way. For this model such a debate is centrally an argument between proponents of rival interpretations of some body of data. Unfairness can arise here from a number of sources; from massively unequal funding of the parties so that the scale of expert advice available to each is very different, from the domination of research by a few experts who place work in the field along rigid lines so that rival interpretations are never explored, and from administrative rules which impose secrecy or which place certain key factual claims in the debate beyond argument. The first source of bias is very common where the debate occurs within the context of a public inquiry. The proposer is often a large private or public body with its own research staff and able to buy expert opinion from outside as well, while the objectors may be individuals or small protest groups hastily thrown together and having no research skills or money to buy opinions. Such inquiries also often exemplify bias from the third source, as they are often held under rules which make it impossible for some of the data to be discussed because it is secret, or which make it impossible to question certain claims. A notorious example of this last is road-building inquiries where the need for the proposed road cannot be discussed, merely whether it is the best route. Bias of the kind identified by model 2 may be subtle, or it may be quite explicit, but in either case it does not require investigation of the psychology of individual experts. It is a public, overt question whether bias exists, and when it is found it may be remedied by public methods such as altering the rules of public inquiries, allocating funds more evenly and ensuring that no-one dominates the research area which is relevant to the debate.

Another problem for model 1 was its simple-minded division between advice and policy, which we saw to be untenable. Here again, model 2 performs better. On model 2 the advisor can be seen as much more of an advocate, actively engaged in the policy debate. The sort of values that figure in such a debate are generally so mundane and ordinary that only the wildest eccentric would want to question them. These values are shared by the parties to the debate, but can be expected to be also held by any of the experts they consult. The expert's task is to offer and defend interpretations of the data which, when coupled with these values, lead to the policy option favoured by his master. The interpretation is the key item, it is this which is disputed not the value judgements. The expert can no longer pretend to be above the conflict, saying 'I just give the facts; what values are used to turn them into decisions is not my business'. He will generally accept the background values shared by the debate's parties so that if he is convinced that a particular interpretation which favours one side is the best, then he will himself regard the policy option supported by that side to be the best. The expert is, therefore, inside the debate and cannot help but be there. There is nothing wrong in seeing an expert as an advocate. His task is the perfectly proper one of discovering and defending interpretations of the data which are in accordance with scientific method, to take extreme examples, he must not destroy recalcitrant data or invent data supporting his position, and which also serve the interest of his master by yielding the policy conclusions he wants when conjoined with background values. This would be pure ritual if it were not for a rival group of experts seeking to serve a master who favours an opposing policy. The battle is then fought by trying to discover which of the expert groups provides the best interpretation, the rival motivation of the paymasters ensuring that the debate about this is thorough and deep.

References

Collingridge, D. (1980). *The Social Control of Technology*, London, Frances Pinter/The Open University Press.

Collingridge, D. (1982) 'Evaluative reasoning and the factual falsification of preferences', *Philosophy* (in press).

EPA (1972) *Health Hazards of Lead*, Washington, US Environmental Protection Agency.

EPA (1973) *EPA's Position on the Health Effects of Airborne Lead*, Washington, US Environmental Protection Agency.

Ethyl (1972) *Comments on EPA's Proposed Lead Regultions*, New York, Ethyl Corporation.

Ethyl (1973) *Critique of EPA's Position on the Health Effects of Lead*, New York, Ethyl Corporation.

Hinton, C. (1977) 'The birth of the breeder', in Forrest, J. (ed.) *The Breeder Reactor*, Edinburgh, Scottish Academic Press, pp. 8-13.

Lawther, P. (1980) *Lead and Health*, London, Department of Health and Social Security.

Popper, K. (1968) 'Epistemology without a knowing subject', in van Rootselaar, B. and Staal, J. (eds) *Proceedings of the 3rd International Congress for Logic, Methodology and Philosophy of Science*, Amsterdam, pp. 333-73; reprinted in Popper, K. *Objective Knowledge*, Oxford University Press, pp. 106-52.

Popper, K. (1972) 'On the theory of the objective mind', in Popper, K. *Objective Knowledge*, Oxford University Press, pp. 153-90.

Schumacher, E. (1973) *Small is Beautiful*, London, Blond and Briggs.

8 Flexibility

Chapter 2 tells us that decisions under ignorance (i.e., decisions where not all the conditions necessary for the application of Bayesian decision rules are satisfied), cannot be justified and may always prove to have been mistaken. This sceptical conclusion was enlarged in chapter 3 where it was shown that no preference sentence may be justified, so that no decision of whatever variety may be justified, a decision being the expression of a preference for the option taken over all those rejected. The only escape from total scepticism about making decisions is to try to construct a critical theory of decision making; one which admits that choice can never be justified but there can, nevertheless, be reasons for favouring one option over another, because one has stood up to criticism better than the other.

With this aim in view, a critical theory of preference was developed in chapter 6, which can accommodate the impossibility of justifying preference sentences by showing how these sentences may be criticized, and reasons for selecting one preference sentence over another given in terms of their performance under critical scrutiny. To make a decision is to act upon a decision maxim which is a preference sentence of form 'no other option which is open pref Q', and such maxims may be tested according to the methodology for the testing of preference sentences of any variety developed in chapter 6. This was, of course, the topic of the previous chapter. There is now only one major problem which must be overcome before we have a fully developed critical theory of decision making, and its solution is the task of the present chapter.

The Need for Flexibility

The problem has already been touched upon in the previous chapter. It is at what point in the critical process should a decision be made? If a decision maxim is highly corroborated when it is subjected to critical scrutiny and is then acted upon, for all its earlier success the maxim may be falsified by some later test. The decision may, in other words, be shown to be mistaken after it is taken, and no amount of success in passing tests in the past can guarantee that this will not happen. Does this reduce decision making to arbitrariness and the critical process to a mere decoration? I think that it need not. Any critical debate is essentially open-ended; there is no time when the debate may be terminated and its conclusions etched into tablets of stone. Some points within the argument may appear to be settled for a very long time, it is true, but this must not be taken as a conclusive indication that these issues will not be opened up again in the future. Closing such a debate at any time can therefore be seen only as an arbitrary and unreasonable act. The problem, of course, is that deciding to implement a decision maxim because of the high degree of corroboration it has achieved in past tests appears to be such an arbitrary closure of a critical debate. At the moment, the maxim may be highly corroborated, but it may fail the very next test to which it is submitted. If this test is performed after the decision is taken, there is nothing that can be done, except to mourn fate.

In so far as this is a true picture of decision making, acting upon a decision maxim would indeed seem to involve the arbitrary act of halting debate about the maxim, in which case the whole purpose and value of the debate seems to be brought into question. Happily, however, this dismal conclusion is based on an over-simple view of decision making. Any decision involves the investment of resources, both tangible and intangible, and the simple view above assumes that these are irrecoverable once the decision is implemented. This being so, the argument runs, no response can be made if the maxim implemented is later falsified, so continuing the debate after the decision's implementation is a mere decoration of no rational purpose. But all decisions are, in reality, reversible to some extent, and what is more there are generally many steps which can be taken to increase the ease with which a given decision may be reversed. It is simply not true that the resources invested following a decision are irrecoverable; some of these resources may always be retrieved if the decision is found to have been in error and the extent of these recoverable resources may generally be increased in a wide variety of ways.

In making decisions, therefore, there is no necessity to call an arbitrary halt to the critical debate. Comparison of the various options being considered must be seen as a continuous process, beginning when the options are poorly articulated and little understood; proceeding as the options become clarified as more information is digested, until one option is selected because of its high degree of corroboration and the ease with which it may be corrected if this is called for in the future; and continuing after the option is implemented so that if a better option is discovered it may be substituted for the one originally selected. The critical process does not halt when the decision is made — it must continue because later criticism may always show that some other option is superior to the one chosen. The ability to respond to this discovery must be retained by making decisions which are easily reversed.

In some cases the critical process may proceed for many years after a decision has been made. The original decision to allow the addition of lead to improve the quality of British petrol was made, after a review of the potential hazards, in the early 1920s. Hazards were then thought to concern only those occupationally exposed to the leaded fuel, such as garage attendants and policemen; the small quantity of lead spread around the country from vehicle exhausts was not thought to represent a health hazard to the general public. The total mileage travelled was so small that any exposure from this source of lead was sure to be much below exposures from already existing sources such as industrial emissions, food and drink. To protect occupationally exposed workers the maximum level of lead in petrol was set at 0.84 g/l.

What could not possibly have been foreseen was the great increase in car ownership and mileage, so that petrol consumption has increased enormously, and with it the quantity of lead scattered into the environment from vehicle exhausts, now about 12 000 tonnes/year. Nor could the results of clinical and epidemiological studies of children pointing to the possibility of neural damage leading to hyperactivity, loss of concentration, drop in school performance, and lowering of IQ from exposure to environmental lead. The evidence is nowhere near conclusive,[1] but in its light the Government revised the regulations from 1973; progressively lowering the limit to its present 0.40 g/l, to guard against the risk of lead from this source being a health hazard. Thus 50 years after the decision was made to allow up to 0.84 g/l lead in British petrol scientific effort has pointed, in a way quite unexpected in the 1920s, to the danger that the unexpectedly greater exposure of the child population might pose a risk to its health, and the decision was accordingly revised.

This may be formalized in the now familiar way:

L = No option which is open pref allowing a maximum of 0.84 g/l lead in petrol

V_B = $(x)(y)$ (x is a fuel whose use may be a health hazard and y is a fuel whose use is not a health hazard $\supset y$ pref x)

F = Petrol containing 0.84 g/l lead is a fuel whose use may be a health hazard and petrol containing 0.40 g/l lead is a fuel whose use is not a health hazard

$$V_B \cdot L \rightarrow \text{not } F$$

so the acceptance of the factual F is a falsification of the maxim L, V_B being a background preference sentence adopted throughout the period, held by the Government which originally allowed the limit of 0.84 g/l and by all Governments since who have reviewed the issue of lead in petrol.

There are two points to be clear on about the revision of a decision like this. It might be argued that it is inappropriate to call the decision based on L wrong or false or falsified, because this is to apply hindsight in an invidiously unfair way. The decision makers in the 1920s could not have foreseen the growth in petrol consumption, any more than what scientific advances would reveal over the ensuing 40 years or so. They did their best, and it is hard on them to call their choice wrong or erroneous. That is not, however, a point of any great significance. The important thing to realise is that facts ascertained after the decision was made showed that it was in need of revision and that this

[1] It cannot, of course, be reviewed here. A good overview is provided by Lawther (1980).

revision was possible. The refining industry was able to produce petrol of the quality required by existing vehicles with lower levels of lead, although this was expensive — for costs see Collingridge and McEvoy (1981). Whether we adopt the convention of calling the original decision a good one at the time, which was later found to require change, or of saying that the original decision was falsified and shown to be erroneous is simply a convention of language upon which nothing more than clarity rests. To call it erroneous and shown false has the danger, it must be admitted, of seeming to cast aspersions on the quality of the original decision and the abilities of those who took it, but it has the great advantage of reflecting the logic of the situation as formalized above. For this reason, I shall speak in this way; although it must always be remembered that to call a decision mistaken in this way is to say nothing about the abilities of those who made it. They may, for all later discoveries, have done their very best with a difficult and intractable decision problem.

The second point is of more importance. It is that the revision of a decision in the light of facts discovered after it is taken in no way implies that the original decision was arbitrary. To think this is to slip back into justificationist patterns of thought. If the decision to allow a maximum of 0.84 g/l lead in petrol is dubbed arbitrary because not all the relevant facts were known at the time it was taken, this can only be because the decision could not have been justified in the absence of some relevant facts. To think in this way, however, is to assume that all decisions are either justified or arbitrary; it is to forget that some decisions are neither because they are criticizable. As we have seen, the decision about the original 0.84 g/l limit was criticized, found wanting, and eventually revised in the light of this criticism. For this reason, the decision can never be accused of being arbitrary. In case the idea that absence of full factual information implies arbitrariness persists, consider the following points. In the first place, there is no way of being sure that all the relevant facts have been identified and gathered in, a point emphasised in chapter 3 in the discussion of the factual falsification of preference sentences. Secondly, if the facts available do not justify the selection of one option over its rivals, they cannot justify delaying the choice until adequate information is available rather than making the decision now with what information happens to be in hand (see Collingridge, 1980, pp. 25-7). Finally, it would be practical madness to confine decisions to those where adequate information is available to justify one option over the others, even allowing the possibility of such justification. Such a policy would confine action to the sort of decisions which are involved in puzzles and games. If some relevant facts are missing, the rational way to proceed is to choose in such a way that any error in the decision may be discovered quickly, and the decision may then be revised easily, and to initiate a search for falsifying information once the decision has been made.

An immediate consequence of this view is that decisions cannot be seen as point events; they must be seen as a *process*. On the Bayesian approach decisions are point events, so that given the state of knowledge about outcomes, options and pay-offs at some particular time and the decision maker's preferences at that time, his decision can be assessed as rational or irrational. The process by which the information was acquired and the preference developed is of no interest; once they are settled a Bayesian algorithm can be applied to give the correct decision. It is quite otherwise from the viewpoint of the critical theory of decision making. Given the information and objectives of one time it is not possible to determine the correct decision, nor to assess the real decision as rational or irrational. This is not a function of the point decision, but depends partly on how the decision maker is prepared to act in the future. Will he, that is, search for information able to show that his original decision is wrong, and if he finds it, will he be able to revise his decision in the light of the discovery? The decision is not just the selection of an option, but this plus a search for information in the future and the ability and resolve to act on this information if it is found. The decision is, in short, a process and not a point. This seems a much more realistic view of complex decision making than that offered by Bayesian theory. It also promises power for the critical theory of decision making, because the more aspects of real decision making which can be explained theoretically, the stronger the theory. But more of this in chapter 9.

In the case of the original lead additive decision, for example, the decision cannot be assessed simply from the information then available about the health effects of lead and the economic benefits from its use, and the preferences of the decision makers. To judge the position of the decision in the dimension irrational–rational it is necessary to ask how diligently the search for unexpected, subtle health effects was carried out and what steps were taken to ensure that the transport system could adjust to reductions in the level of lead additives if this were found to be better than maintaining the levels allowed originally. We shall return to a general discussion of these issues in chapter 10. I have discussed both of these problems as they affect the decision to allow lead additives in petrol elsewhere (Collingridge, 1980, chapters 3 and 12).

The Measurement of Flexibility

Several authors have proposed measures for flexibility (Hashimoto, 1980; Marschak and Nelson, 1962; Merkhofer, 1977; Pye, 1978; Rosenhead and Gupta, 1968; Rosenhead *et al.*, 1972; Rosenhead, 1978; Schekermann, 1978; Stigler, 1939) but all of them are restricted to very well-structured decision problems, where, for example, all states of the world can be identified. Some of these measures also require the assignment of probabilities to states of the world. The kind of decision problems that have been of interest throughout this work, however, are all ones that have to be made under ignorance, so these measures of flexibility cannot be applied. This section therefore aims at a measure of flexibility which is less restrictive and more applicable to the kind of messy problems we normally face in the real world.

The central idea behind such a measure is a simple one. Consider a system that interacts with the environment surrounding it in ways that confer various benefits and impose various costs on the system's controller. The controller receives signals that tell him how the system is behaving and he can alter its behaviour by adjusting one or more of a number of decision variables of the system, each adjustment taking time to become effective. We may think of the controller as steering the system through the environment by means of the system's decision variables. The pay-off over time is a function of the interaction of the system and environment, but in the cases which are of interest to us this cannot be predicted because the controller has to make decisions about the system's decision variables under ignorance. If the controller has to choose which of two systems to steer he cannot, therefore, base his choice on knowledge of the payoffs he will receive from each system. His choice can only be based on his knowledge of the system, not on its interaction with the environment. One system may be more easy to steer than the other; in other words errors in one system's behaviour, its delivery of costs instead of benefits, may be more easily corrected than errors in the other. This will be so, for example, when the systems are identical except that one delivers more signals about its present state to the controller; or where one has more decision variables; or where one has the same number of decision variables as the other but the system responds more quickly to changes in them. The controller should obviously choose the system that is more easily controlled; whose errors can be identified and remedied more easily, so that the pay-off over time is less sensitive to error – in other words, the most flexible system. Flexibility is thus to be judged from the system itself, no information about how the system will actually interact with its environment being needed.

This is the thinking behind the measures proposed here. A decision is easy to correct, or highly flexible, when – if it is mistaken – the mistake can be discovered quickly and cheaply and when the mistake imposes only small costs which can be eliminated at little expense. Deciding under ignorance requires a premium to be placed upon highly corrigible options. The critical debate about the decision maxim which was finally implemented may then continue after the implementation of the maxim. The maxim's opponents may, that is, continue their search for facts which falsify the maxim, because if these are found the decision can still be revised. The various elements relevant to an option's flexibility are as follows:[2]

(a) *Monitoring*. The search for facts capable of falsifying a decision maxim

---

[2] The following discussion leans heavily on Collingridge (1980, chapter 2). For the relationship between the measures proposed here and those of other authors see Collingridge (1979).

after it has been implemented may be called *monitoring* the decision. The minimum period from the decision to the discovery of error may be called the *monitor's response time*. Options that can be monitored cheaply should be favoured because monitoring costs are inescapable in decision making under ignorance. In the rest of the discussion of this chapter monitoring costs will, however, be reckoned as zero, which is a simplification that can often be made in real-world decision problems. The alterations necessary to accommmodate non-zero monitoring costs should, however, be fairly straightforward. Options that have a low monitor's response time should also be favoured. If a decision is mistaken, it pays to discover the mistake quickly. A major part of chapter 10 is devoted to how it may be ensured that decisions are effectively monitored.

(b) *The cost of error*. When a wrong decision has been made, costs — though not necessarily monetary ones — are imposed; indeed it is these costs which constitute the error. The cost of an error is the decision's *error cost*, which is generally a function of time. If no corrective action is taken, we may speak of *uncontrolled error cost*, remedial action reducing this to a *controlled error cost*. Options with a low controlled error cost should be favoured if a decision has to be made in a state of ignorance. If the chosen option proves to be mistaken the mistake need not involve the bearing of great costs.

(c) *Time for correction*. A remedy for a discovered error generally takes time to operate fully. The period from the remedial action to the elimination of error cost may be termed the *corrective response time*. The sum of this and the monitor's response time is the *gross response time*. Options with a low corrective response time should be favoured in making decisions under ignorance. There are three reasons for this. Remedying a mistaken decision quickly means that error costs are eliminated quickly and benefits from an improved decision are obtained early; remembering that early benefits are to be valued more highly than postponed benefits. Secondly, ignorance often extends to the effectiveness of the imposed remedy. When this is so, a remedy with a low corrective response time may be discovered to be ineffective more quickly than a remedy with a high corrective response time. This means that another, and perhaps more effective remedy, can be substituted more quickly. The sooner the substitution, the lower the error cost. A low corrective response time thirdly leaves the decision maker with more options once the discovered mistake has been remedied, as will be shown below.

(d) *The cost of remedy*. The cost of applying a remedy for a mistaken decision may be called the *control cost*. Low control cost is obviously a desirable feature of decisions made under ignorance, but, in addition, where the effectiveness of the remedy is not known favour should be given to remedies having a high variable:fixed cost ratio. If the remedy is found to be ineffective, then all the fixed costs are generally lost, but some of the variable costs will be avoidable once another remedy is substituted.

Having identified the factors relevant to the flexibility of a decision under ignorance, the relationship between them may now be considered. It is useful to regard the first three factors as determining the decision's flexibility, control cost then being seen as the cost of imposing a remedy which exploits the decision's flexibility. A number of remedies will normally exist once monitoring has revealed a mistake, but often their gross response time and controlled error costs vary together. When this happens these two factors pull in the same direction and the set of remedies may be said to be *well behaved*. Ordinal measures for the decision's flexibility can then be applied; the two simplest being [MIN (response time)]$^{-1}$ and [MIN (controlled error cost)]$^{-1}$.

The idea behind these measures is quite simple. The flexibility of an option measures how easily it *may* be corrected, paying no regard to the cost of correction. The two factors that determine corrigibility are gross response time and controlled error cost. When these vary together for a set of remedies, a low controlled error cost being associated with a low gross response time, the ease of control may be measured by the least time in which it is possible to remedy a discovered error, or the lowest error cost which the mistake can impose. These measures are ordinal because they enable decisions to be ordered with respect to flexibility, although differences and ratios of flexibilities so measured have no significance. We can say that one option is more flexible than another, but not by how much.

A final point that should be stressed is that flexibility generally costs money, so that there is a tension between ease of correction and control costs. This tension is at the heart of many decisions made under ignorance.

In my earlier discussion of flexibility (Collingridge, 1980, chapter 2) I showed that there are four equivalent ways of viewing the need for favouring flexible options. As discussed above, a flexible option is one that is easy to correct if it proves to be mistaken, so that we may speak of it as having a high *corrigibility*. Since it is easy to correct, the long term pay-off from the decision is relatively *insensitive to error*. I argued also that such an option is one that is *flexible* in the usual sense of the word in that it keeps the future options of the decision maker open. Lastly, any decision may be seen as an attempt to control a system in the way I have indicated above, and favouring flexible options is equivalent to preferring systems which are easy to control, or have a high *controllability*. The measures developed above for flexibility may be used for corrigibility, insensitivity to error, and controllability as well, since these are all equivalent views of the same feature.

I have also shown how scenario analysis may aid the assessment of flexibility (Collingridge, 1980, chapter 9). The aim of this sort of analysis is to identify decisions that may be made now that will produce a satisfactory outcome over a wide range of future states of the world. These are to be favoured over decisions that produce a satisfactory outcome only under a narrow set of future conditions, although this preference may have to be traded against cost. A satisfactory outcome in the future is said to be *insensitive* to decisions of the first sort, and scenario analysis aims to compare this insensitivity. Not surprisingly, insensitivity estimated in this way may be taken as a guide to flexibility, and so as a guide to the other measures to which this is equivalent.

Having seen how flexibility may be measured, it is now appropriate to ask how the trade-off between flexibility and control cost is to be made. The answer is through critical debate. The choice of an option implies a particular trade-off between flexibility and control cost which may be expressed in a preference sentence, which may be criticized in the usual way by opponents of that option, and the trade-off may be adjusted in the light of this criticism. Where rival decision maxims are being debated, the final selection should be made according to the degree of corroboration achieved by each maxim as it proceeds through the process of criticism. Flexibility is not another, separate criterion in addition to degree of corroboration, rather the degree of corroboration attained by various maxims determines where the trade-off between flexibility and control costs should lie.

The Roots of Inflexibility

The theme of my earlier book, *The Social Control of Technology*, was that all major decisions about technological change have to be made under ignorance so that flexibility is demanded, but that as a technology develops it tends to become increasingly inflexible, or harder to control:

Decisions about the control of technology have to be taken under ignorance. They ought, therefore, to be made in ways which do not prejudice the future control of the technology; in ways which keep future options open; in ways which make error easy to detect and correct, so that the long-term performance of the technology is insensitive to error. But major technologies simply do not behave like this: as they become more developed and diffused, they become more difficult to control, earlier mistakes become harder to rectify, future options are closed, and decisions become more and more sensitive to error. *Decisions about the control of technology do not seem to be made in a rational way*. Given the damaging social costs which modern technology can inflict, this is a problem of the very greatest importance. We desperately need to understand the origins of the resistance of technologies to control, so that ways of countering it can be discovered and applied in order to improve the quality of decision making in an area so vital to us all. (Collingridge, 1980, pp. 41–2)

Through a number of case studies I investigated some of the roots of this resistance to control. Those discussed were:

(a) *Entrenchment*. Entrenchment is the resistance to control which arises from the adjustment of surrounding technologies to one which is developing, so that changing the latter eventually involves widespread changes to all sorts of other technologies (which is very expensive and which cannot be done quickly).

(b) *Competition*. Competition is an exceedingly powerful generator of inflexibility. When competition involves developing technologies with long lead times a disastrous pattern of decision making can occur where each party develops the technology as a hedge against anyone else developing it, so that all the rivals finish up using the technology, even if it proves to have large social costs. Competition therefore makes the control of the technology very difficult; each side seeing itself as being forced to adopt the technology whatever its social cost, because the cost of not having it when a rival has it is even higher.

(c) *The hedging circle*. A good example is provided by the planning of the energy system. Two approaches exist to forecasting future energy demand. The first is based on a projection of historical relationships between economic levels and energy consumption, whilst the second makes a detailed study of the improvements which are likely to be made in the efficiency with which energy is used in a very wide variety of ways. The first method gives a much higher forecast than the second. Accepting the low forecast involves the risk that the expected improvements in efficient energy use will not happen, so that demand for energy will exceed supply. This will take many years to remedy and for this time energy supplies will restrict economic growth. Proponents of the high energy future argue that this risk is too great, and that the liberal assumptions in the high energy forecast must be used to avoid the danger of under-supply. In this way future energy provision is generous, so that there is an abundance of cheap energy, which destroys any incentive for users to invest in ways which make its use efficient. The improvements in efficiency cited by the low-energy forecasters therefore do not happen, and the decision to increase energy supplies appears to be vindicated. In this way, avoiding the risk of under-supply entails that very little is learned about efficient energy use, because the incentive for it vanishes. Because little is learned, the shift to efficient use and low energy consumption always remains a risk too great to take and so energy consumption continues to rise. A low-energy future is thereby made unattainable.

(d) *Lead time and unit size*. Economies of scale are often thought to favour very large units of production, even where this means a longer lead time for their commissioning. Flexibility is enhanced by small units and low lead times, so that concentration on economies of scale can produce a highly inflexible production system; one which is hard to control and whose performance is very sensitive to errors in demand forecasts.

(e) *Dogmatism*. Dogmatism is the use of *ad hoc* stratagems by proponents of a particular decision maxim to avoid its criticism, and is a common source of poor decisions concerning the control of technology.

Having identified these roots of inflexibility in technologies, I suggested some ways in which their effect might be mitigated. Work in this direction I consider to be of the very greatest urgency, and much remains to be done.

References

Collingridge, D. (1979) *The Fallibilist Theory of Value and Its Application to Decision Making*, Ph.D thesis, University of Aston.

Collingridge, D. (1980) *The Social Control of Technology*, London, Frances Pinter/Open University Press.

Collingridge, D. and McEvoy, J. (1981) 'The cost effectiveness comparison of control strategies for environmental lead', *International Journal of Environmental Science*, 16, 139–46.

Lawther, P. (1980) *Lead and Health*, London, Department of Health and Social Security.

Hashimoto, T. (1980) *Robustness Criteria for Planning Water Demand/Supply Systems*, Laxenburg, International Institute for Applied Systems Analysis.

Marschak, T. and Nelson, R. (1962) 'Flexibility, uncertainty and economic theory', *Metroeconomica*, 14, 42–58.

Merkhofer, M. (1977) 'The value of information given decision flexibility', *Management Science*, 23, 716–27.

Pye, R. (1978) 'A Formal, decision theoretic approach to flexibility and robustness', *The Journal of the Operational Research Society*, 29, 215–27.

Rosenhead, J. (1978) 'An education in robustness', *Journal of the Operational Research Society*, 29, 105–11.

Rosenhead, J. and Gupta, S. (1968) 'Robustness in sequential investment decisions', *Management Science*, 15, 18–29.

Rosenhead, J., Elton, M., and Gupta, S. (1972) 'Robustness and optimality as criteria for strategic decisions', *Operations Research Quarterly*, 23, 413–31.

Schekerman, S. (1978) 'Robustness of discrete decisions to the worst case distribution', *Journal of the Operational Research Society*, 29, 159–65.

Stigler, G. (1939) 'Production and distribution in the short run', *Journal of Political Economy*, 47, 305–27.

PART III
COMPARISONS

9 Critical and Bayesian Decision Theory

Part I of this work consists of a number of criticisms of the justificationist model of decision making and of Bayesian decision theory which represents the principal articulation of the justificationist model. Having developed a rival account of decision making in Part II, it is now time to consider whether these same criticisms apply to the new theory, or whether the new theory can find satisfactory answers to them. In this chapter I hope to show the latter; that the critical theory of decision making avoids all the major problems of Bayesian theory identified at the beginning of the book. This will occupy the first section; the second will consider to what extent Bayesian theory and methods may be subsumed under critical theory, so that they may be seen, not as general methods of making decisions, which is how they are now presented, but as methods appropriate to a special class of decisions. I hope to show that Bayesian methods may be retained in this way as special tools appropriate for a narrow set of decision problems, general tools, of course, being provided by the critical theory of decision making.

Critical Decision Theory Avoids the Problems of Bayesian Theory

It will be remembered that the principal objections to Bayesian theory and the justificationist model of decision making on which it is based are:

(a) Its scope of application is very narrow.
(b) It incorporates a naïve view of individual preferences which does not stand up to examination.
(c) It fails to give a satisfactory account of social preferences which are required for public decision making.

It is now necessary to show that these objections do not apply equally to the critical theory of decision making, a necessary condition for the superiority of that theory over Bayesian views.

Scope of application

The application of Bayesian decision methods is possible only when all states of the world have been identified; when the set of options considered is known to be complete; when all pay-offs are known; where all of the decision maker's preferences have been considered; where all relevant data has been collected;

and where all possible interpretations of this data have been compared. The reason for these severe demands, of course, is that Bayesian theory attempts to show how decisions may be justified. Even granted the logical coherence of Bayesian theory, the justification of a decision is a very difficult and demanding task. There are no half-measures in justification, all the conditions required by Bayesian theory must be fully met; if one option has been left out of consideration, or if one pay-off is not known, or if one state of the world has not been identified etc., then justification is at once ruled out.

The power of the critical theory of decision making is that criticism and critical debate is possible where the decision problem does not enable one option to be known to be superior to all the others which are open. As Popper shows so adequately, it is possible to criticize where justification is impossible, and this is true as much in making decisions as in science. Forgetting for a moment the theoretical objections to Bayesian theory, its methods may be applicable to decisions under certainty, risk and restricted uncertainty, but it can have no application to decisions which have to be taken under ignorance, where one or more of the above conditions are not met. Placing all theoretical objections to Bayesian theory aside, therefore, still leaves the theory quite unable to accommodate decisions under ignorance. But the critical theory of decision making can be applied to decisions under ignorance, as the examples of chapter 7 make clear. The decision maxim in question in each of these examples cannot hope for justification from Bayesian techniques, since the decisions are all under ignorance, and yet it is possible to criticize the maxim; to search for facts which, when coupled with background preference sentences, show the maxim to be false. If such facts are discovered, the maxim must be regarded as criticized or falsified, if none are found despite an energetic search, the maxim is corroborated. It must be remembered, however, that corroboration can never amount to justification, as no matter how great the degree of corroboration of a decision maxim, it may be falsified in the very next test.

It must, therefore, be concluded that criticism of decision maxims is possible in many cases where justification through Bayesian decision rules is not possible. The critical theory of decision making may be applied to at least some decisions under ignorance where the conditions necessary for the employment of Bayesian theory are not satisfied.

The reason for this greater strength of critical decision theory may be seen in another way. Bayesian theory tries to show how decisions may be justified and this calls for the identification of the *best* option. This is a severe demand, and it is not surprising that the best option can only be identified when a very powerful set of conditions is met. Where Bayesian theory prescribes 'search for the *best* option', critical decision theory says 'search for a *better* option'. An agent may suggest acting on the decision maxim, 'no option is preferable to Q', thus posing the critic the task of falsifying the maxim by finding facts which, together with some background preference sentences, entail that some option

P is preferable to Q. The agent is then free to defend his original opinion by arguing that the factual claims of his critic are false and the debate may continue to consider such factual issues as we have seen in a number of examples. There is never a need to discover the *best* option; the critic succeeds if he can find an option *better* than Q; the agent succeeds if he can defend Q against criticism of this sort. Critical decision theory therefore frees the decision maker from the enormously restrictive burden of having to find the *best* option, so that its scope of application is wider than that of Bayesian theory.

Individual preferences

Decisions require information and preferences, and so can be justified only if the preferences involved are themselves justified. Thus, the justificationist model of decision making requires a person to be able to justify the preferences which figure in his decisions, and for this reason privileged access to preferences is assumed. In the same kind of way that a person knows when there is a pain in a limb or a tickle in a toe, he knows what his preferences are. This assumption was criticized in chapter 3 on two grounds. Any attempt to justify a preference sentence leads to an infinite regress, and it is possible for factual sentences to falsify preference sentences. The regress means that justification is impossible, as seeking to justify one preference sentence leads to attempting the justification of some other preference sentence, and so on *ad infinitum*. The logical point that preference sentences may be negated by factual sentences means that any body of preference sentences stands in jeopardy from the discovery of some true factual sentence which falsifies it. It can hardly do, therefore, to claim that the preference sentences are justified, or worse, that they are justified because of the agent's privileged access.

This is damning to all forms of the justificationist model of decision making because, as we have seen, the model requires preference sentences to be justified. Far from being an embarrassment to the critical theory of decision making, however, this scepticism about preferences forms the very basis of the theory. If it is impossible to justify any preference sentence, then these must be assessed by being exposed to criticism along the lines explored in chapter 6. Once we have seen how to criticize preference sentences, it is a very simple step to realise how decisions may be similarly criticized. A decision is action following acceptance of a decision maxim, which is simply a preference sentence of the form 'no option which is open is preferable to Q', which can, as such, be subjected to the critical machinery appropriate for any preference sentence, a line of reasoning explored in chapter 7.

Giving up the idea of privileged access to preferences is a profound move for many of the intractable problems which beset Bayesian decisions theory stem from its acceptance of this doctrine. In particular, I hope to show in the next section that the problem of social preferences has its origins here.

Social preferences

Social preferences are preferences that are used in the making of public, or group decisions. Chapter 4 explored various ways in which the justificationist model has attempted to explain the existence and binding quality of social preferences by presenting them as based on some kind of fair aggregation of the preferences of those composing the group or society. The problem is how this aggregation can be performed in a rational and non-arbitrary way, and it was argued that all attempts to date have failed to show how this is possible. The attempts of welfare economics were found to come to grief on the impossibility of separating issues of the quantity of a commodity from issues of its distribution between members of society. The attempt to put issues of fair distribution and equity on one side and develop some measure for social wealth which was constant and able to be shared out in various ways, therefore comes to grief.

The modern attempts of the utilitarian and the social contract traditions within social philosophy to account for social preferences were also considered in the ideas of Harsanyi and Rawls. The brave attempts of both authors to explain the existence and binding quality of social preferences were found to fail on a number of counts. Both theories adopt the device of a veil of ignorance, knowledge of social positions and powers being imagined away. Harsanyi considers an individual choosing between societies where each has a number of social levels yielding a particular utility to those existing at that level and treats this as a straightforward decision under risk. He argues that it is in the selfish interests of the chooser to value the societies by the sum of the fraction of the individuals who occupy each level multiplied by the utility they enjoy in virtue of their occupancy.

He will, therefore, choose to belong to the society with the highest value of this sum, but this is just the society in which he has the highest expected utility. Rawls, on the other hand, argues that a group of agents deciding what rules of social justice to adopt under a similar veil of ignorance would protect their own selfish interests by employing maximin, agreeing to value a society by the utility enjoyed by its least well off member.

The two principal criticisms of these arguments are that in each case the evaluation of the societies depends upon the attitude to risk of the chooser(s) and that they both fail to explain the binding quality of social preferences.[1] Harsanyi's argument requires the chooser to be risk neutral, but other attitudes to risk are, of course, possible. A risk averse decision maker will give more weight to levels of society with a low utility, and a risk seeker more weight to levels with a high utility. This destroys the objectivity which Harsanyi supposes to exist in the choice of society, because the origin of this objectivity is the supposition that all rational choosers will agree on what is the best society.

[1] To this may be added Harsanyi's need to make inter-personal comparisons of utility, but this may be put to one side for present purposes.

But if different attitudes to risk affect the choice and there is, as the justificationist model assumes, no way of arguing about what is the correct attitude to risk, the choice can hardly be held to be objective. It is a function of the choosers' individual, subjective attitudes to risk. Rawls' choosers, on the other hand, are assumed to be infinitely risk averse, so they employ maximin in selecting rules of social justice. As before, the possibility of different attitudes to risk destroys any objectivity in their selection.

The second principal difficulty is that neither account manages to offer an explanation of the binding quality of social preferences. The theories of Harsanyi and Rawls are within what is known in philosophical ethics as the objectivist tradition. For them, social preferences are objective in the sense that they can be agreed upon in a way which is independent of the agents' varying individual preferences. The problem facing all objectivist theories, including these two, is that of explaining the binding nature of social values. Some connection must be made between the agent's private, selfish values and objective social values if the latter are to govern behaviour in any way, for this requires contact with the selfish springs of human action. This is supposed to be accomplished by the veil of ignorance. Under the veil it is in the private selfish interests of those choosing between societies to evaluate each society by the arithmetic mean of the utility enjoyed by each member of society, if Harsanyi is right, and by the utility of the worst off member of the society if Rawls' account is favoured. But in each case the valuations made under the veil of ignorance, where they serve the choosers' private interests, are assumed to apply under more normal circumstances, where they may no longer serve these private interests. What cannot be explained is why these evaluations should remain unaltered when the veil of ignorance is lifted. Evaluations motivate an agent and guide his behaviour only to the extent that they serve his selfish interests. When the veil is lifted what once served an agent's selfish interests may no longer do so, so the evaluations made under the veil may be expected to change.

The agent may, for example, find himself gifted with great wealth and influence when the veil is removed. Under the veil it may have been to his selfish advantage to prefer a society where utility is more equitably distributed to the society which he now discovers himself to belong. This preference judgement no longer serves his selfish interests, however, as it threatens his privileged position. These interests are served by valueing the society he belongs to more highly than one with a more equitable distribution of utility. So what is to prevent the reversal of his original judgement? It will not do to stigmatize the change as 'unfair', as the question simply returns in the quest for reasons why the agent should refrain from being unfair. If it is unfair to exploit knowledge of one's social position in this way, what is wrong with being unfair?

To this sorry tale the problem posed by Arrow's impossibility theorem must be added. What this shows, it will be remembered, is that there is no way of aggregating individual preferences for societies into a social preference that does not infringe one of a number of perfectly reasonable requirements, for example that no one person shall be a dictator in the sense that if he favours one social state over another then this is reflected in the social order. Despite enormous efforts, there still seems no escape from this result, at least one which is compatible with the justificationist model of decision making.

It must now be shown that the critical theory of decision making can offer an account of public preferences which escapes these problems. On this account the transition from private to public preferences is not through the aggregation of varying private values, but is by *persuasion*. Imagine that X supports some preference sentence, V, which is so strong that it cannot be deduced from background preference sentences. V may be a decision maxim, but need not be. If Y objects to V what can he do? We may suppose X and Y to share some fund of mundane preference sentences, which may be called background sentences. If Y is to argue against X's evaluation his arguments must employ preferences, but to what preference sentences may he appeal? If Y employs preference sentences that are unique to himself, his arguments will have no impact on X, whilst if he uses X's preferences he himself will be unconvinced. What he should use, therefore, are preference sentences common to himself and X, or background preference sentences. Y may search for facts which, when coupled with some background preference sentences, falsify V. In pointing to such facts Y shows X's system of preferences − V plus the background preferences − to be factually incorrect, a defect which requires the rejection of V or else some arguments supporting the rejection of one or more of the background preference sentences involved. If V proves resistant to such attack, it is corroborated and both X and Y must admit that it has acquired a certain success. Success may accumulate sufficiently to convince Y that V is, after all, acceptable. Starting with different private values, the process of critical debate leads to agreement; agreement which confers a public status on the preference sentence V. This is how the transition from private to public preference ought to be seen, not as some sort of fair summation of immutable private preferences.

Several examples of such debates have been analysed in chapter 7 where they were indeed found to have this structure. It was noted there that all important issues in debates about preferences concern facts, something very hard to explain if the doctrine of privileged access to preferences is maintained. In rejecting this, the critical theory is able to explain this puzzle. The preferences appealed to in a critical debate are background preferences, common to both parties and usually so mundane that they remain implicit in the arguments put forward. The key elements are factual because the final outcome of the debate turns on what factual sentences are accepted.

Thus, a group decision is rational, not if the individuals' immutable and autonomous preferences, revealed by privileged access, are correctly and reasonably balanced, but if everyone is given the opportunity of arguing for the preference he favours, and if the minds of his fellows are sufficiently open to allow his arguments to alter their own preferences. Rationality does not consist in finding a fair compromise between fixed positions, but in using persuasion to alter positions in the hope of a consensus. This is not to say that the debate should continue until a consensus has been reached, as this would be hugely expensive in many cases where the debate concerns a decision. If flexible decisions are made the unanimity rule may be waived in a way that is not arbitrary, because the dissenters may continue their fight after the decision has been made. If the original decision is flexibile, there is a point in arguing for its reversal. We have seen in the case study on lead in petrol in chapter 7 how decisions may be made without consensus, even though any critical debate about what to do aims at consensus through persuasion.

This account of public preference also avoids the problem of attitude to risk upon which Harsanyi's and Rawls' theories foundered. People may have different attitudes to risk, but this is merely one of the preferences which they can debate about in the hope of a consensus. Attitudes to risk are not, that is, to be regarded as subjective and therefore beyond public discussion, for they are not. Attitude to risk may be argued about publicly in the same way as any other preference claims.

The problem of forging a connection between public values and private, selfish interests in order to explain the binding nature of the former is also overcome. The transition from private to public preference is mediated by persuasion through critical debate. In this way people with divergent preferences can come to agree on some particular preference sentence, this agreement promoting the value to a social one. But agreement in this way is the result of each agent coming to realise that the preference sentence agreed upon favours his own private, selfish interests. There is, therefore, no more of a gap between social preferences and action than between private preferences and action.

This point is sufficiently important to deserve closer attention. Traditionally opposed to objectivist theories of value such as those of Harsanyi and Rawls are subjectivist theories. We have seen how objectivist accounts have difficulty in explaining the binding quality of values, but subjectivist theories accomplish this very simply because they see an agent's values as an expression of his inner feelings, wishes, desires and motives. A central theme in the history of philosopical ethics is the tension between these rival types of theory. The tension exists because subjectivist theories have been able to explain how value judgements can guide action, but have not been able to find any room for reason in ethics; whilst objectivist theories have found it easy to explain the role of reason in evaluation, but impossible to explain why the outcome of this reasoning should exercise any control over our actions. What I hope to show now is that the theory developed here has characteristics that are typical of traditional theories of both sorts, and that it can, therefore, account for the connection between values and action and also explain the need for evaluative reasoning. It will be best to start by a brief discussion of the failures of subjectivist and objectivist theories.

Rather than enter upon a tedious, and probably fruitless, search for a final definition of 'subjective', we can best begin by considering the crudest subjectivist theory, according to which value judgements are merely reflections of inner feelings of approbation or disapprobation. Such a theory holds that:

$A =$ The value of an object for a person is solely determined by the feelings of approbation or disapprobation which the object causes in the person

A explains the connection between value judgements and action very neatly, for there is no more reason to ask why a man seeks what he values and avoids what he thinks worthless, than there is to ask why he seeks pleasure and shuns pain. Where the theory fails is in finding a role for reasoning about values. At the root of this failure is a view such as B.

$B =$ A person has immediate and complete knowledge of his own feelings of approbation and disapprobation

Since a person's feelings of approbation and disapprobation determine what value he places on things, B tells us that a person can have immediate knowledge of his own values. He knows immediately whether his feelings are of approbation or of disapprobation, and in either case he knows immediately the degree of his feelings. It follows from A that he also knows immediately the value of whatever it is that produces these feelings. But if this is so, then there is no need to reason or to argue about values, any more than there is need to offer reasons for or against 'I am in pain'. We can see, therefore, that the very way in which the theory connects judgements with action precludes it from finding any room for reasoning about values.

All traditional subjectivist theories of value have found themselves in a similar situation. In order to forge a connection between value and action, a person's values have been held to be a function of his likes, dislikes, desires, aversions, longings, loathings and so on; a collection we may subsume under the generic term 'interests'. At the same time it has been thought that immediate knowledge of such interests is possible, and, as before, the combination of these two claims has precluded the possibility of reasoning about value judgements (see, for example, Blanchard, 1961, p. 89; Nowell Smith, 1954, p. 210 and 320; Toulmin, 1958, chapter 3).

Turning now to objectivist theories, we may best begin with a typical theory of this sort, one which holds the utilitarian principal that:

$C =$ The value of an object is determined solely by the sum of the happiness or unhappiness which it produces for people

This theory has an obvious place for reason, since reason is needed to determine how much happiness and unhappiness an object produces. The theory cannot, however, explain why values exert control over our actions. In judging that an object is valuable, a person is judging that it will produce a great surplus of happiness over unhappiness, but this, by itself, gives him no cause to cherish the object, or to seek its possession, or to advocate its adoption. He will do so only if he happens to possess a subjective desire to promote the general happiness of the human race.

We saw above how the assumption that immediate knowledge of interests is possible precludes any subjectivist theory from finding a place for reason. We can now see how this same assumption prevents any kind of objectivist theory from linking value and action. Any theory that explains this link must do so by showing how value is a function of an individual's interests – his desires, feelings, longings etc. If immediate knowledge of such interests is possible, then an individual has immediate knowledge of his own values. It follows that a person's opinions about his own values are final and beyond question, a state of affairs quite incompatible with any objectivist view of value.[2] In other words, given the assumption that immediate knowledge of interests is possible, no objectivist theory of value can explain the authority which value judgements have over action.

Two responses to this problem have been traditionally explored. The first maintains that the value of an object is determined by some objective property, and then adds that, as a matter of fact, men favour and desire objects with this property. Bacon makes such a suggestion when he argues that self-interest is the sole determinant of value, and that people happen to seek what is in their own interest. Although this kind of move succeeds in linking value and action, it must fail, since the link it forges is only a contingent one. It hardly does to say that people just happen to seek what is valuable and avoid what is valueless. The link between value and action must be a necessary one.

The second kind of response to the problem of getting an objectivist view to explain the authority of value judgements is typified by Frankena's proposal (Frankena, 1958). He argues that we must distinguish justifying reasons from motivating reasons. Stating an objective evaluative fact may, he argues, provide a reason that justifies a value judgement, although it may fail to provide a motivating reason because it is irrelevant to the interests of the person to whom it is addressed. This suggestion is not, however, very helpful. Suppose that an objective evaluative fact justifies us in accepting that of two actions, P and Q, P is the better. Suppose also that the same evaluative fact fails to provide a motivating reason to anyone, which is quite possible on Frankena's account. When we are thinking about whether to do P or Q, this means that the evaluation 'P is better than Q' is completely irrelevant to our decision. This is, at least prima facie, paradoxical. Unless someone can persuade us that such a striking situation is really possible, we must reckon it as contradictory. Unfortunately,

---

[2] This is mentioned by a host of writers. Frankena (1958) mentions most of them. To his list may be added Blanchard (1961, pp. 34–5), Monro (1967, p. 105) and Stace (1973, pp. 41–3).

Frankena says nothing to so persuade us. It would seem, therefore, that traditional objectivist theories of value cannot, after all, explain the connection between value and action.

We find, therefore, that the traditional inability of subjectivist views of value to find a place for reason, and the traditional failure of objectivist views to explain the authority of value judgements over actions both stem from the same assumption. This is that immediate knowledge of our own interests – our desires, aversions, longings and loathings etc. – is possible.

The theory developed here, of course, explicitly denies the possibility of such immediate knowledge or privileged access, and so is able to explain both the role that reason plays in evaluation and the link between evaluation and action. Preference falls under the generic term 'interests' as defined above (i.e., preferences guide actions). There is no more need to explain why a man strives for what he prefers than there is to explain why he seeks pleasure or avoids pain. My theory resembles subjectivist theories, therefore, in its ability to explain the authority which values have over actions. An agent strives for what he prefers, but he can never be sure what his real preferences are. Reason is, therefore, required if the agent is to test his guesses about what his preferences are, and I have tried to show how these tests should proceed. In its ability to find room for reasoning about value judgements, my theory resembles objectivist theories of value.

It remains only to comment on Arrow's impossibility theorem. It poses no problems for the account of social values which follows from the critical theory of decision making. The theorem shows that there is no social welfare function that does not offend against at least one of a set of reasonable requirements that might be placed upon a democratic, fair and unbiased way of moving from a set of individual preference orderings of social states to a social ordering of social states. But the very use of a social welfare function betrays the belief that social ordering of social states must be a function of how the individuals in the society order the social states. This aggregation view of social preference is a necessary part of the justificationist model of decision making, because it is hard to see what else could justify a social ordering except that it in some way represented a fair balance of the individuals' ordering of social states. It is, however, quite otherwise once the critical theory of decision making has been adopted. Social preferences can no more be justified than individual preferences, so the need to somehow construct the former from the latter vanishes. Instead, social preferences are the expression of a consensus of individual evaluations brought about by critical debate through which the individual agents, all with different ends, come to recognise that there are some preferences that they have in common, some which further the selfish ends of each of them. In denying that social values are an aggregate of individual preferences, the critical theory of decision making effectively side steps the difficulties posed by Arrow's result. The result is logically cogent, but it need not disturb an upholder of the theory, just as the so called problem of induction is logically impeccable, but causes no embarrassment to followers of Popper, who sees no need for science to employ induction.

To summarise this first section; the critical theory of decision making gives a more satisfactory account of how decisions ought to be made than Bayesian decision theory because it avoids all the problems which Bayesian theory generates. In particular, the critical theory has a wider scope of application than Bayesian theory, and it incorporates a much more satisfactory account of individual and social preferences. The obvious question to ask at this point is whether Bayesian theory must be rejected altogether in favour of the newer account, or whether it may be retained for a special class of decision problems. This is the topic of the next section.

Strategic and Tactical Decisions

I hope to show in this section that Bayesian theory need not be altogether rejected in favour of critical theory, but that it may be retained as providing methods for the solution of a special and rather narrow class of decision problem. In this way, critical theory may subsume Bayesian theory, which now appears as a special, limiting case of the more general account of how decisions ought to be made.

Consider again an example from chapter 2 concerning the question a firm faces of whether to launch a new product or to drop it. The decision is represented, it will be recalled, as one under restricted uncertainty, or even risk, having the matrix below in Table 9.1.

Table 9.1 Decision matrix for launch of new product

Decision	Pay-off (£000)	
	10% market share (0.7 chance)	2% market share (0.3 chance)
Launch product	100	−50
Drop product	0	0

A moment's reflection, however, reveals that the decision is not under such happy circumstances at all, but is under ignorance. Instead of just two options, there are an apparently endless number, involving various disruptions to the firm. The firm might cease to market anything, selling its assets and investing the proceeds in an enormous variety of ways; the plant for the new product might be razed to the ground for the insurance money, two products might be launched together, the firm might be sold off to the highest bidder who may then be free to make the decision about the product, and so on and so on. So why is there the temptation to disguise the decision as one to which Bayesian methods can be applied?

The key here is to realise that the issues raised by the product's pending launch are of two kinds. Some issues are *repeating* — they arise whenever the firm is deciding to launch a new product, and from many other decisions the firm may consider too. Other issues are *non-repeating*, because they arise just from the decision about the product launch and nowhere else. How much profit might be expected from the options to launch and to drop given various states of the world is clearly a non-repeating issue, peculiar to this product and to no other. Whether the firm should sell off its plant for investment money, whether it ought to be sold, whether products shall be launched singly or in pairs etc. are, on the other hand, all repeating issues. Any decision by the firm concerning the launch of a product, and many other of its decisions too, raise these issues just as much as the decision of the matrix above. Efficient decision making calls for a separation of repeating and non-repeating issues, for the former can then be answered once and once only instead of a dozen times a week. Decisions about whether to burn the firm's plant, to continue in present ownership etc. ought to be settled by the appropriate decision makers at the appropriate level in the firm, leaving non-repeating issues to be settled as they arise.

In the example, the repeating issues are more general than the non-repeating ones, so that decisions about repeating issues form a framework in which decisions about non-repeating issues may be clarified and answered. Once all the repeating issues are considered, it may, for example, be decided that the firm is to continue marketing its usual product range under existing ownership and according to the customs it has developed, whereby, for example, products are launched singly. This having been settled, the decision about the launching of the product is much more amenable. Within the content of these decisions about the repeating issues there may only be the two options of the matrix in Table 9.1, and pay-off must be reckoned as profit. The repeating issues may here be regarded as relevant to *strategic* decisions, which once taken determine a framework for a whole set of lower order *tactical* decisions whose determination requires consideration of non-repeating issues. It is just because of their strategic role that the issues involved in strategic decisions repeat as they do, for they affect a whole class of tactical decisions. This is a very common feature of decision making and in no way special to the somewhat artificial example considered in the discussion.

Gambling provides another example. A decision whether to place a particular bet raises repeating issues, like the morality of gambling, the offence it gives to religion, the undermining of the spirit of enterprise etc. etc., and its own non-repeating issues, concerning how much will be invested at what return and what risk. If all these questions were answered together gambling would be a very time consuming exercise. As before, efficient decision making calls for separate answers to the repeating and the non-repeating issues. The ethical, religious and social acceptability of gambling ought to be considered once and decisions made which will be unaltered, at least until criticism exposes their flaws. Once an individual decides that gambling with the aim of maximizing his income is acceptable, then he can forget the soul searching this may have involved and concentrate upon the non-repeating elements of the gambles he is offered, that is, upon balancing his investment with returns and risk. As before, the settling of the moral issues to allow gambling may be seen as the making of a strategic decision which sets the framework for a whole series of tactical decisions about the value of individual gambles.

Strategic decisions, typified by those of the two examples, are likely to be complex and open-ended. Once they are settled, tactical decisions are very much more straightforward. Indeed, strategic decisions will always be under ignorance because they concern the structure and objectives of organizations or the moral worth of some human activity, but tactical decision problems may be so simplified that they may meet the requirements for the application of Bayesian decision rules (i.e., they may be under restricted uncertainty, risk or even certainty). This is the key to finding a role for Bayesian theory within the wider compass of critical decision theory.

All decision maxims ought to be open to criticism and rejection if found to be mistaken, but often this can be accomplished by submitting a whole set of tactical decisions to criticism at once, because they depend upon the same presumptions. Thus if non-gambling is discovered by critical debate to be preferable to gambling, all decisions an agent might be faced with concerning bets are criticized together and at once. If critical debate shows that selling the firm's assets is preferable to keeping the firm going, then any decision like that to launch a new product, which presupposes the firm's continued existence, is criticized. If debate shows the best option to be allowing gambling or continuing the firm's life, then some tactical decisions presupposing this may be answered without exposing them individually to criticism. They have, after all, been exposed collectively, for their presuppositions have been considered in a critical debate. In other words, because the repeating issues in the decisions have received critical attention, it is not necessary to expose the non-repeating issues to criticism. In the case of the product launch, for example, it may be that once strategic decisions are made the decision to launch or not is represented by the matrix of Table 9.1. There is no need to criticize the entry of the pay-offs, because how the firm determines the values of its various activities has been debated and it has been decided that the firm shall seek to maximize its monetary profits. Other options may exist, but not ones compatible with the firm's strategic decisions.

Since criticism is not required of such tactical decisions, they may sometimes be settled by the application of Bayesian decision rules. In fact, this is how Bayesian decision procedures are often introduced. It is, for example, admitted that a firm might not want to maximize its profits and that someone might have a moral objection to gambling, but these problems are glossed over when we are asked to imagine decisions facing a profit maximizing firm or a rational gambler. These are easily tackled by Bayesian theory, but the reader is encouraged to stop there — all inquiries about how the firm ought to decide whether it should maximize its profit, or how the potential gambler is to decide upon the acceptability of betting being pushed down by the admiration evoked for the smooth operation of Bayesian procedures. These strategic decisions, of course, cannot be handled by Bayesian theory and call for critical decision theory. Thus, Bayesian theory is only able to be used for tactical decisions because of the applicability of critical theory to the encompassing strategic decisions.

It is important to recognise that benefits may only be expected from the application of Bayesian methods to tactical decisions if the strategic decisions that make this application possible have been made in accordance with the critical theory of decision making. If this is not the case, if, for example, some of the key strategic decisions are taken by an autocrat who is totally deaf to criticism, using Bayesian methods in making tactical decisions is mere decoration which can generate benefits only by accident. To apply Bayesian methods to tactical decisions while paying no attention to the quality of the strategic decisions involved is to engage in a totally spurious fine-focusing. This is, however, a common enough event. Bayesian theory is often seen as the decision maker's friend, because it may be applied with relatively little intellectual trauma to the decision maker. In other words, it presents no threat or challenge to the decision maker. All that is required, or so it is believed, is a list of options and states of the world and outcomes for each option/state pair. Once the decision analyst has elicited the decision maker's subjective probability distribution and utility function and explored the possibility of acquiring more information, the decision maker can be told which option yields the highest expected utility. The analysis offers no challenge or criticism of the decision maker or his organization; it merely claims to free him from confusions which prevent him from seeing what his best choice is. The inherent friendliness of the analysis is emphasised quite nicely in a recent review:

If the decision maker does not feel that (the decision analysis) has captured his knowledge and concerns and that it has produced a course of action he believes in then the decision analysis has failed. But this is rarely the case. (Howard, 1980)

When Bayesian theory is seen in the light of the present discussion, this cosy view must fortunately come to an end. The decision analyst has no justification for considering only the tactical decisions of the organization he is seeking to help; he must also pay attention to the strategic decisions that the organization has made in the past and to the methods employed in their making. He must consider, for example, how open the organization is to criticism of its objectives and values; whether the flow of information through the organization promotes or suppresses criticism and whether the organization has the flexibility to respond to criticism. This is a theme to be explored in more detail in the next section, but it is clear that these issues are much more challenging and threatening to the decision maker than the issues raised by the traditional application of Bayesian methods to tactical decisions. This seems to me a wholly good thing — a decision theory which challenges a decision maker to think about his place in the organization and the way the organization guides itself through a troublesome environment seems to me superior in every way to one which feels discomfited when its results deviate significantly from what the decision maker already wants.

The Responsive Organization

In chapter 7 it was noted that any normative theory about how decisions ought to be taken has a double aspect because it must also try to explain at least some aspects of actual decision making in the real world. Making decisions is a more successful way of getting what you want than, say, waiting passively or praying. It is by no means foolproof, as the bankruptcy courts show, but if someone wants something the obvious thing to do towards its achievement is to make whatever decisions seem likely to bring the goal nearer. Decision making tends to work; it is better at doing what it intends to do than anything else we have yet thought of. This success needs to be explained, and any normative theory must try to show that it is the result of decision makers behaving in something like the way the theory says they ought to behave. In this way the theory can explain why making decisions is so exceptionally successful without resorting to coincidence or denying the success as illusory.

This said, the obvious question is to compare the explanatory power of Bayesian and critical decision theory. To what extent, then, can the success of decision making be explained by arguing that people employ something like Bayesian decision methods? The problem, of course, is the extremely narrow scope of Bayesian methods discussed at length in chapter 2. While many organizations may well be able to use Bayesian methods at the level of tactical decisions, none of the strategic decisions that they face can hope to benefit in this way, the conditions for the use of Bayesian methods being so stringent. No organization has ever had, or will ever have, enough information to be able to apply Bayesian methods to its strategic decisions — all of these are decisions which have to be taken under ignorance. Yet the organization's strategic decisions are of far greater importance to its success or failure than the tactical decisions that depend upon them. Whether a firm should stay in its traditional line of business or launch into new ventures; whether it should continue in existence at all; whether it should aim to maximize its profit or merely see the avoidance of loss as a restraint on its pursuit of wider objectives, are strategic questions of far greater importance to the success of the firm, or the firm's decision makers, than the tactical decisions whether to launch this particular product or whether to spend so much on advertising a particular line.

Thus Bayesian theory cannot hope to explain the success of organizations, for the really important decisions which decide the success of an organization are ones to which the theory cannot be applied. This should be no surprise, because Bayesian theory appeals to an extremely modest set of factors. Decisions are seen as point events. Given the options open to the decision maker, the information about the states of the world and the decision maker's utility function at the time the decision is taken, Bayesian theory isolates one option as the best. This is true even where a sequence of decisions is being considered because Bayesian theory represents this as the point selection of the best decision strategy. The theory says nothing about how the decision maker's preferences ought to have been formulated, nor about how the information used in the decision ought to have been collected, nor does it lay down any rules about what the decision maker ought to do once his decision has been made, implemented and the pay-off received. The theory is, therefore, silent about these features of real world decision making. As far as Bayesian theory goes it just does not matter how the information was collected, how the decision maker's preferences were developed; whatever the story behind these, the success of a decision is simply a function of what information happens to be available at a particular time, and what the decision maker's preferences are at that time.

This means that Bayesian theory tends to avoid some of the most pressing questions about decision making. These are questions, not about the individual decision maker and his preferences and information, but about the institutional setting of the decision maker. Before a decision reaches a minister, managing director or other senior decision maker in a form sufficiently precise and well-defined to be a contender for Bayesian analysis, the issue has passed through all kinds of institutional filters, information gatherers and analysts (maybe for several years) and the decision can be no better than the competence of these various actors allows. There is plenty of room for all kinds of bias and distortion to infect the decision; options may be deliberately neglected; analysis may concentrate on those features where the option favoured by the analysts is clearly superior, neglecting aspects that would be damaging to their favourite; information may be suppressed, or merely not sought, if it is expected to be embarrassing; the institution may effectively prevent expressions of dissident opinion about what its values and objectives ought to be; and the very way the problem is posed to the senior decision maker may actually take away a good deal of his freedom of choice.

If all these biases exist, and more, it is irrelevant to Bayesian theory. The senior decision maker has the preferences he has, however these have been developed and shielded from rival views, and he has so much information available, no matter its origins, and from these Bayesian theory allows the decision maker to identify the best option. The success of the decision is, according to the theory, a function of the point information and point preferences of the decision maker, and depends in no way upon the origins of the information or the preferences. It seems clear that the success or failure of an organization is heavily dependent on the way information flows through its veins and the way its members may criticize its aims and objectives. By refusing to take issue with these factors Bayesian decision theory therefore prevents itself from explaining how organizations succeed and how they fail.

What, then, of the explanatory power of critical decision theory? We already know that it must be greater than the explanatory power of Bayesian theory, but there is more to say. On this view, a decision is a process and not a point event. It begins with the hazy formulation of a set of options; continues as these become sharper or more precise, so that they become more testable; continues in a critical debate about what is the best option until a decision is finally taken, but the process still continues because the chosen maxim may continue to come under criticism and the decision is sufficiently flexible to be reversed if this criticism is successful. Critical theory therefore accounts for the success of real world decision making in a much richer way than its Bayesian rival. For this reason critical theory immediately inquires into the institutional setting of decisions in a way avoided by practitioners of Bayesian decision analysis. If the institution allows the distortion of the decision problem in any of the ways sketched above, then its decisions will tend to be unsuccessful. Critical theory, therefore, highlights the flow of information in an organization, the freedom of its members to explore what others think of as inferior options, the ability of the organization's members to criticize the objectives and values which the organization has and so on. In addition, monitoring of decisions is required for success and with it the maintenance of flexibility so that the institution may respond to the discovery of error even after a decision has been made. Failure to monitor or to ensure flexibility of operation will, therefore, lead to unsuccessful decision making. The tendency of organizations of all sorts and all sizes to refuse to recognise earlier decisions as wrong is, of course, notorious and must be counted by the critical theory of decision making a major source of ineffective decisions. In the next chapter, some of the institutional obstacles to maintaining flexibility will also be examined, and these too are sources of unsuccessful decision making.

A successful organization may be said to be a *responsive* one, because it encourages criticism of its objectives and operations and because it maintains the ability to response to criticism which hits its target by favouring decisions which are flexible. On the view of decision making developed here, an *unresponsive* organization, one which stifles criticism and sees no need to make flexible decisions, will tend to be unsuccessful in doing what it wants to do.

References

Blanchard, B. (1961) *Reason and Goodness*, London, George Allen & Unwin.
Frankena, W. (1958) 'Obligation and motivation in recent moral philosophy', in Melden, A. (ed.) *Essays in Moral Philosophy*, University of Washington Press, pp. 1–56.
Howard, R. (1980) 'An assessment of decision analysis', *Operations Research*, 28, 4–27.
Monro, D. (1967) *Empiricism and Ethics*, Cambridge University Press.
Nowell Smith, P. (1954) *Ethics*, Harmondsworth, Penguin.
Stace, W. (1937) *The Concept of Morals*, London, Macmillan.
Toulmin, S. (1958) *The Place of Reason in Ethics*, Cambridge University Press.

10 Critical Decision Theory and Partisan Mutual Adjustment

Partisan Mutual Adjustment

The final chapter of this work considers the relationship between critical decision theory and the view of the political decision making process offered by Charles Lindblom (see principally Lindblom, 1963, 1965, 1968) and known as *partisan mutual adjustment*. Lindblom attacks two related ideas about decision making. His first target is what he calls the *synoptic ideal*. This calls upon a decision maker to identify which of his values is relevant to the problem in hand; to then undertake a comprehensive survey of all possible means of furthering these values, to then list the consequences or possible consequences of adopting each of these means and in the light of this to finally select the means which maximizes the attainment of his values. This ideal is, of course, upheld by the justificationist model of decision making discussed at the beginning of the present work. Such a synoptic view of the decision process is required in order to be sure that the option finally chosen is justified. Bayesian decision theory also upholds the synoptic ideal, which is hardly surprising considering its roots in the justificationist model of choice. Lindblom's second target is the widespread belief that the co-ordination of decisions made by agents having different interests and values requires a supreme policy maker to undertake the co-ordination. Co-ordination, he argues, is vastly more efficient in the absence of a central co-ordinator. Let us first consider Lindblom's attack on the synoptic ideal of decision making.

His first argument is that the ideal is not adapted to man's limited intelligence; that meeting it poses an insuperably difficult intellectual task, except for the sort of decisions found in games and puzzles from where proponents of the synoptic ideal generally draw their examples. We have seen this to be true of Bayesian decision theory, where the comprehensiveness it demands reduces the scope of its application to near vanishing. In addition, Lindblom argues, the synoptic ideal is not adapted to inadequacy of information. In chapter 2 Bayesian theory was seen to be able to cope only with a very limited degree of uncertainty, up to what was called restricted uncertainty. Beyond this lies ignorance, where Bayesian theory finds no application, except under the very special circumstances outlined in the previous chapter. All real world decisions, except those about games and the like, have to be made under ignorance, revealing the great difficulty that Bayesian theory has in coping with poor information. Because the synoptic ideal is so demanding of information, it is not adapted to the costliness of analysis. In the real world, acquiring sufficient information to apply Bayesian theory would generally be hugely costly, not just because gathering information is itself expensive, but because delaying a decision until all the relevant information has been acquired is very costly. This is well illustrated by the case study about lead in petrol in chapter 7. There is as yet insufficient information for a consensus about the health effects of lead from petrol, and reaching such a happy state of agreement may well take many years. Acquiring further information is expensive enough, but its cost is dwarfed by the cost of delaying a decision until a consensus is reached. If lead from this source is harmful, then the cost of delay is many years of accumulated, and perhaps irreversible harm. The risk of bearing this cost must be taken into account in deciding whether to reduce lead emissions from vehicles now, or to wait until more is known about their health effects. But Bayesian theory is of no help here.[1]

This brings us to Lindblom's fourth criticism of the synoptic ideal. If the ideal cannot be met in a particular case, for example because of lack of information, the ideal is quite silent about how the decision is to be made. The ideal operates in an all or nothing way; if a synoptic view has been taken then it states how a decision is to be made, but if some part of a complete view is missing, the ideal says nothing about what should be done. This is certainly true of Bayesian theory. We saw in chapter 2 that it demands a great deal of information about what options are open, about data and its interpretation, about states of the world, pay-offs and the decision maker's preferences. If some of this information is missing, Bayesian theory ceases to be applicable in any form (except where sensitivity testing is possible, but this is of very little assistance). All the theory does is produce the hopelessly expensive prescription 'find the missing information'.

The fifth criticism also mirrors a point that was made earlier in chapter 3 in the discussion of the factual falsification of preferences. The synoptic approach calls for the decision maker to single out all values that are relevant to the decision problem at hand, but there is no way of knowing that no value has been over-looked, save for a complete review of the decision maker's values, which is quite impractical.

The two final criticisms of the synoptic ideal made by Lindblom are closely related. The ideal is not adapted to the open-ended nature of many decisions that have to be made, particularly at a political level. The consequences of political decisions of even modest importance have ramifications throughout society and to ask the politician concerned to survey the whole of these consequences is to ask the impossible. The impossibility of such an overview means that political decisions are nearly always serial in a way that contradicts the synoptic ideal. Public policy problems like the treatment of criminals, the

[1] As I have argued in Collingridge (1980, chapter 2).

maintenance of peace, unemployment, education, traffic congestion and so on, are never solved in a once and for all way by means of a synoptic overview. Instead, a more modest view of part of the problem receives attention today, some other part coming into prominence tomorrow, and so on more or less *ad infinitum*.[2]

Having considered these arguments against the synoptic ideal, the positive side of Lindblom's account of decision making may now be discussed. Lindblom argues that decision makers have found all sorts of ways of coping with the problems that prevent them from ever acquiring a synoptic view of their problems, the principal strategy being what Lindblom calls *disjointed incrementalism*. This has the following important features:

(i) *Margin dependent choice.* Decison makers do not attempt a synoptic survey of the problem they have to tackle. Instead, attention is focused on the differences between alternative policies and between these and the status quo. There may be options which alter the status quo greatly, but the magnitude of the innovation makes it impossible to trace out the consequences of the option throughout society and to make intelligent comparisons between these and the consequences of rival options. Such options are, therefore, not considered; analysis is confined to the *marginal* differences between the options and between the options and the status quo. Radical policies are simply not assessed, and options are ranked in order of preference of the incremental differences between them. Such an approach frees the decision maker from the impossibly heavy burden that the synoptic ideal seeks to place on his back, and thus represents an adaptation to his limited intellect, the cost of analysis, and the lack of information with which he has to cope.[3]

(ii) *Restricted number of options considered.* The synoptic ideal calls for a listing of all possible options, but considering such a huge, and open-ended list is impossibly demanding in terms of intellectual effort, money and information. The problem is eased if only options which are incrementally different are considered, but surveying all of these is still a formidable task. Decision makers therefore restrict themselves by considering only a few of such options.

(iii) *A restricted number of consequences of each option considered.* Having limited the number of options to be analysed, the decision maker is still faced with an impossible task if he attempts to trace out all the consequences of each option. Attention is, therefore, confined to a very few major consequences.

(iv) *Ends are adjusted to means.* Fixing upon ends in the way demanded by the synoptic ideal is hazardous because the effort of analysis may reveal that there is no satisfactory way of attaining the chosen ends. For this reason decision makers constantly adjust the ends they seek to the means at their disposal.

[2] For criticism of a somewhat similar demand that decision makers take a synoptic view see the discussion of model 1 and model 2 in Collingridge (1980).
[3] For a related view see Popper (1945, chapter 12).

(v) *Serial analysis and evaluation*. Policy makers never achieve a final synoptic solution to any problem, rather they make a never-ending series of incremental attacks on their problems. For this reason, they do not need to find the 'correct' solution. Their problems are so complex that attempting anything more courageous than a serial attack is simply foolish. This gives the decision maker a great advantage; he can afford to neglect aspects of his problem in the knowledge that he can return to them in the future. A serial attack also prevents the policy maker from discovering the final solution to yesterday's problem, a real possibility given the rate at which many political problems change and the time required for the discovery of a synoptic solution.

(vi) *Analysis and evaluation is remedial*. An important feature of real-world decision making is its remedial nature. Policy makers are much less concerned with guiding society to some well-defined future state than with finding quick solutions to easily identified social ills. As with the other adaptations, this focus on remedying ills brings about a great simplification in the decision maker's task.

(vii) *Fragmentation of analysis and evaluation*. Policy making is rarely undertaken by one decision maker. Instead, the usual pattern is that different aspects of the same policy problem are considered by a whole number of decision making agencies with different aims and values. This is thoroughly healthy because it means that all important aspects of the problem are likely to receive detailed attention from somebody, even though no one person or agency can attend to the whole problem. The fragmentation of analysis justifies each policy maker paying attention to only part of the problem, because parts one neglects are sure to be taken into account by other agencies with interests different from one's own. Fragmentation also enables the development of specialist skills by agencies whose task is to consider a particular aspect of many policy problems. If a chosen policy has unexpected bad consequences, one of these specialized agencies is almost certain to identify the unwelcome effect and to consider ways in which it might be eased, given the ameliorative focus of policy formation.

In this way, Lindblom suggests, disjointed incrementalism is a strategy that policy makers not only use to overcome the difficulties that stand in the way of following the synoptic ideal, but which they use *successfully*. It is, for Lindblom, a rational way of proceeding, given the kind of problems which policy making faces.[4]

An essential part of the strategy of disjointed incrementalism is that the analysis and evaluation of policies is fragmented between agencies with different aims and objectives. This immediately raises the problem of how the work of each agency is to be co-ordinated so that an intelligent decision may finally be made. After all, it is of no use if each agency investigates a set of options from the standpoint of its own values and using its own specialized resources, if there

[4] The theory of disjointed incrementalism is given in its fullest form in Lindblom (1963).

is no way of gathering all their findings and opinions together at the end of the day so that the best policy option may be identified. But this looks dangerously like a reintroduction of the synoptic ideal. It seems that a central decision maker must be available to gather in the findings of each of the specialist agencies, and making a final choice on the basis of his own values — but this would mean the central co-ordinator achieving a synoptic view of the policy problem. All that has happened is that instead of developing a synoptic view by himself, the central co-ordinator has left this work to a set of specialized agencies, so that each can analyse that aspect where their particular skill resides. He still acquires a synoptic view, not by his own efforts, but by those of his agencies.

But, as Lindblom shows so forcibly, there is no way in which one person may acquire a synoptic view of a policy problem, no matter how reliant that person may be upon specialized information gatherers. What Lindblom must show, therefore, is how the various findings and opinions of the specialized agencies involved in analysing a policy problem can be co-ordinated *without* the existence of some central co-ordinator seeking to achieve a synoptic view of the problem. This he does in his development of the concept of *partisan mutual adjustment*.[5]

Lindblom sees each agency as a group of *partisan* decision makers or, for purposes of exposition, a single partisan decision maker. That is, each agency attempts to further its own ends and reach its particular objectives. To achieve its ends any agency must co-operate in some way or another with many other specialized agencies and with partisan groups which are politically active, such as the cabinet, party leaders, groups of MPs, outside pressure groups, the leaders of pressure groups and the ordinary public. The problem, of course, is that the partisan groups with which the first agency must co-operate if it is to achieve its ends may very well have widely different values and objectives. How then can partisans co-operate; how can they mutually adjust in such a way that their views on whatever aspect of a policy problem they have an interest in are co-ordinated in the absence of a central co-ordinator? Lindblom sees two classes of adjustment. Where one partisan X simply adapts his or her decisions to those already made by another partisan Y, Lindblom speaks of *adaptive adjustment*. If X decides without regard to any possible harm that might be done to the interests of Y the adjustment is *parametric*, otherwise it is *calculated* or in the extreme *deferential* where X actively seeks to avoid injuring Y's interests. The second class of adjustments are *manipulated* ones, where X induces some response from Y as a condition of making a decision in a particular way. There are many varieties here:

(i) *Negotiation* where X and Y induce responses from one another by exchanging information and debating their views.
(ii) *Bargaining* where X and Y both use conditional threats and promises.

[5] The theory of partisan mutual adjustment is given in its fullest form in Lindblom (1965).

(iii) *Partisan discussion* where X tries to effect a reappraisal of Y's position by giving Y additional information and vice versa.
(iv) *Compensation* where X makes the conditional promise of benefits to Y.
(v) *Reciprocity* where one or both of the parties calls in an outstanding obligation, or acknowledges a new one.
(vi) *Authoritative prescription* where X uses authority to demand a response from Y.
(vii) *Unconditional manipulation* where X induces a response from Y by unconditionally altering the advantages and/or disadvantages to Y of various responses.
(viii) *Prior decision* where X makes a decision first to induce Y to respond rather than forego the advantages of co-operation with X.
(ix) *Indirect manipulation* where X manipulates some third party in one of the above ways to induce a desired response from Y.

Lindblom is at pains to show two things; that such methods of partisan mutual adjustment actually occur in political decision making, and that these manœuvres are a more effective way of co-ordinating the decisions made by the partisans than relying upon an all-seeing central co-ordinator. Having considered his attack on the synoptic ideal, the shortcomings of reliance of a central co-ordinator should be obvious, but by what mechanism does partisan mutual adjustment achieve any better co-ordination? Any partisan will pay particular attention to those aspects of a policy problem which affect its own particular interests and motives, a concentration which ensures the development of skills of analysis and negotiation. No single partisan can have a synoptic view of a policy problem, but this is not a ruinous limitation if other partisans pay attention to other aspects of the problem, bringing to bear their own special skills motivated by their own particular interests. Lindblom gives a brief example:

A city traffic engineer, for example, might propose the allocation of certain streets to one-way traffic. In so doing, he might be quite unable to predict how many serious bottlenecks in traffic, if any, would develop and where they would arise. Nevertheless, he might confidently make his recommendations, assuming that if any bottlenecks arose, appropriate steps to solve the new problems could be taken at that time — new traffic lights, assignment of a traffic patrolman, or further revision of the one-way plan itself. He might also have quite correctly anticipated certain other consequences, such as business losses from rerouting customer traffic. Some of these he nevertheless ignores as a consideration in his traffic plan. Instead, he proposes subsequently to alter parking regulations, ease pedestrian traffic in certain areas, or turn to still some other policy to reduce the business losses ruled irrelevant to his first policy problem. The remedial and serial character of his strategy in effect achieves remedies for emerging problems.

In short, if decision making is remedial and serial, anticipated adverse consequences of any given policy can often be better dealt with if regarded as new and separate problems than if regarded as aspects of an existing problem. And unanticipated adverse consequences can often be better guarded against by waiting for their emergence than by often futile attempts to anticipate every contingency as required in synoptic problem solving. (Lindblom, 1965, pp. 150-1)

The whole process of serial remedy is made much more efficient if a large number of partisans are involved in the decision. Each partisan having distinct interests from the others, their multiplicity ensures that no consequences of a decision that may be unwelcome goes unnoticed and unremedied. As well as remedying earlier decisions of another partisan, each partisan may also call the attention of others to problems about decisions not yet made. In Lindblom's words:

The great multiplicity of decision makers in, say, American public policy making can be seen, therefore, as a great strength where problem solving cannot be synoptically accomplished but must be strategically pursued. Multiplicity copes with the inevitability of omission and other errors in complex problem solving. Were there no decision makers with a stake in international trade, we might wonder whether farm policy might not put strains on international trade to which the farm-policy decision makers might themselves be inadequately sensitive; but we know that, if the strains appear, those decision makers who have a stake in international trade will attack them as their own problem. were it not for decision makers with an interest in parks and recreation, we might wonder whether an urban redevelopment board could be trusted to make decisions on the relocation of commerical houses within a city. (Lindblom, 1965, p. 151)

In this way, the remedy of decisions by other decisions, either in anticipation of the ill or following its detection, serves to co-ordinate decisions made by different partisans. Where one partisan fears that some consequence of a decision proposed or already taken by another partisan will harm its interests, it may employ any of the above listed manœuvres to try to induce a change of mind on the part of the other partisan, in an attempt to co-ordinate his interests with those of the other partisan.

An important feature of partisan mutual adjustment is that it tends to lead to agreement about what decisions to make. Through negotiation partisans with widely different aims and objectives can come to agree that some policy is in all their interests. If partisan X wants Y to adjust in a particular way to decisions X has already made, or is seeking to make, there is no point in couching the appeal in terms of X's values and aims. X must try to convince Y that what X wants also serves the special interests of Y, by, for example, presenting Y with additional information or helping Y sort out some muddled thinking about Y's own values. If negotiation fails, X may threaten, or bribe or compensate Y to make what is in X's interests also serve those of Y, using any of the devices listed earlier. Partisans are strongly motivated to reach agreement in this way because the extent to which any partisan can achieve his ends is determined by the co-operation he can achieve with other partisans. This ensures that no avenue of co-operation is likely to be overlooked as each partisan seeks to do the best for himself as he may.

The moulding of values to remove conflict is one element in the political process by which the decisions of the partisans are co-ordinated, but it must be supplemented by the weighing and aggregating of values where conflict cannot be resolved. Lindblom argues that this second process is no less arbitrary than leaving the weighting to a central co-ordinator. Indeed, it is less arbitrary because the weighting given to the opinions of rival partisans may be changed relatively easily if this is thought necessary, and attention may be given to even very weak partisans. The weights may be changed permanently, by a systematic re-allocation of authority, or from decision to decision. The process of weighing conflicting values will, Lindblom argues, tend to attach great weight to widely shared values, to values held very intensely by some partisans and to the values of people having a special concern in the decision. Another important feature of the process is that once a decision has been made, with a set of weights implicitly assigned to the conflicting values of the partisans, the distribution of weight will often be widely endorsed by all parties to the decision. There are two reasons for this; the weighting is accepted simply because it is the one that has emerged from partisan mutual adjustment, so that the adjustment legitimates the weighting, and because some partisans may come to realise, once the enthusiasm of debate has subsided, that the weight given to their values does serve their interests after all.

This ends our account of Lindblom's partisan mutual adjustment, except that we must note his views on the acceptability of partisan mutual adjustment as a way of making policy decisions. Whilst he sees its principal merit in its provision of an intelligent, rational decision process he concedes that there may be occasions where central co-ordination would be more appropriate. The choice between the two approaches cannot be settled in a general way, but will depend on the particular circumstances of the case.[6]

We may now turn to the relationship between critical decision theory and partisan mutual adjustment.

Critical Decision Theory as a Base for Partisan Mutual Adjustment

Many similarities will, no doubt, have already been noted between critical decision theory and Lindblom's account of partisan mutual adjustment. The following are points in common, though I make no claims that the list is exhaustive:

(i) The partisans all face a decision problem, that is under ignorance. Nobody can take the synoptic view, which is necessary for their decision to be

[6] In fact, it is to be settled by partisan mutual adjustment.

CRITICAL DECISION THEORY AND PARTISAN MUTUAL ADJUSTMENT 181

justified. Partisan mutual adjustment is a process designed to cope with the necessity of making choices under ignorance.

(ii) Partisans may learn that their preferences are mistaken through facts brought to their attention by other partisans in a debate.

(iii) Partisan mutual adjustment has no resort to the aggregation of individual values through a social welfare function or similar device.

(iv) No distinction is made between the individual values of the partisans and the resulting social value employed in making decisions. Partisans seek consensus in their individual evaluations of policy and consensus, once reached, confers the status of social value upon the agreed individual values.

(v) Decision making is a continuous and meliorative process rather than the point presented by Bayesian theory. Errors in the form of unwanted consequences are detected by partisans who then remedy the error or pass the information to another partisan who will do so. Detection of error is efficient because of the number of partisans and their diverse interests.

This suggests that critical decision theory may be able to provide a theoretical base for partisan mutual adjustment. An obvious place to begin is the nature of negotiation between partisans. Consider first partisan discussion. We may suppose a partisan Y to be proposing the acceptance of a decision maxim M, of form 'No option is preferable to Q'. This upsets another partisan X who holds that the option Q^1 is preferable to Q. X may appeal to Y by pointing to some factual sentence, F, which together with the shared background preference sentence V, entails 'Q^1 is preferable to Q', thus falsifying M. In this way, X factually falsifies Y's maxim, showing that Y's favoured maxim will have to be revised unless Y can show X that F is false or give reasons for rejecting V instead of M. In either case, as we have seen, the debate between the partisans will proceed to consider factual issues.

All the other manipulated adjustments within partisan mutual adjustment can receive a similar interpretation. Each adjustment may be formalized in the same way. Again suppose Y to propose acting on the decision maxim M, 'No option is preferable to Q'. Y also holds the conditional preference sentence 'If G then Q^1 is preferable to Q', and, of course, believes that G is not the case. X holds that option Q^1 is preferable to Q contrary to Y and so wishes to influence Y not to act on M. X can achieve this by showing Y that G does, in fact, hold or else can act, or get some third party to act, to ensure that G holds. If X succeeds in this, Y must accept falsification of M unless Y can retaliate by acting to restore the original situation. In reciprocity, X calls in an old, or a just-created obligation. In this case, Y may be attributed a conditional preference sentence of form, 'If X obligates Y to protect X's interest, then Q^1 is preferable to Q'. Where X acts unconditionally to alter the costs and advantages of a course of action of Y, Lindblom talks of unconditional manipulation.

Formally, X acts to bring about the state of affairs described by G. Where this involves X making a decision first, the adjustment is by prior decision. Where X invokes authority over Y, we may suppose Y to hold the conditional preference sentence 'If X invokes authority over Y in order to protect X's interests, then Q^1 is preferable to Q'. This is, of course, authoritative prescription. If X attempts to influence Y by paying compensation of K, Y may be attributed the conditional preference sentence 'If Y receives K in exchange for a change in preferences, then Q^1 is preferable to Q'. Lastly, in bargaining, X attempts to influence Y by conditional promises or threats. X tells Y that he will do L if Y acts on M, and Y holds the conditional preference sentence 'If X will do L if Y does Q, then Q^1 is preferable to Q'.

For Lindblom all these devices are equally acceptable within partisan mutual adjustment, but does this remain so if adjustment is analysed from the point of view of the critical theory of decision making? Partisan discussion is perfectly in order, because this is just a critical debate between partisans about what to do. Each party to the debate attempts to find factual claims that can be substantiated by evidence and that falsify a rival's preference sentence or decision maxim. But the same cannot be said of the other methods of adjustment. In all cases except partisan discussion, or critical debate as I would call it, the decision finally taken depends not on the quality of the arguments for and against, but on the relative strength, power and pocket of the partisans. Imagine, for example, an extremely wealthy partisan in dispute with a whole group of much poorer partisans. The rich partisan may be able to compensate all rivals without much personal loss, remembering the declining marginal utility of money, so that success is gained by virtue of pocket not argument. It might be held that buying agreement by paying compensation does give a reasonable aggregation of individual values into a social value, but we have seen how this suggestion fails in chapter 4 and it is not one suggested by Lindblom. Compensation undoubtedly enables the partisans to adjust to each other, but the final outcome of the adjustment cannot be reckoned as any more rational than settling the debate by a toss of the coin.

Similarly, if one partisan invokes authority over the others to gain success. Here, too, the decision finally made is not a function of who has brought forward the best argument, but of who happens to have authority over whom. The same is true if one partisan calls in an existing obligation or makes a new promise in order to fulfil a want, for the decision is then determined by who has what obligations to whom, or by which of the rivals is in a better position to undertake promises for the future, and not on who manages to make out the best argument for their case. Threatening is an even clearer example, where the final decision is determined by factors quite separate from who has the best arguments.

This leaves the whole idea of mutual adjustment between partisans with a very serious problem. If the adjustment between partisans is to be governed only by critical debate which manages to forge a consensus between partisans who are originally in dispute, the scope for adjustment is extremely limited. It is the rare exception, rather than the rule, to find that a critical debate between rivals eliminates disagreement by producing consensus. This, it is true, is the aim of the debate, but it is an aim which is very slow to be reached, if achieved at all. For this reason Lindblom is anxious to stress the many other ways in which partisans may generate a mutual adjustment of their positions. If these are now stigmatized as irrational, the adjustment of partisans in the real world would seem to be a largely irrational process. Critical debate may have produced consensus on some issues, but the remaining ones can only be settled in a way which is arbitrary, a way which reflects only the relative resources of the competing partisans.

Luckily, the solution to this problem is already at hand. A critical debate between partisans can be expected to eliminate conflict and produce agreement on an increasing number of points as time goes on, but time is the enemy of all decision makers; delay in deciding is always expensive and not rarely ruinous. In a typical case, then, debate may have narrowed the conflict between the partisans and may be expected to narrow it further in time, but because delay is expensive a decision must be made before a complete consensus is achieved. The decision at this point may be a reflection, not just of the debate which has gone on, but also of the relative power, influence and pocket of the partisans, but this does not mean that it is arbitrary. Arbitrariness can be avoided if the decision is flexible. The partisans can then *continue* their debate after the decision has been made in the knowledge that their argument is not a decoration but can have an effect on the decision because if it is found to be mistaken it may be revised. Without flexibility, argument after the decision would be pointless, and the decision would then be truly arbitrary.

Seeing critical decision theory as a base for partisan mutual adjustment therefore strengthens Lindblom's account in two important ways. Partisan discussion must be singled out as the only rational method of adjustment, and the need to make flexibile decisions is emphasised. This gives considerably greater power to the idea of partisan mutual adjustment. Lindblom's account seems to be a good description of the sort of thing that goes on in political decision making and his support of its rationality and superiority over traditional views is very important. But any theory of how political policies ought to be forged should have more teeth than this. It should tell us not just how things operate in the real world, but also how their operation could be improved. Lindblom says nothing of this; nowhere does he point to radical defects in the machinery of policy formulation which would have been overlooked but for his formulation of partisan mutual adjustment. The amendments proposed here, however, do just this.

Since partisan discussion is the only rational way by which partisans can adjust to one another, it is to be encouraged. In Lindblom's account this is not so; it is one of a whole tribe of instruments for adjustment and if it proves difficult, something else may be tried. From the viewpoint of critical decision theory, partisan discussion must be stimulated as much as possible, and obstacles to its employment ought to be identified and minimized. In the second place, decisions made in the absence of consensus between partisans ought to be flexible so that they do not bring an end to the process of critical debate. Obstacles to maintaining flexibility must be discovered and ways of avoiding them found. Decisions made at one time may severely limit what options are available many years into the future in a way which cannot be remedied by partisan action (see Schilling, 1961). It is not enough to make decisions about adjustment in the optimistic hope that future problems of adjustment can be settled when and as they arise, because a decision at one time may enforce a rigid and inflexible pattern of future adjustments between the partisans. The decision makers must be aware of such dangers, and elsewhere I have tried to show how they might be predicted, not in detail but with sufficient precision to influence the decision (see chapter 8 and Collingridge, 1980, chapter 9). It is not enough for a partisan decision maker to employ a totally incremental approach, paying attention only to the local, short-term consequences of the options that are available, in the hope that the global, long-term consequences will be investigated and treated by other partisans, because the partisan's decisions may constrain future adjustment along a dangerously narrow front.

Conclusions

In conclusion it may be stated that the critical theory of decision making developed here is able to explain the theory of partisan mutual adjustment while at the same time correcting it in two important ways.[7] First, adjustment through partisan discussion is the only rational way of progressing towards a consensus among the partisans, and as such should be encouraged by, for example, a free interchange of information or the provision of expert support to small dissenting groups. Secondly, the mutual adjustment between partisans ought to be made in a way that maintains flexibility, keeps options open, and limits the cost of the maladjustments that must arise from time to time. This enables critical decision theory to be seen as a kind of half-way house between Bayesian approaches, which demand that a synoptic view be achieved by the decision maker, and Lindblom's partisans who make only incremental decisions, in the light of short-term, local, consequences. On the view taken here, a decision maker does not have to achieve the impossibility of a synoptic overview, but cannot be confined to incremental consequences. The decision maker needs to take a sufficiently broad view of the decision problem to be able to identify major sources of inflexibilities that it might otherwise be impossible to avoid. This does not need detailed forecasting, as I hope to have shown elsewhere, and

---

[7] This sort of correction is an important feature of theoretical innovation, see Popper (1972).

is perfectly compatible with the impossibility of acquiring the synoptic heights demanded by Bayesian theory.

A final point is the light the above relationship between critical decision theory and Lindblom's partisan mutual adjustment throws on the relationship discussed in the previous chapter between critical and Bayesian decision theory. Bayesian theory considers a single decision maker with a particular utility function and particular items of information to hand, which may be added to by acquiring more data, and the theory tries to show how he ought to make a decision on this basis. The institutional setting of the decision maker, the way the organization seeks, gathers and handles information and promotes or stifles discussion of its objectives and values, is something on which the theory is silent. There may be good reasons for handling information in a particular way or for promoting discussion of values, but these cannot be drawn from Bayesian theory. As I have argued in the previous chapter, critical decision theory offers a much richer account of decision making and it can now be seen to be even stronger. An essential part of making any decision under ignorance is the monitoring of the decision's consequences, but for complex decisions there is no single agent able to obtain a synoptic view of the consequences. Efficient monitoring therefore calls for the existence of a whole collection of partisans, each concerned with the effects of the decision on his own narrow interests and motivated to attempt a revision of the decision if it should prove to compromise these interests. Thus critical decision theory says a great deal about the sort of environment in which complex decisions under ignorance should be made.

References

Braybrooke, D. and Lindblom, C. (1963) *A Strategy of Decision*, London, Collier-Macmillan.
Collingridge, D. (1980) *The Social Control of Technology*, London, Frances Pinter/Open University Press.
Lindblom, C. (1965) *The Intelligence of Democracy*, London, Collier-Macmillan.
Lindblom, C. (1968) *The Policy Making Process*, New York, Prentice Hall.
Popper, K. (1945) *The Open Society and Its Enemies*, Vol. 1, London, Routledge & Kegan Paul.
Popper, K. (1972) 'The aim of science', in *Objective Knowledge – An Evolutionary Approach*, Oxford University Press, pp. 191–205.
Schilling, W. (1961) 'The H-bomb decision', *Political Science Quarterly*, 76, 21–46.

Index

Arrow's impossibility theorem, 59–62, 159–60

Bayesian decision theory, 8; criticism, 10; decisions as point events, 144–5; examining all interpretations of data, 29–32; identifying all options, 22–7; identifying states of the world, 22; justificationist model, 7–10; knowing all pay-offs, 27; necessary conditions for employing, 32; need for all relevant information, 28–9; problems avoided by critical decision theory, 155–65; problems of variable interpretation of data, 31; response to institutional effects, 170–1; scope of application, 155–7; use for tactical decisions, 168; use in practical decision making, 107
Bias in decision making, 136

Catalytic converters for lead-containing petrol, 129–30
Certainty, decisions under, 5, 21
Competition, and inflexibility, 150
Conflict, avoidance by moulding values, 180; resolution to attain truth, 73
Consumption, as main pillar of economics, 121, increase following economic changes, 46; related to income distribution, 47; setting tax rates, 52
Corporal Punishment Bill, 114–20
Corroboration of scientific theories, 77–9; later failure of test, 142
Cost of information collection, 8, 28, 174

Data, examination of all interpretations of, 29–32; variability of interpretations, 30–1
Decision making, accounting for bias, 136; adjusting ends to means, 175; adoption of maxims, 97; analysis and evaluation, 176; as means of achieving goals, 169; choice between policies and status quo, 175; closing options, 105; co-ordination, 173; division between advice and policy, 139; fact and value in debates, 112–14; flexibility, 141–51; following rational assessment, 82; importance of critical debate, 183; justificationist model, 3–20; need for later revision, 144; public nature of debate, 110–12; related to methodological rules, 108; responsiveness of organization, 169–71; synoptic ideal, 173
Decision matrices, 12
Decision theory, 10–19
Decision trees, 109, 110
Decisions, correction time, 147; cost of remedying errors, 147–8; costs of errors, 147; monitoring, 146–7; remedied by other decisions, 179; repeating and non-repeating, 166; strategic and tactical, 165–9; under ignorance, 108–10
Deterrence value of corporal punishment, 117–18
Disjointed incrementalism, 107, 175–7
Dogmatism, and control of technology, 150

Economics, Buddhist vs. conventional, 121–2; Schumacher's criticism, 121
Economies of scale, and inflexibility, 150
Energy planning decisions, 22
Entrenchment, and inflexibility, 149
Environmental Protection Agency (EPA), debate vs. Ethyl Corporation, 129–39
Errors, cost of, 147; cost of remedying, 147–8; time for correction, 147
Ethyl Corporation, debate vs. Environmental Protection Agency (EPA), 129–39

Falsification, factual, 40–2; in scientific method content, 71; of decision maxims, 100; of option choices, 104–5; of theories: effect on test sentences, 75, example, 87, protection from, 79–80, 93–5; of universal preference sentences, 87–9
Flexibility in decision making, 141–51; four ways of viewing need, 148; measurement, 145–9

INDEX

Gambling, issues raised by, 166–7

Hedging, and inflexibility, 150

Ignorance, decisions under, 108–10
Income distribution, factors influencing, 48; related to consumption, 47
Information, and decisions under uncertainty, 9; collecting, 28–9; costs, 8, 28; fullness and relevance, 144; perfect, 14; problem of late collection, 28; requirements of synoptic ideal, 174; to judge social values, 51

Justificationist model, 3–20; in Bayesian decision theory, 7–10; in welfare economics, 6–7; regress of reasons, 34–8, 82; scope, 21–33
Juvenile crime, 116–17

Labour, Buddhist v. conventional view, 121–2
Lead in petrol debate, health effects data, 133–4; original decision in UK, 142–3; US debate, 129
Lindblom, Charles, 173

Maximax principle, 57
Maximin principle, 55–7
Maxims, case studies, 106–39; conjunction with preference sentences, 97–8; criticism, 97–139; in decision making, 82; logical relationships, 99; motivation to attack or defend, 113; open to criticism and rejection, 167–8; point of decision, 105–6
Money, marginal utility, 16–18; value, 16
Money pump, 4, 11, 39
Monitoring decisions, 146–7
Motivation, in preference choice, 137

Natural resources, consumption rate, 121; exhaustion, 123–5
Nuclear power, Schumacher's view, 127–8

Optimization, piecemeal, 26
Options, ability to revise, 23, 28; allowance for late choice, 26; cost of extending set, 25; determining complete set, 23–4; future, limited by current decisions, 184; identifying, 22–7; in Bayesian theory, 156; ranking, 4–5, 11; reducing shortlists of, 105–6; restrictions on consequences, 175; restrictions on numbers, 175

Partisan mutual adjustment, 173–80; critical decision theory as basis, 180–4; group structure, 177; types, 177–8
Pay-offs, choice of option affecting, 26; knowledge under Bayesian theory, 27
Philosophical ethics, justification of value judgements, 34–8; related to decision theory, 10, 38
Policy making, using disjointed incrementalism, 176
Popper, Karl, 69; rationality of methodology, 70–4; three worlds, 111; view related to preference theory, 83; views applied to scientific truth, 107
Preferences, 4–5, 11; appraisal of judgements, 111–12; as value judgements, 38; avoiding factual falsification, 40–2; choice of one sentence over another, 95–6; clashes between, 38–42; critical theory of, 82–96, corroboration, 91–3, metatheory, 84–6, protection from falsification, 93–5, test sentences, 86–9; criticism by factual test sentences, 90–1; expressed by consumers, 6; for one theory over another, 80, 83; guiding actions, 164; holding open to criticism, 89–90; individual, 157; justifying, 40; not justifiable, 83; social, 158–64; social justification, 43; sources of error in choice, 84–5
Primary social goods, 55
Probabilities, choice of maximin or maximax rule, 57–8; prior and posterior, 8, 15; related to decision making under uncertainty, 9
Probability distribution, 7

Rationality, and decision maxims, 97; choice between irrationality and, 72; claimed for justificationist model, 4
Rawls' theory of value, 10
Risk, decisions under, 7, 11–12; effect of individual attitudes, 52–3, 161
Road-building inquiries, 138–9

Scenario analysis, 148–9
Schumacher, E. F., 120–9
Scientific enquiry theory, 69
Scientific method, testing rival interpretations of data, 136
Scientific theories, corroboration, 77–9; empirical content, 76–7; Popper's view, 69; predictions, 77–8; protection from falsification, 79–80; question of selective success, 107; test sentences, 74–6
Sensitivity analysis, 27
Social contract theory, 55–9
Social preferences, 158–64; objectivist

theories, 159; subjectivist theories, 161–2
Social values, 43–65; basis in individual values, 44–5; clash with selfish interests, 58; determining social justice, 55; in choice of society, 55; problem of acting against own interests, 53–4; related to lot of least advantaged, 56; social welfare function, 52, 60
States of the world, identifying, 22
Synoptic ideal, 173
Synoptic view of decision problem, 21

Technology, economic dependence, 121; in Buddhist economics, 126; inflexibility, 149–50; intermediate, 125–7; use by developing countries, 125
Test sentences, 74–6
Truth, and search for scientific method, 70–1; connecting Popper's methodology, 72; resolving conflicts in statements, 73

Uncertainty, decisions under restricted, 19; related to information defects, 32
Utility, choice by each individual, 50; comparisons between individuals, 44, 50; maximization, 7, 11; possibility curves, 46–7; related to available information, 29; scale, 6–7, 11, 12–13, 50–1; social, 49–54; weighted measurements, 45

Values, estimating a second person's, 50; governing choice of social welfare function, 60; importance of justifying, 34; in debate about actions, 112–14; in lead in petrol debate, 130, 135; in parliamentary debates, 114; in social preferences, 158; moulding to avoid conflict, 180; personal, characteristics of, 162; regress of reasons, 34–8; traditional responses, 163; social, 43–65

Welfare economics, concept of optimal state, 45; meeting Pareto conditions, 26–7; social values, 44–8; use of justificationist model, 6–7